The Nietzsche Disappointment

The Nietzsche Disappointment

Reckoning with Nietzsche's Unkept
Promises on Origins and Outcomes

Nickolas Pappas

ROWMAN & LITTLEFIELD PUBLISHERS, INC.
Lanham • Boulder • New York • Toronto • Oxford

ROWMAN & LITTLEFIELD PUBLISHERS, INC.

Published in the United States of America
by Rowman & Littlefield Publishers, Inc.
A wholly owned subsidiary of The Rowman & Littlefield Publishing Group, Inc.
4501 Forbes Boulevard, Suite 200, Lanham, Maryland 20706
www.rowmanlittlefield.com

PO Box 317
Oxford
OX2 9RU, UK

British Library Cataloguing in Publication Information Available

Library of Congress Cataloging-in-Publication Data

Pappas, Nickolas, 1960–
  The Nietzsche disappointment : reckoning with Nietzsche's unkept promises on
origins and outcomes / Nickolas Pappas.
   p. cm.
  Includes bibliographical references and index.
  ISBN 0-7425-4346-3 (alk. paper) — ISBN 0-7425-4347-1 (pbk. : alk. paper)
  1. Nietzsche, Friedrich Wilhelm, 1844–1900. I. Title.

B3317.P34 2005
193—dc22   2004029377

Printed in the United States of America

♾™ The paper used in this publication meets the minimum requirements of
American National Standard for Information Sciences—Permanence of Paper for
Printed Library Materials, ANSI/NISO Z39.48-1992.

For Barbara

Have you been wondering why I have stopped writing to you? I have been wondering about it too. . . . If I knew why, I would not wonder any more, but—I would perhaps be sad.

Letter to Malwida von Meysenbug
March 13, 1885
Selected Letters of Friedrich Nietzsche, p. 236

If we are "disappointed," it is at least not regarding life.

Will to Power 16 (November 1887–March 1888)

Contents

Abbreviations and Principal References

Beyond Good and Evil [*Beyond*], translated by Walter Kaufmann (New York: Vintage Books, 1966). All quotations are identified by the number of the section they appear in.

The Birth of Tragedy [*Birth*], translated by Walter Kaufmann (New York: Vintage Books, 1967). Passages labeled with a numeral appear in the body of *Birth*, in the section bearing that number; quotes from "Preface to Wagner" are labeled "PW." Nietzsche's 1886 preface, "Attempt at a Self-Criticism," is divided into sections; quotations are identified by "AS" and the section number.

Ecce Homo, translated by Walter Kaufmann (New York: Vintage Books, 1967). Passages from any part *other than* "Why I Write Such Good Books" are identified by an abbreviation of that part's title together with section number. The opening sections of "Why I Write Such Good Books" are referred to by "Books" and section number; for sections on a book, a short form of that book's title identifies the part (thus *Ecce Homo, Twilight* 2).

The Gay Science, translated by Walter Kaufmann (New York: Vintage Books, 1974). All quotations are identified by the number of the section they appear in.

On the Genealogy of Morals [*Genealogy*], translated by Walter Kaufmann and R. J. Hollingdale (New York: Vintage Books, 1967). All passages are identified by the essay and section they appear in. Passages from Nietzsche's preface are labeled with "P" and the section number. Essays are referred to by Roman numeral.

"On the Use and Disadvantage of History for Life" ["History"], translated by Peter Preuss (Indianapolis: Hackett, 1980). Arabic and lowercase Roman numerals indicate the section and paragraph that a quotation comes from: thus "3.v" denotes the fifth paragraph of section 3.

Thus Spoke Zarathustra [*Zarathustra*], translated by Walter Kaufmann (New York: Viking Penguin Inc., 1966). All quotations are identified by the title of the chapter they appear in or by an obvious abbreviation of that title. Where the chapter is divided into sections, the section number is given.

Will to Power [*Will*], translated by Walter Kaufmann and R. J. Hollingdale, edited by Walter Kaufmann (New York: Vintage Books, 1967). All quotations are identified by the number of the section they appear in.

Charles Darwin, *The Origin of Species* [*Origin*]. Darwin divided most chapters into sections. These will be treated as numbered, and references to *Origin* identified by chapter (Roman numerals), section (Arabic numerals), and paragraph (lowercase Roman). "Historical Sketch" will be referred to by that title, its paragraphs by lowercase Roman numerals; similarly with "Introduction." *Origin*'s concluding chapter (XV) is unclearly divided into sections; references cite only paragraphs.

Preface

The history of philosophy.   Mark Twain's fellow traveler in Italy (*Innocents Abroad*) confounds the museum guide who just showed them a mummy. "Is he dead?" And upon learning how *long* the mummy's been dead: "What do you mean by such conduct. . . . Trying to impose your vile second-hand carcasses on us!" There are people in America who keeled over just this morning!

Something in philosophers has wanted to play the innocent American traveling likewise through history. Trot out any thoughts you have, but don't make us stand respectfully in front of philosophical carcasses that have nothing more to commend them than their age.

So what do you do with the philosophers who belong to history? That question worries everyone who writes a book about Nietzsche; but also everyone who writes about Aristotle, Berkeley, Crescas. . . . Nietzsche's reader faces an additional question: *Does* Nietzsche belong to the history of philosophy? Granted that he's only going to be found in a museum—is that where he deserves to be? Or is he someone special?

Does Nietzsche's reader still have to be his advocate and publicist?

Maybe not: maybe this is the sign that a different kind of book is now possible, that one may begin by pushing back against Nietzsche instead of (yet again) pulling him onto the philosophical stage.

Pushing against Nietzsche does not have to mean abusing him. The purpose of investigating the Nietzsche disappointment is not to berate the man, nor to get free of him in the sense of leaving his refuted corpus in the dust, only to figure out what to do next with his books beyond embracing or rejecting them.

Does the project sound too ordinary? And yet it cannot be taken for granted. It is the effort to achieve a reasonable distance from Nietzsche.

Nietzsche's causal explanations. This book engages Nietzsche in a conversation about causes and origins that he made possible. The main questions in that conversation are "How did the present come out of the past?" and "What kind of future might come out of the present?" Nietzsche insists on making these questions for philosophy. They are questions that philosophy has not let itself ask, or else has snubbed the answers to (by feigning that these are matters of historical interest alone). Nietzsche presses the questions as concerns for a new philosophy, and he offers his own answers.

Nietzsche's answers look sound on their face. But in the specific step at which he claims one phenomenon to cause another, the histories and prophecies show an astonishing tendency to falter. The cause cannot work, or it stands in need of a cause itself. Nietzsche begs crucial questions, sometimes argues in a circle.

That Nietzsche's causal explanations fail, and why they should fail, are the subjects of this book.

Although references to other works of Nietzsche's turn up, the argument will seriously treat three books and one long essay: "On the Use and Disadvantage of History for Life," *The Birth of Tragedy, On the Genealogy of Morals,* and *Beyond Good and Evil.* These are the most overtly historical or prophetic works that Nietzsche wrote.

Nietzsche speaks of being hard to understand. It might be essential to his philosophical project that he be difficult, though this should not go without saying and certainly should not rest on his say-so. Anyway it isn't essential to *this* book's project. I have kept jargon to a minimum and emphasized key points. The division of chapters into much smaller sections is also designed to aid in comprehension.

Sometimes one's best efforts are not enough. The question "Where are we in the argument?" will come up occasionally. So I have inserted summations and recapitulations into the long main chapters as well as into the semi-chapters between them.

How to write about Nietzsche. If this book remains hard to understand in spite of all my efforts, the problem might lie in the sometimes-indirect way it is written.

Why write indirectly? First of all because the explanatory failures in Nietzsche are not obvious. A little like a dream, his books open themselves up to interpretation not when a reader enters them in frontal assault but after a sly reconnoitering.

Moreover it is hard for Nietzsche's reader to keep a steady focus on a single subject like causal explanation. If his own books do not reason in marked-out steps from A to Z, a reading that is sensitive to those books' workings should also not try to maintain an artificial focus. To write about a cluster of intertwined theories and claims one must write in a manner that respects and reflects the intertwining.

Another book on Nietzsche may meet the challenge better than this one has. No good book on Nietzsche will deny that the challenge exists.

One example of the intertwining: two themes that will keep coming to the surface in this discussion are those of Nietzsche's originality as a philosopher and of his birth as a human being. Strictly speaking these subjects do not have to enter the discussion. You can assess a causal explanation perfectly well without once asking about the author's psychology and dreams of originality. But Nietzsche's books connect the issues. In his hands the one does implicate the other; a good reader ought to see that the topics are linked, and ought to ask why they are.

The issue of Nietzsche's originality in turn leads into a method of collage and juxtaposition. In each major chapter of this book I read the work under examination alongside a work by someone else: Descartes's *Meditations* (fleetingly) in chapter 1, Plato's *Symposium* in chapter 2, the Gospel of John in chapter 3. Chapter 4 mainly checks Nietzsche against *Origin of Species*, although it also makes use of Bergson's *Laughter*. The conclusion finds occasion to speak of Augustine's *Confessions* and some other Platonic dialogues.

Nietzsche is writing against these books. *They are his books' shadows.* The Fourth Gospel might be more than anything else the book that *On the Genealogy of Morals* wants *not* to be. *The Birth of Tragedy* presupposes and combats the *Symposium*.

But Nietzsche's opposition to his predecessors compromises his fantasy of originality. He needs the Gospel of John to exist so that the astonishment of *Genealogy* may shine forth. But he also needs it not to exist, so that his thoughts can have the spontaneity and independence he prizes so highly.

The problem of evil.   Here is another example of why talk about Nietzsche's causal explanations should branch off into other topics.

One way of seeing the explanatory failure in Nietzsche's histories is by lo-cating a confusion or predicament in them that parallels the traditional prob-lem of evil.

The traditional argument asks how pain and other evils can be possible in a universe that contains an omnipotent good God. These "good" and "evil" are nothing to Nietzsche. Still his description of the present names a number of phenomena he laments, from an ethic of pity to lies that human beings are equal. These are the evils he has to account for.

And where religious believers find the ground of all explanations in God, Nietzsche attributes every human deed, word, thought, and theory to a posi-tive motive force. (He usually calls this force the will to power, but it goes by other names too.) In short he says enough to generate a mirrored or perverse problem of evil. If pity is as lamentable and sickly as Nietzsche makes it out to be—or guilt, or that figment the "soul"—then how could the vital and healthy will have produced such a thing?

The problem is trickier than these few sentences would indicate. A fair presentation has to touch on the business of the will, on Nietzsche's general theory of religion, and on the dynamics by which he finds psychopathologies entering the human being. Now there is not just one topic in the air but sev-eral, all of them germane to the issue of causal explanation.

Previously published materials. Portions of this book overlap with ma-terials already published or presented.

In May 2001 I presented "Nietzsche on the Bidirectionality of Cause and Effect" to the International Association for Philosophy and Literature meet-ing at Spelman College. One vexatious question from the audience prodded me to enlarge this talk until it became chapter 3; then chapter 3 became the present book. Along the way some ideas found themselves in a short piece for the audacious new review *Brooklyn Rail*: see "Something Is about to Hap-pen," January–February 2002. Other ideas, under the title "The Problem of 'Evil,'" were presented at the Philosophy Colloquium of the City College of New York in March 2003.

"Morality Gags" in *Monist* (forthcoming, 2005) was written after chapter 4, reshaping selections from that chapter to make a freestanding article. The article then brought me to rewrite chapter 4 in turn. I am grateful to Lau-rence Goldstein, the editor of that *Monist* issue, for his kind and open-minded assistance; I am also grateful to the Philosophy Colloquium of the City University Graduate Center, where I read a version of "Morality Gags" in March 2004.

Much of "Psychoanalysis and Film: The Question of the Interpreter" found its way into the latter half of this book's conclusion. It appears in Robert Prince (ed.), *The Death of Psychoanalysis: Murder? Suicide? Or Rumor Greatly Exaggerated?* (Northvale, N.J.: Jason Aronson Inc., 1999), pp. 305–20. "Authorship and Authority" likewise informs the conclusion: it first appeared in *The Journal of Aesthetics and Art Criticism* 47 (1989): 325–32, though it has been subsequently revised and reprinted.

"Plato's *Ion*: The Problem of the Author" was my first publication: *Philosophy* 64 (1989): 381–89. Not until after I sent the initial manuscript of this book to the publisher did I see that my present worries over how to read Nietzsche played a sprightly counterpoint to Socrates' worries about reading and the soul. Going back to that article helped to ripen the present book's conclusion.

Finally, there is "The Eternal-Serpentine" in Christa D. Acampora and Ralph R. Acampora (eds.), *A Nietzsche Bestiary* (Lanham, Md.: Rowman & Littlefield, 2004), pp. 71–82. The overlap is slight, but the pleasure of participating in that project moves me to include this reference.

My readers and my students.   Great thanks of different sorts go to those who read this book in manuscript or heard its contents in the classroom.

Joseph McElroy gave me both the most specific comments of any reader and the broadest. He keeps teaching me how to make my writing think for itself. When a debt is as large as mine is to him, it's a relief to have something concrete to give public thanks for.

Ken Johnson read chapters of this book in early form and brought his many talents—as critic, teacher, essayist—to our discussion of it. In the most sublime sense he is a hard sell; I'm grateful for that.

Hafthor Yngvason is a philosopher of profound gifts and a generous reader, an encourager when I needed one the most. I could not have spoken of transfiguration in chapter 2 without his help, though much larger features of this book have resulted from his comments than he will guess.

Mikhal Dekel read and questioned chapter 3 at length, and showed me implications of it that I would not have imagined. She has read my articles over the past decade, always with a hawk-eye for sense and rigor.

Hundreds of students have heard me develop my thoughts on Nietzsche, at Harvard University, Hollins College, and the City College of New York.

(One stunning example: upon arriving at Hollins I had the good luck to meet Christa Davis—today Christa Davis Acampora, a prodigious Nietzsche scholar—and to direct her in an independent study on Nietzsche.)

David Rigsbee has talked philosophy and poetry with me since January 1989, until it now keeps slipping my mind that he was my student. I can thank him here for "The Skeptic's Notebook," but his thoughts have influenced mine in countless other ways too.

As I grew in my understanding of Nietzsche my students kept rising to the occasion. In 2003 one class responded with delectable intelligence to ideas presented practically in the form they take here. I name Eileen Chanza, Robert Takai, and Jason Woempner, but these were all outstanding students.

Two graduate seminars at the City University Graduate Center also helped this material take form. Gloria Bragdon, Steve Hoffman, and Maria Brincker are sure to see where they contributed in the first seminar; in the second I taught Lori Yamato, Michael Lamb, and a dozen other hugely gifted students. Damien DuPont, Ellen Fridland, and Kristian Kemtrup took this latter seminar; I learned from them then, and in deeper ways when they became my teaching assistants.

Finally, this is the place to thank Jens Veneman and George Milling-Stanley for invaluable help with Nietzsche's German.

My teachers and colleagues. First among my teachers is Stanley Cavell, for a hundred good reasons, including a heartening letter that set this book in motion. The best reason to thank Cavell might be that he took a common enough and noble enough motive energy—the desire to practice philosophy with care—and did not so much pass the motive along as show, the way an experienced mother might show a new mother, *how* to care.

At Hollins College I taught alongside Brian Seitz, colleague for a while but friend for keeps. Brian has read much of this book in manuscript. His *Politology* (written with Thomas Thorpe) will be out soon and will influence many thinkers, as it has already affected this book.

Also at Hollins, I had the stroke of luck to learn from John Cunningham. In chapter 4, I cite his rich studies of sacramental comedy. They showed me what I needed to know about comedy to understand *Beyond Good and Evil*, and what I need to know about metaphor in order to understand anything.

At my beloved City College of New York, I owe many and various debts to the philosophers John Greenwood, Michael Levin, Claudine Verheggen, and David Weissman, and to Joshua Wilner in English, one of the most acute readers of Nietzsche I have ever met. Therese Davis, in our Department of Philosophy, has done me endless kind favors over the past decade, many of them during the writing of this book (so that I *could* write it).

The president of City College, Gregory Williams, works hard to encourage scholarly activity by the school's faculty. His support for me made the completion of this book possible. I am happy for the chance to thank him.

My family.   Without my wife Barbara and our daughters Sabina and Sophie, any number of beautiful things would be impossible. Their delight at this book's progress and publication is so pure it is almost selfish. Above all, I am grateful to them for constituting a little world, an inner community that sometimes resembles the outer world but that governs itself, as the outer one does not, according to principles of joy and kindness.

Introduction

Voluntary.   The hard thing is to approach Nietzsche personally enough but also impersonally enough.

Nietzsche's causal lapses.   Disappointment can be one's first response to Nietzsche. His new fans rush to live out the mocking and self-obsessed amorality that they take to be his doctrine, until the liberation fades and they sag back down into ordinary life tasting the ashes of love gone dead (Bergmann 82–84).

Years along you might read a long passage aloud that makes you look up saying, "Sometimes he does sound like a blowhard, doesn't he?"

But after these disappointments there is another one ahead, more intellectual: the disappointment that despite his abundant gifts Nietzsche will not deliver what he promises with respect to the past or the future. For a philosopher so preoccupied with history he leaves gaps in his accounts of the causes of things. For a philosopher as focused as he is on the future of humanity, he leaves the way to the future equally unspecified.

The complaint in more specific terms.   Nietzsche observes a human phenomenon, altruism for instance. He observes that philosophers prevent themselves from understanding the phenomenon by rendering it eternal. A behavior has been lifted out of its historical context and reconceived as an abstraction, so that altruism "as such" arises from the free will, in compliance with one's observation of moral principles—and more such nonsense (*Beyond 2*).

In his critique of morality, Nietzsche therefore makes the eternal historical. He reinserts the timeless essence into time. What is now "given" had once looked very different, and someday it will have a new look barely imaginable today.

How Nietzsche pictures these transformations happening is a matter of controversy; *that* he takes them to happen is not. That Nietzsche uncages essences to run free and mutable over the plains of time is evident pretty early on to every serious reader.

Thus one of the great potential disappointments is prepared for at the start, with Nietzsche's promises to show the reader that philosophy has willingly fallen—*plunged* really—out of Plato's Heaven and into time's sewer. The disappointment lies in the reader's eventual recognition that Nietzsche's stories about the past and future end up in contradiction, vagueness, confusion.

Here is one example. A problem of evil haunts many of Nietzsche's histories. He establishes a dynamism to explain all actions: sometimes he calls it life, more often the will to power. Then he proclaims that there has been a fall out of life as it should be into life as the present day knows it—and doesn't explain how such a fall could have happened given the existing dynamism. He either does not see or pretends not to see that some further account is demanded by his original explanation; nor does he see (unless with great effort he is pretending not to see) that the conditions of his explanation make that further account impossible.

How could weakness have come to govern strength? The answer hangs open as vacantly as traditional stories of how altruism could ever have arisen out of selfishness.

When he turns from the past to the future, Nietzsche's perverse retelling of the fall with its own problem of evil finds its match in a perverse scenario of redemption. There will be new philosophers; a higher man. And yet by his own account, Europe finds itself packed full of a population so degenerate it shouldn't be able to produce a single good philosopher, let alone a higher breed of humanity. How can the same forces that debased modernity also bring new forms of morality into the world? Nietzsche does not say.

What makes Nietzsche's failures *disappointments*? He does not keep his promises—but then too the reader believed those promises. Could this theory letdown be closer than it looks to the first-time reader's dashed hopes after trying to live the thrilling ethos of a Nietzschean warrior? Maybe the disappointment is not just intellectual; in which case understanding it calls for psychological exploration.

History and origins.   The first section of *Beyond* suggests how elusive a question of first cause can be. Nietzsche asks about the will to truth, a drive that for twenty-five centuries has laid questions before philosophers. "Is it any wonder that we should finally learn from this Sphinx to ask questions, too? *Who* is it really that puts questions to us here?"

The Sphinx of philosophy will fall shrieking before the counterquestion "Why truth?" Nietzsche is telling a new kind of story about modern thought, or a new ending to the old story. But there is a hole in the plot. "The problem of the value of truth came before us—or was it we who came before the problem? Who of us is Oedipus here? Who the Sphinx?" Philosophers have come to a meeting at a crossroads, but without knowing who arrived first and who makes the first move next. And not knowing amounts to not knowing if the rendezvous had to happen. If the Sphinx's question comes before you, *presents itself*, that means a historical process propelled the question to arise, exactly when the right answer can strip the new clothes off the emperor. "Truth? We've been praising it for nothing," and nihilism is here for good. Then the question of truth belongs in a story of inevitable historical processes.

If you come before the question though, that is your doing and your hand knocking at the door. You *decided* to ask whether truth has a value. Maybe nobody else wants to know. You can call it a forced question or even a riddle. "What is the value of truth?" has been put together according to a private scheme and everyone else has to guess its answer.

If Nietzsche came first to the rendezvous, the question about truth's value begins with him and not in any grand historical process. He is telling a story about a stranger who rides into town and sets it on fire.

Not knowing which came first, the question or the questioner, makes Nietzsche's question about the value of truth feel both natural and forced. It flows out of the history of European metaphysics and simultaneously tries to block that history from flowing on further.

Nietzsche had to exist, because *someone* would be thinking these thoughts (so he is an effect); on the other hand he's entirely original (as it were a cause).

Causal inversions.   In *Birth*, Oedipus leads by another route to Nietzsche's odd way with causal explanations.

Nietzsche lifts away the Apollinian reading of the Oedipus story to show its true message.

> There is a tremendously old popular belief, especially in Persia, that a wise magus can be born only from incest. . . . [We] interpret this to mean that where

prophetic and magical powers have broken the spell of present and future, the rigid law of individuation, and the real magic of nature, some enormously un-natural event—such as incest—must have occurred earlier as a cause. . . . It is this insight that I find expressed in that horrible triad of Oedipus's destinies: the same man who solves the riddle of nature . . . also must break the most sa-cred natural orders by murdering his father and marrying his mother. (*Birth* 9)

In *Beyond*, Nietzsche seemed to be contemplating causal uncertainty. Here he is at its mercy. For why go hunting in Persia for the antique folklore to ex-plain Oedipus if you're only going to get the wisdom backward? The super-stition says that incest produces a sage. But if the story of Oedipus contains any general statement, it should be that one who defeats inhuman monsters with the secret of human identity in general will consequently commit the inhuman monstrosity of incest, because he lacks the secret of his identity in particular. Oedipus defeats the Sphinx *before* committing incest. The incest is cause in the Persian tale, effect in the Greek.

This temporal inversion explains why Nietzsche writes that the riddle-solver *also* is the one to violate nature, that timeless "also" hiding the story's temporal order. But this gambit feels like a child's evasion: he's been found out. Was Nietzsche only pretending to explain?

The inner life of the human. Here is a third manifestation of Nietzsche's predicament.

The new Sphinx asks or is asked the value of the will to truth, and the an-swer is almost the same one that the old Sphinx heard: "Man." More precisely Nietzsche's "man of knowledge" is the new answer, though also a fresh riddle. "We are unknown to ourselves, we men of knowledge" (*Genealogy* P.1).

What is truth? The man in front of you. But what man is this? Has some history spawned this curious inward man of knowledge or did he arrive out of nowhere?

The problem of accounting for inwardness comes up explicitly in "His-tory" and *Genealogy*. The existence of the inner life, its role in morality, its relationship to time and history, all face special scrutiny. Where Descartes and Kant take the self-reflective mind to be a given, Nietzsche sets out to show where it comes from.

Here too Nietzsche's causal story runs in two directions. *Genealogy* I says that slave morality brings about the existence of the soul. Eager to outlaw the strong man's actions, slave morality differentiates between the agent and the action, and the subject is that within the person that does not act. Nor does the soul remain a posit: it makes itself true. Slave morality deploys the fiction of the subject, which does not remain fictional, to effect its devaluation of the values of master morality. *Slave morality produces the soul.*

But *Genealogy* I also imagines an already internalized self acting out its resentment. Lacking the expression that deeds offer, this self takes its revenge symbolically. It produces moral assessments whose aim is to bring the master prayerfully to his knees. That is to say that the animal grows itself a soul and then uses that soul to invert the values of the masters. Human beings with inward lives create the inversion of values that constitutes slave morality. *The soul makes for slave morality.*

The origins of humans. The start of self-consciousness, later to become "second nature" to the human, is a new birth. What about the old birth? (Freud heard "Where do babies come from?" garbled in the Sphinx's riddle; why not in the new Sphinx's question too?)

Beyond is the book in which Nietzsche most often looks ahead toward "exceptional human beings" (242), reckless philosophers he calls "attempters [experimenters]" (42). "Many generations must have labored to prepare the origin of the philosopher" (213) and his book performs part of the labor. So it is not surprising to find *Beyond* circling around the topic of procreation.

Only "procreation" turns out not to mean what you think. Nietzsche helps himself to the language of pregnancy and birth but makes it metaphorical. A genius is "one who either *begets* or *gives birth*, taking both terms in their most elevated sense" (206). Circling back to the genius Nietzsche says there is "one which above all begets and wants to beget, and another which prefers being fertilized and giving birth" (248)—*metaphorically speaking.*

For some readers, the keenest Nietzsche disappointment comes from sentences like these. They burst with language that promises to cut through philosophers' intellectualism—language of sex and pregnancy, violence, exploitation—and then winds up being strictly figurative: intellectualism all over again.

Nietzsche calls for prophecy and talks like a prophet. In every way he frets over the problem of a future being, except that then he won't talk about the reproductive path to that being. When he says he wants "giving birth" to have an elevated sense, he sounds too squeamish to think about the *un*elevated sense.

He sounds squeamish again talking about women. Despite Nietzsche's sarcasm about romance (237) and sexual fulfillment (232), he barely acknowledges the biological outcome of women's relationship to men. All this "sex" and hardly a word about babies.

The source of the disappointment. The examples given in this introduction are condensed. Assessing the Nietzsche disappointment means enlarging them and others like them, finding where Nietzsche calls for causal accounts and then leaves them out of his books or even renders essential causal accounts impossible.

Thus chapter 1 reads "On the Use and Disadvantage of History for Life" with a close eye on its provocative treatment of inwardness. That "life" that the title speaks of, being a motive force behind all actions, bears responsibility for this inverted human who represents the antipode to life, as surely as (the faithful weep) God made a world that has evils in it.

The conundrum may explain why "History" presses to expose the origin of the historical animal, which is to say the *inward* animal, and yet cannot begin the one story it was set on paper to tell.

Chapter 2 finds *Birth of Tragedy* stumbling over the appearance of Socrates, the one creature who can chase Apollo and Dionysus away from the magnificent ancient culture they engendered—but also the one creature who, if Nietzsche described that culture rightly, could not have come into existence there.

Could Socrates have made himself?

Chapter 2 juxtaposes Nietzsche's Socrates to the one in the *Symposium*, where Plato, establishing Socratism as the beginning of philosophy, gives Socrates an unaccountable birth. Nietzsche wants to stage his own beginnings as a philosopher in *Birth*; to that end he takes on Socrates; but his rebellion against Plato becomes indistinguishable from obedience when he remains just as silent about the birth of Socrates as philosophy had ever been.

The argument of chapter 3 is more nuanced: it treats that great nuance-riven book *On the Genealogy of Morals. Genealogy* is the most successful of Nietzsche's books at conceiving a human existence apart from, before, what is called morality. It repeatedly asks how modern morality could have happened—or tries to. For however the question is formulated, it comes to look unanswerable, and the answers slip into claims of reciprocal causation and other question-beggings.

The disappointment of *Beyond Good and Evil* has already been touched on. Chapter 4 reads *Beyond* as Nietzsche's look ahead, to see how causal explanations might fare when they address the future instead of the past. As surprising as Socrates was in Greek antiquity, the coming philosophers are also supposed to be, when they crawl out of the mucky sea of modernity to stand on future shores. Their power to re-create morality requires them to come unexpectedly.

But nature abhors a surprise. Stanley Cavell is right to say "Where Emerson speaks of *revolution*, Nietzsche speaks of *evolution*" (Cavell 2004, 213)—and yet what kind of evolution can this be? Nietzsche wants something Darwin cannot provide, a fast-as-magic act of nature that kicks today's philosopher into the middle of next week. So he invokes Darwinian mechanisms but also denies them.

Why this disappointment, then, whether it is a disappointment *by* Nietzsche or *in* his reader? The disappointment calls for some explanation.

If the further explanations focus on Nietzsche, they will try to say what blocks him from finishing his own stories. *Something* needs to be said: Nietzsche's silence when the time comes for clear talk about origins or outcomes begs for an explanation. What fears lurk in Nietzsche's desexualized birth stories? Why does *Genealogy* keep coming back to the figure of the priest as source of all existing human phenomena, as though a priest had more to do with birth than a woman could?

This is one way to use psychoanalysis on the relationship between reader and writer. The author acts as the analysand, and when something *off* appears in the writing the reader probes for a deeper explanation.

As productive as it can be, however, such an application of psychoanalysis is only one among many. To assume that a reading has no choice but to insert the reader into the analyst's place, and lay the author on the couch, is to impoverish the uses of psychoanalysis and vulgarize its meaning.

For if the stock psychoanalytic approach assumes a confession in the writing, what kind of interpretation could bloom out of *confessional reading*? The reader who asks "Why this disappointment?" might not only point that question at Nietzsche but also wonder "What am I getting out of this disappointed feeling?" and "What can I do next with it?"

When reading turns confessional it might take new directions. Disappointment with Nietzsche is not his reader's endpoint but a new fact in need of further interpretation. (See conclusion.)

Nietzsche's theory of causality.   Psychological explanations are premature if this line of reasoning rests on a mistake, if there is nothing wrong with Nietzsche's treatment of causation.

Nietzsche makes so many overt remarks about causality, the objection might say. Don't those remarks account for the causal lacunae in Nietzsche's own histories and prophecies?

As presented in *Nietzsche's Perspectivism* the causal theory seeks to end philosophy's adoration of causal necessity (Hales and Welshon 85–110). Nietzsche "repudiates specific claims about causality and causes and effects;

he . . . rejects the lawfulness of causality; and he rejects the claim that causality is a necessary relation" (86). Philosophers have taken a before-and-after and convoluted it until the convolutions mystify them and the mystification enchants them. Thus in some unpublished writings (*Will* 550, 629, 631), Nietzsche argues that regularity has been misinterpreted as revealing laws that compel one event to bring about the other (Hales and Welshon 93).

Unlike Hume, Nietzsche then diagnoses "necessity" as the projection of human perspectives into nature (*Twilight* VI 3). Still less like Hume he seeks to replace causality with some version of the will to power (Hales and Welshon 94, 98–99).

But Nietzsche sometimes preserves the causation that he seems to be repudiating. His hints at a radical alternative to scientific causation clash with other passages that proclaim necessity in nature. Or maybe causality has its place within Nietzsche's theory of perspective (Hales and Welshon 86, 94).

But first of all, even if Nietzsche's stories omit or invert causal connections in a way consistent with his theory of causality, that consistency will not shield him from criticism. For if his books' strategies *call* for causal connections—if Nietzsche claims slave morality to have succeeded master morality and claims it so paradoxically that the reader asks "How?"—then not supplying those connections mars the books regardless of what a theory says.

If a theory of causality implies that you leave out certain causal explanations, that could even doom the theory. If Nietzsche wrote so ungrammatically that you could not understand him, it might intrigue you to find him criticizing grammar (*Beyond* 20; *Genealogy* I.13). His suspicions about grammar might explain incomprehensible writing. But they would not justify that writing, nor make you forgive Nietzsche his writing and keep reading him, unless you were excessively deferential to such justificatory theories.

Second, whether Nietzsche's anticausality justifies the lapses in his causal stories depends on what causality he's attacking. Does he mean to retain ordinary talk about causes and analyze it as talk about will to power, or would he rather eliminate the vocabulary of causation from ordinary talk? His notes sometimes press in one direction and sometimes the other: see *Will* 632, 634, 641, 664, 688, 689 (Hales and Welshon 99; Schacht 1983, 175).

If Nietzsche's point is to eliminate only the extravagant metaphysical interpretations of ordinary causal ascriptions, the causal theory will not excuse lapses in his causal practice. For on that interpretation his theory has no quarrel with statements that one thing caused another one and no quarrel with the use of those statements in explanations. He just doesn't want to see philosophical hay made of those ordinary statements. All well and good; but then he has no reason to leave the same statements out of *his* philosophy.

Nietzsche's enthymeme.   The appeal to a causal theory to justify faulty causal attributions separates some readings of Nietzschean causation from others. On one side the gaps in his causal explanations emerge as intentional, on the other they are flaws.

There is also a second way in which describing Nietzsche's silences (his falling silent) determines the intention that is being ascribed to him. For not speaking, like nonbeing, is said in many ways. Not telling the argument's conclusion can be called plain old "not finishing," but also an enthymeme. "Enthymeme" more typically names an argument with missing premises but can also refer to one from which the conclusion is omitted.

David Allison proposes that the dominant trope in Nietzsche's post-*Zarathustra* writing is aposiopesis, self-interruption (Allison 1990, 1994). In this narrower species of enthymeme one stops, as if overcome, before reaching a conclusion. (Arthur Quinn's invaluable *Figures of Speech* informs this book's treatment of aposiopesis and of all other tropes.) Moses apologizes to God for the worship of the golden calf: "This people have sinned a great sin. . . . Yet now, if thou wilt forgive their sin—; and if not, blot me, I pray thee, out of thy book which thou hast written" (*Exodus* 32:31–32).

Self-interruption is more striking than the bare omission of a conclusion and attributing this trope to him gives more credit to Nietzsche. He would like to tell his readers more but he can't go on.

There are other ways of reading the telling unwritten last words of an argument. If one acts like a person arguing but leaves the conclusion unsaid, you *might* deliver the enthymeme aposiopetically with the strain of the unnamable finish choking the pen's throat, but you don't *have* to, you can simply stop urbanely before your conclusion as if holding a door open, bowing to the reader, "After you."

Faced with an inconclusiveness as dramatically prepared as the grand enthymeme that constitutes Nietzsche's corpus, the task therefore is to see if these repeated moments at which the history unravels should be read as points at which Nietzsche's antimetaphysical strategy falters, or as openings like the opening of a door.

CHAPTER ONE

—⌒⌐

"On the Use and Disadvantage of History for Life": First Temporalizing, Then Temporizing

Time and life. This long essay contains the closest thing there is to Nietzsche's theory of time. Accordingly, it is the first thing to read when assessing his historical and prophetic books.

To attribute a theory of time to "History" is to say that it wrangles with the question, "Where does a sense of time come from, and how does it inform the life of the temporal entity known as the human being?"

"History" investigates the experience of time with one eye always on the biological impulse that its title calls "life," apparently a dynamic motive force. In this respect again the essay is the right introduction to the present study, which will repeatedly encounter "life" or surrogate posits.

A caution to the reader. Nietzsche quotes Goethe approvingly: "Whatever has a beginning *deserves* to have an undoing; it would be better if nothing began at all" (3.v).

To be born is to wind up ceasing to be *and* to deserve that fate. Everything goes wrong at the moment of birth, as if the sensitive viewer ought to look away from that event. Also (taking Goethe's last clause in one natural way) as if it would be better if everything had always existed.

Descartes's birth. Descartes asks whether he came to exist thanks to his own efforts, because of his parents, or because of some other being less perfect than God. If all those alternatives fail, did he come from God (*Meditations* III, paragraphs 29–36)?

Along with the first and third possibilities, Descartes rejects the second. Because parents lack the power to maintain him in existence once he has begun to be, they can't be his real cause. At most one's parents account for an event in the past, "birth," but exactly because they fulfill that temporal function they cannot account for the timeless aspect of existence.

Anyway, parents only make the body's birth possible. "I am a mind," says Descartes (III.36).

Untimely meditations.   Nietzsche published his book of essays under the title of *Untimely Meditations* (*Unzeitgemässe Betrachtungen*). They are meditations because like Descartes's sequence they catch mental activity as it happens; untimely not in the sense of being time-*less*—Nietzsche does not meditate on *first* philosophy as Descartes did—for these essays belong to a time, just not to their own.

Three of the book's four essays address prominent Germans. Nietzsche's essay on David Strauss is a public flaying; those on Schopenhauer and Wagner adore their subjects, not really against the spirit of the age but as if understanding the age more deeply, from the inside.

Sixteen years later, reviewing the essays, Nietzsche will admit their solipsistic character. "Schopenhauer as Educator" could have been called "Nietzsche as Educator," for it was about his past. "Wagner in Bayreuth" gave readers Nietzsche's vision of his own future (*Ecce Homo*, "The Untimely Ones" 3).

"Both [essays] speak of me alone," he writes to Peter Gast in December 1888. "Psychologically speaking, neither Wagner nor Schopenhauer makes an appearance there" (Middleton 333). "Confessions about myself," he calls the essays in a letter to Georg Brandes earlier in 1888 with equal unembarrassment about his solipsism (Middleton 286).

Only the second *Meditation* does not address itself to a person. Nietzsche uses "History" to speak of two concerns that subsequently never disappear from his writing. First he examines the practice of history. What has the study of the past done for human beings thus far? Second, because history in *his* time has asserted itself as scientific, Nietzsche launches an untimely strike against historical science, also but more slyly against any science at all.

A couple of lifetimes after "History" appeared, certain distinctions that Nietzsche occupies himself with feel time-bound. You might even consider the overarching subject of the essay to be dated. Today it makes one nervous to speak of studying history "objectively" or of "knowledge for its own sake." Like the debates that Kant diagnoses in his Antinomy, these positions have the stodgy flavor of a superseded era.

In this respect the essay's timeliness, like the first *Critique*'s, partly falls victim to its own success. Kant drove so much speculation out of metaphysics that his own act of expulsion feels otiose. And a great reason that one rarely boasts of historical objectivity today is Nietzsche's own essay.

Even when Nietzsche's conclusions do sound familiar he reaches them along unexpected paths. The workings of his argument become clearer when they are separated from its taxonomy of historical modes (antiquarian, monumental, critical).

"Life."   Somewhat as the "Dionysian will" also did in *Birth* a few years before, the "life" in Nietzsche's title approximates what he will later call the "will to power."

(Peter Berkowitz overstates the case when he says the "aim of Nietzsche's histories is to discover and display nonhistorical or enduring knowledge about human nature." But to the slender degree that this sentence describes "History" it is with reference to "life": Berkowitz 28.)

The Dionysian will and the will to power do not account for the same actions that "life" does, but all three pose as motives for human behavior *that differ from self-preservation*. The essay's first words cite Goethe's authority: "Moreover I hate everything which merely instructs me without increasing or directly quickening my activity [Tätigkeit]." Egoism interprets life as a thing one preserves and husbands. This liveliness gets increased and quickened.

When Nietzsche says in the same first paragraph that human beings need history "for life and action [zum Leben und zur Tat]," the "and" indicates a hendiadys. These are not separate goals when life is action and only ever ought to be.

Nietzsche's "History" only describes "life" twice (3.v, 5.i), and the second characterization is negative (see "'Life' and scientific history" later). So the closest thing to a definition appears at 3.v, when Nietzsche speaks of "life alone, that dark, driving, insatiably self-desiring power [jene dunkle, treibende, unersättlich sich selbst begehrende Macht]."

An egoist would never use "driving" or "insatiable" to describe ultimate motives. Egoistic motives have goals (they do not drive the body onward), and they yield upon achieving their goals (they are satiable).

The description of life as "self-desiring" finally hints that every lively desire yearns for both its present satisfaction *and* its further arousal. Against a tradition of hedonic calculi that dates back to the *Republic* (583c–586b), Nietzsche eschews any analysis of action according to which one starts with unwanted desires and moves to relieve them, finally bidding both the desire and its concomitant pleasure a glad goodbye. For Nietzsche pursuing the de-sired thing does not boil down to escaping the desire, even if philosophers in-terpret the rushes of desire that way. Life that seeks to put its desires to rest is *economical*: it wants to settle accounts. The desire that Nietzsche speaks of goes on desiring its own desirousness. It seeks no endpoint (Schacht 1983, 242), it has fallen in love with those climbs and plunges lamented by Plato and Epicurus.

Varieties of history.   The three species of history all exist in order to serve "life" even if they work against life. For history has this persistent trait of bringing mixed effects to civilization.

Human memory retains experience, as the minds of many other animals do, but also understands that the experience being remembered belongs to the past and will not come again. In this respect history originates in a gloomy insight.

But Nietzsche does not lament the poignancy of memory. Culture can't grow in the darkness that enfolds animal memory.

> Only so far as man . . . limits that unhistorical element; only so far as a bright lightning flash or light occurs within that encircling cloud of mist—that is, only through the power to use the past for life and to refashion what has hap-pened into history, does man become man. (1.v)

Nevertheless memory loads the human down with the "ever greater weight of the past" (1.ii). Understood as a quantity of memory and a mass of habit and tradition, history becomes unbearable: "with an excess of history man ceases again, and without that cloak of the unhistorical he would never have begun and dared to begin" (1.v). History in the precise sense, *a cultural practice of sorting and interpreting memories*, arises to relieve the strain of rec-ollection.

As memory exercises the double effect of raising the human above the an-imal and crushing the human into a condition beneath animals' dignity, so too the traditional forms of historical practice benefit human life when they take on the burden of the past productively, but also threaten to damage that life. It is this essential similarity among the species of history that Nietzsche emphasizes. The time he spends arranging traditional histories into monu-mental, antiquarian, and critical makes the distinctions among these forms appear to be his subject—as if he wanted to rank one above the rest. But the taxonomy only exists to multiply his examples of *the ambiguity of history as such*. What matters more to Nietzsche than any difference between two forms of history is the general truth that each form has a proper task. Each "is justified in only one soil and one climate: in every other it turns into a noxious weed" (2.viii).

Rather than praise or condemn a type of history, Nietzsche digs for the forms of culture and personality that bring out its most beneficial effect, then too for the context that turns the medicine into a drug. Like jungle roots that need to be cooked just right to feed and not poison, all three forms of history issue in contradictory effects.

Thus monumental history can inspire heroic deeds (2.ii) or break them under the weight of its examples (2.vi). Antiquarian history's preservationist instinct (3.i) can keep a past time alive and healthy but also make the present culture a waxwork museum, the antiquarianism declining into mindless love of the past (3.iii). Critical history serves suffering people by showing them how to battle against an oppressive past—exposing the old errors of a ruling class—although it threatens to let the genie out of the bottle to destroy more than it meant to (3.v).

In every instance "the unhistorical and the historical are equally necessary for the health of an individual, a people and a culture" (1.iv). Every history does its part but also has to stop doing its part.

The double effect of all these histories is not a problem in itself. History *may* serve life but is not compelled to. It was not designed for a purpose. When the brilliant deeds that monumental history sets before the present threaten to shame and hobble that present, monumental history has not failed in the way that a wheel might fail its maker, but at most the way that upright posture, though freeing the human forepaws, also brings aches to a back forced to balance on one end. No failures where no successes were planned, only multiple effects.

Scientific history.   "And now a quick glance at our time!" (4.ii).

Any timely thinker can tell you things are different today. That is practically the message that God put timely people on earth to deliver. A timely observer will especially want to tell you that *history* has changed. No more propaganda! From now on it will be history itself—that's what you could mean by the "demand that history be a science" (4.ii), that history fulfill its proper function without concern for its origins (e.g., in flattery of kings) or cultural effects.

The modern demand that history be treated as an independent discipline compromises Nietzsche's account of historical practices as tactics for managing the burden of memory. There is no longer a pure "relation between life and history. . . . Now life is no longer the sole ruler and master of knowledge of the past" (4.ii). History "as such" appears to have earned itself an entirely different category from the other forms of historical inquiry, now that knowledge for its own sake has become the purpose of history.

Nietzsche said of monumental history that it resists truth telling—"in order, at the expense of the cause, to present the effect monumentally" (2.iv)—but scientific history will not let any external purpose suspend the pursuit of truth. It interprets its own unconditional demand for knowledge as proof that it stands free of the purposes of "life and action." But Nietzsche points out that scientific history grows more fruitfully in one type of historian than in others, just as the other forms of history also do (see 6); that scientific history produces cultural effects just as the others do (7); that it further resembles the other histories in torturing facts to fit its interpretations (6).

Modern history also manifests a cultural origin and orientation as pervasive as those behind the unscientific histories. In its case, the bias derives from loyalty to the Christian culture that spawned it. For scientific history's obedience to a linear conception of time boils down to Christian anticipation of the apocalypse dressed up in secular jargon (8).

The practitioners of scientific history may have run into more mischief than other historians did. But the mischief did not happen because scientific history bears no relationship to life, rather because it has denied that relationship, not seeing that it too "is justified in only one soil and one climate" and has been planted in the wrong ground.

For all the differences between Nietzsche's philosophizing and Kant's, Nietzsche's discussion of scientific history deserves the name "critique." They both object to a view not on the grounds of its simple falsehood but because it's been inflated, out of the context in which it held true, into an unconditional claim purporting to hold true in every context and every time. Scientific history does not recognize that it has a place and one particular home. By bringing it back within the fold of traditional historical practices, Nietzsche can transfer everything he said about monumental, antiquarian, and critical histories to the modern species. So historical science too constitutes a stratagem by which human beings try to handle the weight of their memories; it too is a regimen of intellectual diet and exercise in the interests of "life"; it too must be judged according to how deleteriously it affects life when it strays from its place.

History temporalized.   To *temporalize* (it is a nonce-word) shall mean: to situate a concept in time when it had previously not been considered temporal. Nietzsche temporalizes when he says that "the origin of historical education . . . *must* itself be historically understood, history *must* itself dissolve the problem of history" (8.ii).

"Life" and scientific history.   The insistence on knowledge for its own sake that characterizes history-as-science creates new threats to life.

Nietzsche gives "life" a second and more detailed description (5.1), this one negative where the first (3.v) had been direct. He announces five effects of historical excess that undermine life: (a) the intensification of the difference between inner and outer; (b) the encouragement of present people's delusion that they are more just than historical persons were; (c) the degradation of instinct; (d) the enhancement of moderns' view of themselves as latecomers; (e) the cultivation of irony.

If the five effects of excessive history threaten life, then life ought to contain the threatened phenomena. If excessive history attacks life by degrading the instincts, life must be instinctual.

That third effect works obviously enough; so too (d) and (e). You don't need Nietzsche's help to find it depressing that you feel like a latecomer or that you act out every passion inside the costume of irony's quotation marks. It is so easy to see how (c)–(e) work against life that they don't imply much of a specific nature about Nietzsche's "life."

Effect (b) is more curious. What does feeling more just than one's predecessors have to do with *not living*? Why should Nietzsche consider faith in humans' growing justice a danger? It can't be because faith in moral progress is false. Falsehood does not imperil life.

Is it the vanity of today's judgments, then? Observers look back at American slavery or much further back at Athenian imperialism. They are struck by past people's blindness to their own cruelty. The modern observers puff themselves up as more decent human types. They give themselves credit for higher moral standards in the act of identifying the slave-owners' unreflectiveness.

And perhaps the self-satisfaction in contemporary moralizing makes the vain imagine that their merit inheres in their moral judgment, in the sensitivity and the psychological nuance of that judgment.

Like critics of the arts who secretly infer from their power to grade a work of art their superiority to its maker, moral critics equate their virtue with their ability to see other people's vices. The critics who live in these last days satisfy their moral sense by thinking "That's bad," and enjoying the flexion of that judgment instead of actually doing something good.

When thoughts bring the same gratification as thoughtful acts, they lack the old imperative to act. So the worst consequence of elevating oneself as a judge of one's forebears is this new habit of locating one's merit in a mental domain. Thought withdraws from action.

Effect (b) thus inclines toward (a), the inwardness that Nietzsche diagnoses among the Germans of his day (4). Both dangers distract modern historical humans away from bodily movement and toward the fidget of mental activity. Where there had been life there is now only thought.

Inwardness has a history. "Inwardness" ("Innerlichkeit") amounts to a discrepancy between thought and action. The cultivation of inwardness (so close to the self-consciousness that Descartes described and drew on) is the greatest sin that Nietzsche accuses scientific history of committing. But this major accusation will also become the great impossibility in his account: it is a problem of evil that prevents him from advancing beyond the Cartesian picture he'd like to reject.

Nietzsche's critique begins impressively. In the first of many lifelong analogies to digestion, he compares scientific history to an indiscriminate eating organ that takes in more food than the organism can assimilate.

> In the end modern man drags an immense amount of indigestible knowledge stones around with him. . . . Knowledge, taken in excess without hunger, even contrary to need, no longer acts as a transforming motive impelling to action and remains hidden in a certain chaotic inner world which that modern man, with curious pride, calls his unique "inwardness." (4.iii)

Inwardness comes of having too much time on your mind.

Thus inwardness is a historical phenomenon in two senses. Its content derives from the human's relationship with the past, and its form has a past and an origin.

With the latter claim Nietzsche temporalizes the inner life as he temporalized scientific history. Human beings did not arrive ready-made in a condition in which inner and outer withdrew from one another. They *researched* themselves into that state, until today, in this excessively historical Europe, people have *become* what Descartes said they always essentially *were*:

> Crumbled and fallen apart, on the whole half mechanically divided into an inside and an outside . . . I may perhaps still have the right to say about myself *cogito, ergo sum* but not *vivo, ergo cogito*. (10.v)

Descartes was right—but only about the minds of moderns.

The condition Nietzsche describes, in which thought does not flow from living but exists on its own terms and for its own sake, ought to strike all observers as a degenerative state. "Empty 'being' but not full and green 'life' is guaranteed me; my original feeling only guarantees that I am a thinking, not a living being" (10.v).

What "History" calls "life" is missing from modern existence. Any activity that the present human *does* muster, "unalive [unlebendige] and yet uncannily active" as it is, will look peculiar. It is the modern German who "cannot be judged at all by an action and remains hidden as an individual even after this deed. He must . . . be measured by his thoughts and his feelings" (4.v). In other words, Descartes had it backward. That degree of self-consciousness or inwardness that is needed for launching the *cogito* does not lead onward to more certainties and thence to knowledge for its own sake. If Descartes thinks he has found an argument that proceeds in that direction, out of solipsism, his belief only shows how ontological ordering falsifies temporal order. Look at what really comes after what and you won't be able to swallow philosophy's fairy tales any more; for the self-consciousness with which Descartes gets the *cogito* started, and then the movement toward knowledge, *is itself the legacy of the pursuit of knowledge* (4). Knowledge-seeking brings inwardness, not the other way around.

The Cartesian memory.   "I am a thinking thing," Descartes keeps saying. Thinking means doubting, understanding, affirming and denying, willing and refusing, imagining and feeling (II.8); also desiring (II.9); also knowing and failing to know (III.1). Also *remembering*?

In the first paragraph of *Meditation* I, Descartes speaks of beliefs he has held since early youth and his long suspicion that many of them are false. But the mere persistence of those beliefs does not yet constitute memory. Memory presumes that things were different once; and the problem with the adult Descartes's inheritance of his old mistakes is precisely that they have not changed. They persist with animal innocence about time.

Maybe for this reason, Descartes says nothing about memory when describing his naïve past. Whatever faculty persists in false belief needs to be tamed, maybe purged. Memory, however, participates in returning the mind to knowledge. Descartes finishes *Meditations* II, in which he's convinced himself that he knows his mind better than his body, with the resolve to imprint this new understanding on his memory (II.16). Something has happened, at last he knows something, and now there is useful work for his memory to do.

The book's final paragraph mentions memory again, as a method by which Descartes can preserve himself from falling into error again. This time memory even answers the skeptical argument about dreaming: the difference between waking perceptions and dreams, Descartes says as he concludes, is that events in dreams are not connected by memory to the rest of one's life in the way that waking experiences are (VI.24).

It has been alleged for some time that the *cogito* itself smuggles memory in as an unstated assumption. Thus Arthur Lovejoy writing in 1930 argued that Descartes had built memory into the self's reality (Lovejoy 305). Regardless of what Descartes thinks he is doing, he is actually demonstrating the existence of a *remembering* thing (see Wiener 483).

Time and consciousness.   The relationship between time consciousness and self-consciousness proposed in "History" mirrors a philosophical tradition's treatment of time—meaning that it resembles that treatment but also reverses it.

Augustine associates time with interiority in *Confessions* XI when he decides that past and future have their only being within the soul. Past objects enjoy a present life in the form of memory, present things in the form of objects of sensation, and future things live as hopes or expectations; and hope, sensation, and memory are mental acts.

Kant follows Augustine's lead when he associates time with the "inner sense" (*Critique of Pure Reason* A33/B49–50). Insofar as rational beings are self-consciously thinking things, they will be aware of the continuing passage of time.

The Kantian intuition of time is given in all experience, but Nietzsche asks what experience the intuition could have come from. Kant and Augustine explain the experience of events as past on the basis of the existence of the inner; Nietzsche identifies the experience of things past as that which came to *give* human beings an experience of the inner.

The History of history.   Descartes's *Meditations* (a book later translated into German as *Betrachtungen*, the same word Nietzsche chose for his title) opens deep inside a mind as it tries to clear out misinformation. (But see Zuckert 55n1 for a non-Cartesian reading of *Betrachtung*.)

Partly in a strategic contrast to Descartes, Nietzsche tells a parable at the start of "History" proper (after its three-paragraph preface):

> Consider the herd grazing before you. These animals do not know what yesterday and today are but leap about, eat, rest, digest and leap again; and so from morning to night and from day to day . . . enthralled by the moment and for that reason neither melancholy nor bored. It is hard for a man to see this, for he is proud of being human and not an animal and yet regards its happiness with envy because he wants nothing other than to live like the an-

imal, neither bored nor in pain, yet wants it in vain because he does not want it like the animal. Man may well ask the animal: why do you not speak to me of your happiness but only look at me? The animal does want to answer and say: because I always immediately forget what I wanted to say—but then it already forgot this answer and remained silent: so that man could only wonder. (1.i)

Philosophy begins in wonder, as it did long ago, not with doubt; but like Cartesian doubt the Nietzschean wonder begins with a reflection on the emergence of the human.

The dangers of the past and the future.   Nietzsche's illustration also directs itself against that Christian conception of time that he finds at work behind scientific history (8.i–ii). The appeal to happy animals evokes the Sermon on the Mount: "Think of the crows that neither sow nor reap nor gather into barns. . . . Think of the lilies how they grow" (Lk. 12.14, 27; cf. Mt. 6.26 ff.).

In the Sermon, as in "History," human thinking suffers by comparison with the relationship to time that natural lives have. The birds and lilies that Jesus tells his hearers to consider are blessed with the heedlessness of Nietzsche's grazing herd, except that—which is some difference—they are said not to heed the *next* day:

> Therefore do not be anxious about tomorrow; for tomorrow will worry about its own; the day's evil is enough for that day. [King James: "Sufficient unto the day is the evil thereof."] (Mt. 6.34)

After all it was concern for the future that initiated all suffering. "Your eyes shall be opened, and ye shall be as gods," the serpent promised Eve and got her thinking ahead (Gen. 3.5). So human beings come closer to the tree of life if they renounce some of their desire for knowledge about the future.

When Nietzsche attributes animals' happiness to their amnesia, he is replying to Scripture that the present day finds itself more aggressively invaded from the past than from the future. If philosophers could only tell themselves an honest story about their lost paradise, they would mark the fall not by punishments directed ahead—

> thou shalt surely die (Gen. 2.17);
> in sorrow thou shalt bring forth children (Gen. 2.16);
> in the sweat of thy face shalt thou eat bread, till thou return unto the ground (Gen 3.19)

but by the more implacable sentences "I remember" (the word unknown to the forgetful animal) and "It was" (a saying not yet learned by the child who "has nothing past [nichts Vergangnes] to deny": 1.ii).

Christianity.   The truth has gone untold, its tale pointed backward, because Christianity suppresses origin stories. Nietzsche blames Christianity for its surreptitious control over modern scholarly history (8.i–iv), also for its silence about its institutional dependence on the Roman Empire (9.vii). Standing by a cover story about the Fall is more of the same hide and seek.

Though it begins in the fullness of time and ends at the Second Coming, Christianity denies temporal movement (8.i). By reifying the future as a fixed place that already exists ("tomorrow will worry about its own"), Christianity has robbed time of its fluidity. It expects a conclusion to history that will retroactively trivialize the cares of the present. The present acquires the flavor of a *foregone conclusion.*

Nietzsche draws the moral about "life and action":

> A religion which, of all the hours of a human life, takes the last one to be the most important, which predicts an end to life on earth as such and condemns the living to live in the fifth act of the tragedy . . . is hostile toward all new planting, bold attempting, free desiring. (8.i)

Time for the Christian is a hand of solitaire played so close to its finish that there are almost no choices left, let alone bold ones. And trusting the biblical promise of only apocalypse ahead, modern history waits; tallies the past's facts.

But what if the apocalypse already happened?

(Nietzsche is a man by a Dead End Ahead sign shouting "Look out behind you!")

No story of history.   Nietzsche turns coy when it comes time to tell a different story. He starts with the appurtenances of parable but then abandons them. And the untellability of the story he's chosen will turn out to reflect its theoretical impossibility.

Consider these animals. They graze, which is to say that they eat without farming, as if in a garden. If Nietzsche had a story to tell, its next episode would bring the herd to the brink of history. One beast moves apart from the others. It remembers. Then it remembers too much—but it's plain enough where a story like that one ought to lead and just as plain that this one will not go there. Rather than continue his parable Nietzsche abandons the concrete setting, abandons his audience, he abandons any pretext of a narrative.

The paragraph opens with a familiar "you," addressing the reader before whom the herd is grazing, as if *you* are now about to see the thoughtless ruminators transformed. Then "you" fade out of Nietzsche's example. He talks about the herd and its pleasures and ease of mind; the next time he mentions an observer it is in the third person, a man ("Mensch") is watching the animals. The transition out of animality is over.

History *has* a beginning; you were about to watch it happen; now you won't.

As Nietzsche's paragraph moves from you to a generalized human, it passes from the occasion for action in an imagined past to action's aftermath in the necessarily imperfect present. There is no tale of how history began, only the observation after the fact that *it must have begun*. Every time people see a herd grazing or a child at play they experience something that they interpret as the memory of a fall. ("It is hard for a man to see this.")

The observation is compromised. The human looks at the animal with mixed feelings, because it still counts for something to be human, only not enough to compensate for the pain and boredom that animals could not even be trained to guess at.

The observers have sunk into such debasement that the sentiment inspired by these apparent memories of a lost Eden ("eines verlornen Paradiesen": 1.ii) has to navigate between the worst of the deadly sins, pride and envy (1.i).

The observation is also *epistemically* compromised. Looking at animals invites the conclusion that there must have been a fall instead of triggering an actual memory. The event in need of being remembered is the birth of memory; to contain *that* event, memory would have to have begun in the time before memory. But once the time before memory is lost it is not available for recollection.

The upshot is a fallen state with no fall that started it. The present feels imperfect, so something else must have happened: end of story. Nietzsche does not look directly at the step into humanness. He can only look past that moment and across a gulf into animality, conjecturing someone's crossing the gulf.

A step must have been taken. Everything went wrong, but in a fictitious moment.

Likewise no story of "life."   If the problem with the origin of history is something missing from the past like an ancient event left untold, the problem with the origin of inwardness lies in the present, whenever the self-consciousness of modernity is thought to arise. It is the question of a persistently recurrent fall to set alongside that of a unique past occurrence, for both begin with memory.

"History" has been speaking of a monistic motive force that it calls "life"; Nietzsche calls inwardness the threat to that force. But how can antilife be possible if life grounds all actions and phenomena? Is inwardness still a sign of "life"? Does "life" indeed account for everything? (See Müller-Lauter 25–26 for a suggestion of questions much like these.)

The problem is that monistic explanations falter as fast as monotheistic ones once they are asked to explain oppositions. If a single God presides over both good and evil, people ask where the evil could have come from. Depending on how you interpret *that* monism, it collapses into either vacuity (everything is good), or dualism (positive evil exists) that embarrasses the monism.

A problem of evil in Descartes. For Descartes the vexing evil is error. If his arguments in the first three *Meditations* ensure that the mind can know truths, how do false beliefs ever happen? The argument ought to imply that one makes no mistakes at all (IV.4).

Glancing back at this problem a second time, Descartes introduces a "new problem" associated with it (VI.16). Even granted that the will ought to confine itself to accepting beliefs only when it understands their truth, he has to explain why false beliefs enter the mind in the first place. How can God's goodness be compatible with the deceptiveness that seems to reside in the mind-body compound (VI.18)?

The existence of inwardness distinct from the body makes it possible for Descartes to answer. Body is divisible, mind is not (VI.19), and the divisibility of the body means that every sensation travels through links before it reaches the brain. Those links can fail: the nerves' signals to the brain are intercepted when the body undergoes trauma or disease. Thus ghost pain in an amputated foot results from damage to the nerve that ought to run from foot to brain. The brain can't tell that the nerve's original terminus did not send the message (VI.22–23), any more than a letter's recipient can tell whether the letter came straight from the return address or stopped along the way.

Because of the essential difference between body and mind, the indivisible mind is not designed to detect the types of mistake that a body falls prey to.

Now suppose you wanted to go beyond Descartes. What frustrates Descartes about the circumstances of his birth (he says) is the quantity of error that his younger self took in. But at least that frustration means that replacing the errors with truths will let him make up for the misfortune of contingent birth.

Suppose that being a philosopher born after Descartes added the fact of his existence to your frustration over having been born when you were. Born after Descartes and (*qua* philosopher) because of him, you register your frustration by casting him aside as a blunder of philosophy's youth.

Does Descartes begin with self-consciousness—"I am thinking the thought about my thinking"—to prove what strikes him as most essential, that he exists? Then you scorn that mere existence. It is no more than an etiolated self-consciousness could demonstrate, but in that respect it's already a symptom of bitted and bridled life. Descartes's starting point becomes the endpoint of a temporal process.

But it was as a starting point that Cartesian self-consciousness showed the way out of a problem of evil. Mind-body dualism left room for error. If inwardness represents no dualism given in reality but is the ingrowth of a single force then it cannot play an explanatory role in accounts of what is better or worse. The Cartesian theodicy fails if inwardness comes into being, because then inwardness does not belong to some order separate from the body.

Meanwhile the problem of evil has not disappeared. The worse status of inwardness itself needs accounting for.

The origins of inwardness. "With baptism in the Dionysian religion of life, the problem of evil is washed away" writes one Nietzsche commentator (Thiele 79). But even if Nietzsche steps free of old snares about moral evil because he can see both "evil" and "good" as signs of "life," he falls into a new snare. The question becomes whether "life" accounts for the inwardness that he calls a threat to life.

Suppose you answer that it does. Sometimes the drive to act is blocked. The stymied motion acts itself out on the inner stage. Just as you feel your fear more intensely when something prevents you from running, so too will you become more conscious of the knowledge you have taken in when it does not stir you to act.

The apparent *opposite* to action, namely the theorist's contemplative abstention from action (an abstention and a mode of contemplation that Nietzsche has identified as a danger to life), is explained in terms of the principle of action. This is how life causes inwardness.

Now "life" looks vacuous. If it accounts for activity and inactivity equally well, there's no point urging the principle of life that is action. Contemplation is one more sign of activity. "Ought" implies nothing.

Moreover Nietzsche was talking nonsense when he called inwardness a *danger*. How can interiority be both one more manifestation of life and a threat to it? If all is the expression of life, then life is always and everywhere enhanced.

For inwardness to endanger life it must derive from some other source. But how can "life" account for a contradictory motive force? If everything is powered by this vitalism, nothing could even come into existence that combats it.

It is not fair to press Nietzsche too hard at this point. He says much less about "life" than he'll say in later books about the will to power, that still problematic proposal for a universal motive force. At the same time it would be misguided to overlook the problem. A structurally similar worry comes up again in *Genealogy* when Nietzsche declares the victory of slave morality even though he has declared the very idea of that victory to be absurd. The problem comes up in *Birth*, when Nietzsche celebrates the Dionysian and Apollinian impulses for having borne and begotten every phase of Greek civilization, and yet also claims that Socrates appeared spontaneously.

Whether the explanatory gaps undermine Nietzsche's philosophy or pose merely apparent obstacles to it, the fact remains that he repeatedly runs into trouble when he has to say where something undesirable could have come from.

Trouble with origins. Nietzsche temporalizes but then temporizes.

Nietzsche temporalizes by introducing history into hosts that had sealed it out. Where the demand for knowledge once enjoyed unquestioning obeisance he asks about its origins. He finds the conditions that gave human beings the inner life that philosophers treat as a given.

And yet the story of history's origin either cannot be told or never does get told. "Life" purports to account for all behaviors, yet Nietzsche warns against its collapse in the face of an inwardness that life both *had to have* caused and *could not have* caused.

History as root. By itself the nondelivery of a story of history does not show that Nietzsche is defensive about origins in general. Maybe he just initiated a project he couldn't finish. Here and there he might contradict himself—that happens.

But Nietzsche's defensiveness about origins turns up in other places too, for instance in the slippery way he applies common metaphors to historical inquiry.

If memory is the ground out of which a culture grows, then the practice of history is the culture's burrowing root that feeds off that memory. So "History" sometimes uses "Wurzel" to denote the nourishing function of history and to acknowledge its naturalness.

Between Jesus and the imperial institutions of Christianity, Nietzsche writes, "there is a very earthly and dark layer . . . from which Christianity drew that earthy taste and bit of soil which made possible its continuation in this world" (9.vii). Even after the Roman Empire disappeared it continued to deposit its effects over Europe, and those effects built up into a rich topsoil of cultural memory on which Christianity draws. When early Christianity practiced its own brand of history it sent a tap root down into those accretions and drew strength from them. Historical practice functioned as a life-sustaining root.

The historical practice that Nietzsche has in mind as Christianity's choice is probably the antiquarian variety. He has already described antiquarian history with self-aware figurativeness:

> To use a somewhat stretched metaphor [or: to speak with some freedom of metaphor, Mit einiger Freiheit des Bildes gesprochen]: the tree feels its roots [Wurzeln] more than it can see them; this feeling . . . measures their size by the size and strength of its visible branches. (3.ii)

The tree's natural organ metaphorically denotes a cultural practice that sustains individuals and their collectives. So it is that Nietzsche can write, again regarding antiquarian history, that its practice in the right context brings people comfort with their own culture, akin to "the contentment of a tree with its roots [Wurzeln], the happiness of knowing oneself not to be wholly arbitrary and accidental, but rather as growing out of a past as its heir, flower and fruit" (3.i). Persons, institutions, whole traditions digest their memory—history is the feeding organ—and turn it into action.

Nietzsche calls the historical basis for an institution its root even in those circumstances in which one finds the institution's life deplorable. When oppressed people need to fight free of unjust governance, they attack with critical history. Then the institution's past "is considered critically, then one puts the knife to its roots [Wurzeln]" (3.v).

Meanwhile Nietzsche also says things like this: "The stronger the roots of the inmost nature of a man are, the more of the past will he appropriate or master" (1.iv). In that sentence the roots antedate the past (a century later insurance companies will use the word "preexisting"). The roots belong to the person's nature, "die innerste Natur." But if roots are nature, the accumulated past that history brings is something else. When nature bequeaths you strong roots you can master historical events, which are therefore *not* natural. "Root" acquires a contrary sense, signifying a natural human power instead of a power that history supplies.

Later Nietzsche reformulates the same opposition: "The historical sense, if it rules without restraint . . . uproots [entwurzelt] the future because it destroys illusions" (7.i). Culture and nature are working at cross-purposes. If the historical sense does the uprooting then it must be *something that kills roots*. The root is now a natural source of power, as the remainder of the paragraph shows: "Each man who is forced no longer to love unconditionally, has had the root of his strength cut off [die Wurzeln seiner Kraft abgeschnitten]" (7.i).

Natural strength has roots; uprooting is what the historical sense does to nature.

Later Nietzsche sets the historical sense squarely against nature. "One knows after all what history is capable of," namely "of uprooting [zu entwurzeln] the strongest instincts of youth" (9.ix).

It is not just that history sometimes roots and sometimes uproots; nor only that the root of life is sometimes a name for the cultural context in which a phenomenon arises, and sometimes a source of natural strength opposed to culture. There is a third implication of Nietzsche's metaphor mixing: a root sometimes digs into the *past* and sometimes into a *perpetually contemporary nature*. The historical sense that weakens life does so by weakening those roots that have no history.

In other words, Nietzsche's vacillation over what to call a root (history or natural strength) betrays an inconsistency in his thinking about a source of "life." Sometimes the source of life lies in the past—the person, the culture, has an origin in time—then suddenly sometimes it does not.

It is as if *having a past*, the thought with which Nietzsche threatened history, felt like a threat to him too. He wants to visualize a source of power that has no history. Against his historical sense a metaphysician's ambition is also hard at work, that expects to find the only real origins not in the lost reaches of time but in the present.

The historian against the solipsist. The three other essays in *Untimely Meditations* begin in Nietzsche's personal motives. Does "History" stand apart spoiling comparisons between this book and Descartes's *Meditations*, that is, as two tangles with solipsism?

Not at all. Nietzsche is writing "History" as a historian and wondering what use or disadvantage *he* will be, for his own life if not for anyone else's. He keeps his essay wound up tight to the high pluck of self-attending self-consciousness. The closing section even permits itself a confession:

> In tracking down the dangers of history we have found ourselves most severely exposed to them . . . and precisely this treatise, as I will not conceal, shows its modern character, the character of weak personality . . . (10.ii)

Throughout "History" and despite his capacity for these looks at himself, Nietzsche sounds like the overbred historian he is—as at the very start of the piece, when he reads the word "moreover" in Goethe and thinks of Cato's call to arms against Carthage.

"Moreover I hate everything . . ." and so on says Goethe in the quote Nietzsche uses to begin his essay. Nietzsche cites Cato's *ceterum censeo* to make sure his readers notice which word he put first. As Cato concluded every speech in the Senate with "Moreover I am of the opinion that Carthage be destroyed" until it was, Goethe is imagined as having tagged his tribute to activity onto every other sentiment he ever expressed.

Nietzsche can quote him no matter what Goethe might have been saying before the "moreover." The problem of pure knowledge has plagued modern culture too long already. The conversation has long been under way.

And Nietzsche has had to carry around the entire tradition that lies behind an act as slight as adding "moreover" to something else you were saying. He came late to the conversation.

To arrive late means to arrive after the beginning. It tortures the late arrival to speak of origins, because starting anywhere other than at the beginning of everything amounts to a weakness or failure. As a partial fantastic defense against his own weakness, Nietzsche identifies himself with preexisting men. He was here before he was even here; and he will outlive himself. The solipsist's first problem is to have come into existence. "What his existence basically is—a never to be completed imperfect tense" (1.ii).

Four Thoughts between Chapters

Disappointments thus far: summary. "History" aims to put historical science in its place; Nietzsche assesses historical discourse as an expedient the human species evolved for digesting the mass of memories it had to consume. From history he turns to knowledge in general, and from knowledge to that unusual self-aware animal that knows.

Ultimately Nietzsche wants to confront modern philosophy's conception of the human. The Cartesian legacy needs to be replaced by a philosophy that dares to speak of living and not merely thinking, a *vivo* argument grounding life instead of the *cogito.*

Nietzsche therefore launches an attack on the mentalism that has dominated philosophy. Where philosophy understands the inner life as an ahistorical given, Nietzsche sketches a history of its birth. Where philosophy interprets time as an effect of the mind's functioning, Nietzschean philosophy makes time and the experiences it contains the cause, mental functioning—self-conscious inwardness—the problematic effect.

But the *Meditations* shadow "History" more tenaciously than Nietzsche expected. His parable about a start to history presents not an event you could call a fall (into history, inwardness, humanity) but only the persistent illusion of the fall's aftermath. And even if the story did arrive at some conclusion, Nietzsche would have to call the outcome—inhibited "life"—impossible, for a problem of evil dogs the Nietzschean *vivo* reminiscent of a problem the *cogito* had faced.

Where does "life" come from, anyway? Where does it draw its strength? It might be natural for Nietzsche to reach for the image of a root as the life-sustaining organ; but he wields the metaphor with anxious inconsistency. Sometimes he conceives the root as a human life's pipeline to the sustenance that culture has to give, while in other moments the root denies culture, connecting to a strength that comes from nature.

Nietzsche's inconsistency means that he cannot decide whether "life" has an eternal and changeless origin or a specific origin in time.

This early in the discussion, any background story for the disappointment has to be loose. There is something about being a latecomer to philosophy that obsesses Nietzsche. He is right to close his essay with a self-criticism about its instantiating the psychic ills it diagnoses, for Nietzsche is highly conscious of the weight of philosophical history that precedes him. He projects himself onto Wagner and Schopenhauer when writing his essays about them; he does not quite manage to project himself onto the history of modern philosophy.

One goal of the coming chapters will be to expand and illuminate this sense one gets from Nietzsche, that he has come along late—contingently, only happening to be born when he was—and can't bear that knowledge.

Disappointment-fact. "The Nietzsche disappointment" taken in the subjective way promises to begin and end with a reader's bad feeling. But like other feeling-words—"care" and "complaint," "expectation"—"disappointment" can describe a condition unaccompanied by feeling. You can care for the sick without caring about them and expect the bus with no sense of expectancy; and disappointment does not have to refer to blocked desire. When Ajax throws his javelin at Hector in Pope's *Iliad* (VII), that wary Trojan "shrinks, and bending low / Beneath his buckler, disappoints the blow"—meaning that he thwarts the blow, not that anyone feels let down.

Most neutrally one might call disappointment the negation of an appointment. One who is appointed is elevated to an office, named to a post. Mail carriers have appointed rounds. The Nietzsche disappointment that is not a Nietzsche-feeling, therefore, begins in his failure to arrive at a meeting.

Chapter 1 describes missed appointments in its claim that Nietzsche sets a standard and does not meet it: that when it comes time for him to deliver the causal story he called for, he balks. Nietzsche says that history needs a history but doesn't give one. Inwardness signifies life gone aberrant, but he describes a "life" whose aberrations there can be no explanation for.

So the disappointment that is an appointment that did not happen concerns Nietzsche's program for a temporalized philosophy and the obstacles that stop him from reaching it.

As with other failures to arrive in an appointed place, one reason for the present disappointment is a failure to leave another place. Nietzsche's inability to achieve untimeliness begins with his attachment to those old haunts, philosophy in general and Cartesian philosophy especially. He scorns philosophy but falls back into a philosophical problem of evil.

If the disappointment-fact comes to look as if it's really there in Nietzsche's books, the discussion will have to continue with some further explanation. One might say for instance: "If Nietzsche had not been straining to outdo his own human limitations he would have served up a more coherent causal account." On such a reading, Nietzsche balks because the thought of causes and origins, like a bitter madeleine, brings him the unwelcome reminder that he occupies one place in history among others. He has been acknowledging his own historical placement but also resenting it.

But so far explaining Nietzsche's missteps has to remain sketchy. For one thing he is writing *about* history in "History," not writing history. He is not likely to leave elaborated historical accounts incomplete in an essay that attempts no elaborate history. Nietzsche's main enactments of history—in *Birth* and *Genealogy*—will offer more opportunities for watching him approach historical explanations and back away again.

Disappointment-feeling. Reading Nietzsche as the disappointment calls for one kind of explanation of his reader's chagrin. Your disappointment lies in his failure to supply a history for history, and you trace the roots of his failure to (for instance) his defensiveness about belonging to one time rather than another.

In general you explain the disappointment-fact by telling why something failed to happen.

But you would also explain the *feeling* of disappointment by telling how someone came to expect what did not happen. You might ask "Why do Nietzsche's writings disappoint?" not as if sitting on the tribunal that judges him, but really wanting to know: Why does it matter so much that Nietzsche did not produce his origin stories?

Could the problem be that you appointed Nietzsche to that same superhuman status he imagines for himself? That would complicate your complicity. What makes his failure bother you so much is also what makes him fail. Fantasizing his own superhumanity Nietzsche evades the causal explanations that his own revaluation of philosophy demands; and as his reader, fantasizing his superhumanity, you fully expect those causal explanations and you take it to heart when they don't arrive. Whence the feeling of disappointment on top of the disappointment-fact.

Divine intervention. The two long chapters ahead cover *Birth* and *Genealogy*. Despite the detail, their tendencies of argument should be clear enough. The subject is always Nietzsche's causal explanations regarding the past and future. The signs of trouble largely remain the same too: groundless assumptions of an ultimate cause; inexplicable falls out of innocence; problems of evil; impossible redemptions on the way.

Do you want to call Nietzsche's conceptual tangles farcical restagings of Christian theology? That is not a bad strategy, but it does call for some investigation of the divinities that appear in his books. If he is secretly writing like a divine then his reader needs to understand what he has to say about divinity.

Accordingly one of the subjects in the coming chapters is divinity. Nietzsche's readers need to approach the topic attentively. Nietzsche proclaimed the death of God but is not what you'd expect from an atheist. He does see how the language of divinity gets abused; on the other hand he does not eliminate that language from his writing. All the important kinds of history seem determined to turn mythic, replete with divine action. Gods will not stay out of the Nietzschean cosmogony: it's as if he insisted on having some relationship to them.

Indeed, something might emerge in the coming chapters about who Nietzsche thinks he is, which very much has to do with what he thinks a god is, and what he thinks gods have to do with him.

Chapter 2 explores how far Nietzsche goes with a sympathetic conception of the divine or the mythical. Where Schopenhauer contented himself with metaphysics Nietzsche determines to retranslate philosophy into mythic language. The translation nets him mythic epochality: he can make tragedy appear out of nothing.

In this respect *Birth* is *meant* as a mythic treatment of tragedy's origins. There is no disappointment because Nietzsche makes no false promises.

Nietzsche temporalizes things as far back as the birth of tragedy. He does not start temporizing until Socrates shows up.

Moreover, Nietzsche's inability to account for Socrates is built into the ambition behind *Birth*. Nietzsche wants to establish his own importance to philosophy's history, comparable to Socrates' importance. Yet Socrates remains the touchstone for Nietzsche's status. The great problem becomes whether to put Socrates back into some mythic era (in which case he could not have been the one to ruin tragedy) or to keep him in the epoch that the present occupies (in which case he dwarfs any present competitor).

The problem of where to put Socrates finds its symbolical representation in the problem of accounting for his birth. Nietzsche evokes gods of unimaginable fertility, but even they cannot have made the baby Socrates.

—◦

The Birth of Tragedy:
The First Philosopher

Abstract. This chapter considers Nietzsche's mythologizing. It asks what *Birth* intends to do with Apollo and Dionysus—which is mainly: to account astonishingly for the astonishment that is tragedy—then passes from gods to that half-god the philosopher Socrates (can he cross over into myth too?), finally to the would-be philosopher, would-be half-god, "who was to be the father of this book" (AS 1).

Philosophy begins by separating itself from myth, or it did in Thales' hands. Meanwhile Nietzsche's career as an author begins, in *Birth*, with his declaration of himself as a philosopher. But his way of making himself a philosopher involves rediscovering the magical motion behind phenomena that myth makes possible and that philosophy had abolished.

This new way of establishing philosophical authority lies behind what could look like the merely illustrative maneuver of attaching gods' names to Schopenhauer's metaphysical categories. And it is in keeping with his mythologization of philosophy that Nietzsche soaks *Birth* in images of impossible fertility. In his hands, the names "Apollo" and "Dionysus" re-create the possibility of an age decisively different from the present.

There is a kernel of truth in calling Nietzsche nostalgic: he sees the past as fundamentally *gone*. Divinely fertile as they are, Apollo and Dionysus underwrite the unrepeatable birth of tragedy. If *Birth* treats births in general mythically, and all the more so the birth of tragedy, the effect is to shield tragedy's origins from the prying eyes of the present.

Nietzsche intentionally provides no causal explanation of tragedy's beginnings: in this respect he stands opposed to Aristotle's account of tragedy with its valorization of the causal relation. Moreover, Nietzsche is speaking as a Dionysian and appeals to Dionysus to separate tragic Greece from the present, to fracture causal accounts by rupturing the temporal continuity they presuppose.

Nietzsche opposes Thales by refusing to connect the tragic age to the present age. Nietzsche's refusal to tell where tragedy comes from is therefore not a failing. He wants to set the two ages apart, the Socratic present from its mythic forebear.

This elaborate exoneration of Nietzsche on the subject of tragedy's beginning does not end the discussion but only sets up another accusation. For his claim of discontinuity between pre-Socratic and post-Socratic, the split coming *at* and *in* and *because of* Socrates introduces the question: *Why Socrates?* And the question of Socrates—his birth, his possibility—both *must* be answered and *can't* be.

It must be answered because the distinct difference between then (tragic age) and now (theoretical age) calls for an explanation and cannot be explained mythically (constituting as it does the end of myth).

But the question of Socrates *cannot* be answered because it leads into a problem of evil, also because for all his efforts Nietzsche keeps deifying Socrates. Socrates is neither Apollinian nor Dionysian, even though the two impulses are supposed to account for all phenomena. They represent the sum of what a mythologized nature can create—so he is not even natural.

Sometimes Nietzsche shows that he feels the problem of a Socratic evil in his effort to escape it: the stratagem of a Socratism before Socrates.

More often his explanation of Socrates is resolute nonexplanation. Echoing Plato's *Symposium*, *Birth* calls Socrates a demon, no ordinary human and possibly a god. And adopting Plato's conception of Socrates only blocks the possibility of his birth all over again. Socrates resembles the god Eros; but how could Eros have been born?—out of what motive?

Nietzsche skirts comparable impossibilities in his own account of Socrates, because of his unstable desire to be another Socrates, *another first philosopher.* To become another Socrates, somewhat as he will be another Zarathustra, Nietzsche both becomes Socrates and repels the possibility of becoming him.

First philosophers.   Where does philosophy come from? What makes someone the first philosopher?

Aristotle credits Thales with initiating natural philosophy (*Metaphysics* 983b20). Five centuries later, Diogenes Laertius calls Thales the first to study astronomy and predict solar eclipses (*Lives of Eminent Philosophers* I.23), the first to specify the sizes of the sun and moon, and the first, "according to some people, to discourse on nature" (I.24).

Presumably it is for all these reasons that Thales was "the first who was named [*ônomasthê*] wise"—that is, the first named among the Seven Sages of antiquity (I.22).

And before Thales? In one Homeric passage, the only lines of cosmogony in either epic, Oceanus is called "the origin [*genesis*] of the gods" (*Iliad* 14.201, 302) and "origin of all" (14.246). Plato (*Cratylus* 402b; *Theaetetus* 152e, 180c–d) heard the metaphysics in that verse; to Aristotle it sounded just like Thales (*Metaphysics* 983b27). (Sallis 2005, a strong influence on this and other sections of the present chapter, looks probingly at the Homeric lines.)

Scholars today press further back to Egyptian and Phoenician antecedents for Thales. For Homer too: this passage so out of place in the *Iliad* bears the marks of foreign sources, from the Babylonian *Enuma Elish* to the Akkadian story of Atraharsis (Burkert 1992, 88–92). But something happens first with Thales. As primitive as "All is water" sounds, it signifies the rejection of stories about Oceanus or Apsu and Tiamat, with their waters out of which the world *was once* made. "Everything *was* water," those stories say; "no longer." (Compare *Genesis* 9.11–15: after the great flood recedes to leave the present world, God promises there will never be another.)

The Thalean pronouncement equates the material conditions and the natural laws of the past with those of the present (Vernant 119–122). Being water makes bodies act according to certain principles now and it always did. The past runs continuously into the present by a series of causal links. Philosophy inherits from Thales his abandonment of mythology and postulation of a continuous time unifying all eras.

If Socrates is sometimes cited as a first in philosophy, he owes that distinction not to disrespect for Thales but to Socrates' also unprecedented insistence that philosophy shift its attention from the universe to the values, words, and deeds of the human species (and treat *those* subjects unmythologically too).

Thus Diogenes calls Socrates the one "who introduced ethics" to philosophy (I.14) and "also the first who reasoned about life and the first philosopher put to death after a trial" (II.20).

Nietzsche as philosopher. "It should have *sung*, this 'new soul'—and not spoken!" Nietzsche says of his younger self in 1886's retrospective preface to *Birth* (AS 3; emphasis in original, as in every quote from Nietzsche).

"What I had to say then, too bad that I did not dare say it as a poet . . . at least as a philologist," as anything instead of a philosopher.

But the new soul that wrote the book in 1872 felt compelled to speak as it did, philosophically. *Birth* seeks to establish Nietzsche as that special breed of man, the philosopher.

Before publishing *Birth* Nietzsche tried to change his affiliation at Basel from philology to philosophy with a letter to Wilhelm Vischer-Bilfinger, applying to the vacated chair in philosophy. Nietzsche considered himself more qualified to teach philosophy than philology, his letter said; "and even in my philological studies I was most attracted by those aspects which seemed important to the history of philosophy or to ethical and esthetic problems" (Middleton 76).

The university rejected Nietzsche's petition. He would have to achieve philosopher's status in a book, for example, in one that did not look like a philologist's book. As the letter to Vischer-Bilfinger promises:

> I shall be able, soon enough, to show publicly my competence for an appointment in philosophy: my published works on Laertius Diogenes are in any case also to be taken into account with regard to my aspirations in the history of philosophy. (Middleton 77)

"Also" is half an apology: Nietzsche does not plan to use his extensive work on Diogenes to demonstrate his philosophical standing. Rather something else he is writing, something he will publish "soon enough," namely *Birth*.

The book seemed to do its work. Once he wrote it, Nietzsche says in retrospect, he had "found the concept of the 'tragic.'" Having discovered *that* concept, "I have the right to understand myself as the first *tragic philosopher*" (*Ecce Homo*, *Birth* 3).

A philosophical forebear.   Nietzsche did have precursors, though. When he discovered one, he wrote giddily to Franz Overbeck.

"And *what* a precursor!"—Spinoza! Both of them obsessed with knowledge, they had evolved along separate lines of growth toward essential shared doctrines.

Nietzsche's letter lists the ideas that he and Spinoza both reject, like teleology, but says nothing about Spinoza's incessant talk of God. Later mentions of Spinoza in his books acknowledge the precursor's shortcomings (Richard Schacht's discussion treats all important references: Schacht 1995, 167–186), yet Nietzsche mentions religion only once, obliquely, with a comment about philosophers' being seen as "sots of God" (*Beyond* 205).

Spinoza had famously been called drunk on God. God fills every page of his *Ethics* as completely as He fills every corner of the Spinozistic universe— even if, as the title character observes in Malamud's *Fixer*, this God takes up so much more space than the shtetl's God, and yet that one runs around with both hands full and the Spinozistic one doesn't do much of anything.

The difference between the two Gods explains why Nietzsche should not mind Spinoza's apparent religiosity. Spinoza's God shares barely more than a name with the one who hurries around the shtetl. Nietzsche tells Overbeck that he and Spinoza both deny "free will, purposes, the moral world order, the nonegoistical, evil" (Middleton 177)—all of which rules out a traditional God but squares perfectly with this new philosophical being.

If you can't imagine praying to the being whose existence is compatible with determinism and with a world lacking moral order, so much the better. Spinoza says as much about God as he does specifically to draw your attention away from the God that religions have dreamt up and toward an intelligible surrogate.

Spinoza would say he is merely preserving what makes sense in religions' ideas of God, maybe as Newton would claim to find the meaningful core in pre-Newtonian conceptions of mass and force. Whatever the plan was, it issued in a God without a religion to live in. Such a God is neither the misinterpretation of phenomena (see *Gay Science* 151), because Spinoza's God comprises and does not replace the natural explanation for a natural event, nor the projection of human resentments (*Genealogy* II.20), inasmuch as the philosophical God stays out of moral discourse. Such a God evades Nietzsche's criticisms of religion.

Nietzsche might prefer to call this entity life, possibly the will to power. But he can accept the terminological distance between himself and Spinoza as one of those differences "of period, culture, field of knowledge" that his letter makes allowances for.

"There are gods here too."   The last philosopher Nietzsche was to surrender as a precursor (*Ecce Homo*, Birth 3) is said to have welcomed strangers into his kitchen—they had come to visit the great Heraclitus but found him warming himself at the furnace and hesitated—with the words, "There are gods here too" (Aristotle, *Parts of Animals* I.5, 645a17–21).

The principles Heraclitus finds in nature, especially the fiery principles, will turn up in a kitchen as easily as anywhere else. (Skowron 29–34, the section "Zarathustra und Heraklit," is useful here.) So too the artistic impulses of *Birth*.

Nietzsche's gods belong in the past.   It might amuse Spinoza's pious readers to witness so many gulps of God's name by a philosopher who wants to swear off God. They may take the irony to consist in Spinoza's dogged chase after atheism when his mind remained on God. But he is no would-be unbeliever who keeps God in his heart; Spinoza speaks of God as a service to atheism. He cannily dispenses that name "God" for an unbeliever's purposes, and Nietzsche saw the difference.

Nietzsche's own talk of God should be read even more cannily. Paul Tillich interprets the "Ugliest Man" section of *Zarathustra* as evidence that Nietzsche feels haunted by God (Tillich), making the argument too easy for himself by miles—almost as easy as Billy Graham had been on *himself*:

> Nietzsche was a deep thinker, and when Nietzsche said, "God is dead" . . . it was a tragedy to him, and the last 12 years of his life he spent in a mental institution (Graham)

and yet Tillich and Graham hear something in Nietzsche's writings. (See David Booth for a full discussion of theology and Nietzsche; for the remarkable history of attempts to reclaim Nietzschean insights for the "revitalization" of Christianity, see Steven Aschheim.) Atheism hardly needs champions in the 1880s: so why does Nietzsche belabor the point? And why does he wield more religious language than any freethinker of his time would know, let alone deign to use?

"The 'father' in God has been thoroughly refuted," says *Beyond* 53 (as if that's what you do with fathers, refute them). A remark like that sounds dogmatic to religious readers, but it must also seem otiose to a freethinker.

In later books when the God that haunts him is the Christians', Nietzsche's understanding of divinity blurs into his moral and historical assessment of Christianity. Those are the wrong books to bear in mind when reading *Birth*, lest the Bible-thumping sacrilege that Nietzsche is famous for overshadow the early book's willingness to venerate. *Birth* is a very different book from "later Nietzsche," liberated from his antitheism by its focus on the pre-Christian past.

Ecce Homo is wrong to call *Birth*'s absence of comment about Christianity a "hostile silence" (*Ecce Homo, Birth* 1), in fact that willful misreading takes argument-from-silence into wild new territory. The only religion at stake in *Birth* has seen no serious worship in twenty lifetimes. People are not about to pray to Dionysus, and Nietzsche has no qualms about the political or psychological effect if they did. No nasty asceticism here, for example. So he can look straight at the divine as such.

Perhaps for this reason, when Nietzsche came back to write a new preface to *Birth* in 1886 he spoke freely of the gods that his youthful enthusiasm had evoked. "The disciple of a still 'unknown God,'" he calls his twenty-six-year-old self (AS 3), "one 'who knows' is talking, the initiate and disciple of his god" (AS 4). For that young author the meaning behind all phenomena is "a 'god,' if you please, but certainly only an entirely reckless and amoral artist-god" (AS 5).

The divine is worth speaking of as long as it looks different enough from the divine as widely known.

Spinoza may talk about God because everyone else does. Nietzsche talks about gods because no one else does. They already differ in a way he will later acknowledge, that Spinoza tries to compel his readers' agreement while Nietzsche confronts his readers with disagreeabilities (*Beyond* 5).

Nietzsche's talk of gods, contra Schopenhauer.   Schopenhauer sets the terms for *Birth*'s aesthetic theory—the undifferentiated driving will; the effulgent variegation of appearance—and shows Nietzsche how to explain art with them. And up to a point Nietzsche happily plays the disciple. Aesthetics properly began with Schopenhauer's contrast between music and the other arts. Music, the imprint of will, belongs in a category distinct from the other arts, which address themselves to the phenomenal realm. "This most important insight of aesthetics" (16)—that's the thing a camp-following kind of student says preparatory to extending the master's theory into a new domain.

Even so, *Birth* does more than deliver the Schopenhauerian news. If anything, Nietzsche understates the differences between Schopenhauer's account of art and his own account of the Greek art of tragedy.

First of all, Schopenhauer uses the distinction between phenomena and noumena to hold two art forms apart. He does not let the two metaphysical realms run together, and therefore not the arts that copy them. *Birth* assumes the interplay of both forms of art in tragedy. Although the summary that begins 16 speaks of "two worlds of art differing in their intrinsic essence and in their highest aims," it will also ask—and sweat to make Schopenhauer answer—

what aesthetic effect results when the essentially separate art-forces, the Apollinian and the Dionysian, enter into simultaneous activity? (16)

The question does not apply naturally to Schopenhauer who said nothing of Dionysus or Apollo. He achieved his aesthetic insights "even without this clue to the symbolism of the Hellenic divinities" (16).

The "even without this clue" sounds modest, Nietzsche playing down his own contribution—as if the gods' names accomplish no more than Nabokov thought Freud's plentiful references to Narcissus and Oedipus accomplished for *his* theories.

Even if Nietzsche has a gift for the apposite apotheosis, still, just as young boys who desire their mothers don't have to hail from Corinth or answer riddles, the natural artistic impulses share no more than names with their mythic analogues. Schopenhauer said all that needed to be said. Nietzsche came along to label things.

But Nietzsche's phrase does not have to sound as ingratiating as that reading would have it. Suppose it mattered to the substance of Schopenhauer's aesthetic theory that he forbore finding divine names for those propensities to seek out appearances and the will. Then lacking the name-symbolism represents a failure on Schopenhauer's part.

One thing a name suggests is the possibility of action. A story, even. Schopenhauer's terms of art have no story to move around in; they stay apart, identified against each other and occupying incommensurable metaphysical spaces. The intellect that moves among appearances is prohibited by definition from glimpsing the will behind those appearances. The "Apollinian" (whether called that or not) and the "Dionysian" (ditto) remain in distinct realms.

Now, Schopenhauer's own accounts of the will betray his impatience with the very impediments to thinking he set up himself. John Sallis's *Crossings* finds passages in *Birth* that differentiate Nietzsche from Schopenhauer in this respect.

> For what Nietzsche recognized . . . was how readily and how frequently Schopenhauer crosses and recrosses the boundary, in principle uncrossable, between phenomena and thing-in-itself. (Sallis 1991, 22)

Schopenhauer wants the two worlds to remain ignorant of each other but he cannot sustain the separation. Still he does not contemplate a biological crossing. What if the dreamer's impulse to linger over phenomena and the drunk's impulse to plunge into noumenal insight were to meet and mate and spawn? That is no way to think about realms of being, the commonest way in the world to think about creatures with names.

Miracles. Nietzsche sometimes falls into Schopenhauerian language, positing "tendencies" that generate art (1) or "artistic energies which burst forth from nature herself" (2). He always comes back around to Apollo and Dionysus as mythical personages.

How much does it matter? Phrases like "the ghost of a chance" and "come hell or high water" do not bespeak trust in the supernatural. Nietzsche's Apollo and Dionysus might just be naturalized surrogates for the beings of Greek religion, as Spinoza's God substitutes natural laws for the Being of modern monotheism. "Influenced by Schopenhauer, Nietzsche employed Dionysus as a symbol of the metaphysical will" (Barrack 116); the names merely abbreviate complex natural processes. (Also see Henrichs who comes to very different conclusions, but whose survey of Nietzsche on polytheism is indispensable reading.)

When Nietzsche says "Apollo" or "Dionysus" does he mean something more than Spinoza meant saying "God"?

First of all, there is the significant difference that God is the most transparent name possible for a god, while the Greek gods' names have incomprehensible meanings. Even by comparison with their close counterparts in Roman and Babylonian pantheons, "the names of the Greek gods are almost all impenetrable," as Walter Burkert says in *Greek Religion*. Those gods accordingly "are persons, not abstractions, ideas, or concepts" (Burkert 1985, 182).

That is to say that Nietzsche is drawing on a religious tradition whose deities least reduce to natural powers. They are singularities.

Apollo and Dionysus also mean more in Nietzsche's hands than "God" does in the *Ethics*—Nietzsche does more with divinity than Spinoza does—if "more" means something beyond nature, a miracle. Nietzsche un-Spinozistically begins the first section of *Birth* with an appeal to the miraculous:

> by a metaphysical miracle [Wunderakt] of the Hellenic "will" [the Apollinian and Dionysian] appear coupled with each other, and through this coupling ultimately generate an equally Dionysian and Apollinian form of art—Attic tragedy. (1)

Curiously enough this end-of-sentence belongs not to *Birth* as it originally appeared (1871) but to the almost indistinguishable 1874 version. The two sentences are the same until the words just quoted; the original version ends:

> eventually, at the moment of the flowering of the Hellenic "will," [the Apollinian and Dionysian] appear fused to generate together the art form of Attic tragedy.

One of Nietzsche's few emendations of *Birth* replaces mere "flowering" in its opening paragraph with a miracle, as if to say: This is why I speak of gods.

Schopenhauer's will might not perform miracles but the Hellenic "will" did. Put its name in quotation marks to signal the difference. Nietzsche's embrace of supernaturalizing language, as emphatic as the denial of that language in Thales, makes the art of the deep past a leap beyond what naturalistic theories of the present can account for.

In the same supernaturalizing spirit *Birth* pronounces it "blasphemy" to call tragedy's chorus an image of ancient democracy (7). The metaphysical miracle of Attic tragedy is not to be pawed by hands messed with modern politics. "The chorus of the Oceanides really believes that it sees before it the Titan Prometheus" (7). "In this magic transformation [Verzauberung] the Dionysian reveler sees himself as a satyr, *and as a satyr, in turn, he sees the god*" (8).

If the Dionysian sight and a place in the chorus are no longer available, at least Nietzsche will not douse tragedy with the desacralizing waters of explanation. His task is not to accommodate ancient magic to modern secularism. If anything, the hortatory closing sentences of 20 yearn for the conditions under which modern Germans might hope to become satyrs themselves, the secular yielding that ground it had gained with Thales:

> Yes, my friends, believe with me in Dionysian life and the rebirth of tragedy.
> . . . Prepare yourselves for hard strife, but believe in the miracles [die Wunder] of your god.

The new philosophy begins with these "Wunder."

Religious nostalgia. Now and then Nietzsche's turn to myth reaches an extreme in which he seems in need of being reminded that the gods do not exist. He drops even the gentle ribbing that he gives the Greeks ("presumptuous little people": 15) in favor of what sounds like nostalgia.

Most recently it was Jürgen Habermas who imputed a nostalgic impulse to Nietzsche and a longing for lost authenticity:

> What is *older* is *earlier* in the generational chain and nearer to the origin. The *more primordial* is considered the more worthy of honor, the preferable, the more unspoiled, the purer. (Habermas 126)

For proffering this interpretation, Habermas found himself reproached on all sides (e.g., by Alexander Nehamas 1996 and Tracy Strong 1996; Strong 1988 more generally criticizes the idea of "going back to the Greeks"). Nehamas adduces evidence in Nietzsche to indicate that he does not believe in any original and better state to be returned to; that even the concept of "decline" does not grow naturally in the soil of Nietzsche's thought. He observes regarding *Birth* that "Greek tragic culture . . . was itself, as [Nietzsche] well knows, a late development" (Nehamas 1996, 229). He cites *Philosophy in the Tragic Age of the Greeks*, written in the same period, which equates the early with the crude and uncouth; also *Daybreak* 44: "The more insight we possess into an origin the less significant does the origin appear."

Given the temptation to see Nietzsche as a nostalgist, it is important to reflect upon the passages Nehamas cites, also upon one he does not cite from *Beyond*, in which Nietzsche finds a hidden nostalgia in skeptical thinkers' attack on "appearance."

> The main thing about them is not that they wish to go "back," but that they wish to get—away. A little more strength, flight, courage, and artistic power, and they would want to *rise*—not return! (*Beyond* 10)

Given a bit more strength, the skeptics would not have plumped for the same old nostalgia.

On the other hand as this passage also says, the skeptics' nostalgic impulse deserves some respect for having recognized the failure in modernity.

The word "nostalgia" looks Greek but isn't really. Johannes Hofer coined it in Basel in 1678, cobbling together Greek words for "return home" and "pain" to describe the depression that comes of living in a foreign place. The malady had been observed before Hofer, among Swiss mercenaries stationed abroad; in the eighteenth century it was sometimes referred to as "the Swiss disease" (see Rosen, Werman). That much is straightforward; but the etymology within the word's etymology suggests a contradiction. *Nostos*, "the return home," derives from *neomai*, which can mean something as neutral as "to go" but as early as Homer carries the implication of going *back*; so that *nostos*, though it technically could refer to reaching a place for the first time (*Odyssey* 5.344), quickly took on the narrower meaning of retracing steps.

When "nostalgia" acquired its dominant sense of painful longing for the past, it embroidered its contradictoriness on its sleeve. Unlike Switzerland, the past has to cease to exist before it becomes the object of longing. In fact its disappearance has to be final: nostalgia aims at what distinguishes the past from the present. Does it falsify the past? Most ways of remembering do. The falsifications of nostalgia stand out by heightening the differences between present and past.

The contradiction in nostalgia therefore derives from its simultaneously separating past and present and imagining a path between past and present on which steps get retraced. But in that case *Beyond* 10 reminds you of the insight in nostalgia. The present does not resemble the past. Something happened. This may be why Nietzsche's writings court nostalgia even if—rejecting any continuum from past to present—they do not endorse it.

The legacy of Thales, who equated all epochs to the point of predicting eclipses of Apollo (the sun), will call for special attention with respect to the subject of tragedy's life and death. For now it is enough to notice that nostalgic fantasies of return—continuity between past and present—coexist with the pain born of recognizing discontinuity; to notice that the pain seems to underwrite Nietzsche's conscious plan of whipping up nostalgic temptations, whatever his hidden motives may also be for dangling the Greek world before his readers as vividly as a dieter reviews, with juicy mouth, the recipe for cheesecake.

One thing that makes pre-Socratic Greeks Nietzsche's cheesecake—he will settle for looking at them but he does insist on having that look—is their relationship to their own gods. To believe that such gods existed would warrant the impossible trip into the past if anything did.

In its final section *Birth* expresses nostalgia as clearly as any words can, the two concluding paragraphs playing out a fantasy of time travel:

That [the return of Apollo to modern art] should be necessary, everybody should be able to feel . . . provided he has ever felt, if only in a dream, that he was carried back into an ancient Greek existence.

The dream goes on. Nietzsche's traveler takes in the Apollinian self-control, harmony, the rhythm of the Ionic marketplace—Greece as reconstructed in nineteenth-century Europe's histories—and remarks on the power that Dionysus must have possessed to be able to call forth such extreme counterformations.

Modern Europe needed Nietzsche to make this remark about the Apollinian Greece of historical "memory," namely that it masked and tensed itself against a Dionysian Greece. Nietzsche gives himself the credit for rediscovering Dionysus (*Ecce Homo*, *Birth* 1). So he is the first time traveler.

In the daydreamed past an old Athenian might remind the "curious stranger" that suffering underlay the beauty. "But now follow me to witness a tragedy, and sacrifice with me in the temple of both deities!" The book's final words luxuriate in the fantasy of a past in which Apollo and Dionysus live an existence that is more than metaphorical personification.

Doubling the move of identification that he found in the tragic chorus, Nietzsche imagines himself transposed into a past where he will witness those semisatyrs, the everyday people of antiquity who seemed to have been able to witness the gods.

It is more fantasy nostalgia than nostalgic fantasy: Nietzsche allows himself only to fantasize about the act of fantasizing that Dionysus and Apollo exist. And yet he does close this section with a sacrifice to deities; he does call the Dionysian "eternal [ewig]" and "foundation of all existence"; does name a "law of eternal justice" that equalizes Dionysian and Apollinian powers; speaks twice of the "magic [Zauber]" of those impulses.

Art is a miracle even when natural impulses have made it.

Divine fathers.   Apollo and Dionysus possess more miraculous power than garden-variety gods. Notorious begetters, they bring tragedy to life. Art forms spring up wherever Apollo and Dionysus embraced—and more than art. The two of them explain the frieze of the Parthenon but also the freeze of Spartan civil society (4). Every mental state that goes beyond the ordinary owes its power to these gods who undergo "new births ever following and mutually augmenting one another" (4).

The male gods of Greece could boast a 100 percent success record as studs—"every act has issue" (Burkert 1985, 183)—but the ability of Dionysus and Apollo to impregnate one another surpasses even that sexual fantasy.

The more divinely Nietzsche portrays Apollo and Dionysus the more phenomena they account for. When you refute "the father" in God you deny yourself an explanatory principle of unequaled range. So Nietzsche glorifies the gods of art with new powers, in particular with remarkable generative powers. They "incite each other to new and more powerful births" (1).

Indeed Nietzsche attributes the entire classical pantheon to Apollo.

> We must not be misled by the fact that Apollo stands side by side with the others as an individual deity. . . . For the same impulse that embodied itself in Apollo gave birth to this entire Olympian world, and in this sense Apollo is its father. (3)

What could mislead is the story of Apollo's birth that puts him into the divine family and side by side with the others. Apollo was Zeus's son by Leto, and the third Homeric Hymn tells of the vulnerability in which he was born. Fearing Hera's retribution, every spot on earth denied Leto a place to give birth; then the goddess of childbearing would not come to relieve her birth pangs. For nine days Apollo could not be born, finally managing to only on a technicality.

None of this happens in Nietzsche's story. In the Homeric Hymn the new-born infant god declares that he will declare the will of his father Zeus to men; in *Birth* he becomes Zeus's father.

Dionysus's origin makes his existence even more improbable. Hera deceives the pregnant Semele into asking Zeus to appear before her in undisguised form. The sight reduces her to ashes; Zeus scoops up the imperishable divine fetus, sews it into his own thigh, and in time gives birth to Dionysus. The maternal childbearing that was almost subverted in Apollo's case finds itself altogether replaced in this story. Like his half-brother Apollo, Dionysus almost did not come into existence, by rights should *not* have.

But near-death stories of Dionysus take other forms too, and Nietzsche prefers to invoke

> the suffering Dionysus of the Mysteries . . . of whom wonderful myths tell that as a boy he was torn to pieces by the Titans and now is worshiped in this state as Zagreus. . . . From the smile of this Dionysus sprang the Olympian gods, from his tears sprang man. (10)

On Nietzsche's favored account Dionysus too has sired the Olympians, including (again) his own father. If his association with Apollo has spawned every phase in art's development, "just as procreation depends on the duality of the sexes, involving perpetual strife with only periodically intervening reconciliations" (1), then theirs is an unpredictably fertile coupling: two male gods, half-brothers at their most distantly related, at their closest the same person (is this why Nietzsche sometimes says tragedy was "born from" the Dionysian?: AS 1), the magical son who sires his own father.

Impossible fertility. Prodigious fertility turns up elsewhere in *Birth* as well. It is only half observant to notice the book's metaphors of reproduction without also noticing how often the births it speaks of are magically impossible—"logically impossible," one might object if reading a philosopher more known for logical scruples.

The choral parts of tragedy are "the womb that gave birth to the . . . dialogue" (8). Nature has a "lost son, man" (1).

Birth is magically impossible in another way when Nietzsche forces a metaphor of sexual reproduction only to snatch the sex out of it. Thus non-Greek celebrations of Dionysus "centered in extravagant licentiousness" against which the Greeks shielded themselves (2). So, in a reduplicated *ex nihilo*, the vegetation god comes to represent reproduction without the sexuality that naturally accompanies reproduction; and the Greek version of the god takes on a wholly new form in this essentially original culture.

In the mortal realm, Wagner's superlative paternity finds explicit and impossible form in *Birth*'s original preface, which builds to Nietzsche's description of himself:

> as he [Nietzsche] hatched these ideas, he was communicating with you [Wagner] as if you were present, and hence could write down only what was in keeping with that presence. (PW)

Nietzsche hatched this book. (Which might explain why his teacher Friedrich Ritschl wrote in his journal on February 2, 1872: "To N about his *Birth of Tragedy*: conceived by Mamma.") Wagner fertilized him "as if" present, so perfectly even at a distance that Nietzsche couldn't add anything of his own to the birth.

Such paternity claims make a difference—for see how they can be withdrawn. In the "Attempt at a Self-Criticism" Nietzsche speaks of that earlier version of him "who was to be the father of this book" (AS 1): no more credit to Wagner. Shortly thereafter *The Case of Wagner* will remark in its own preface, "I am, no less than Wagner, a child of this time." Two children, neither one the other's father. And Nietzsche's identification with the Wagner of *Birth*—

> A psychologist might still add that what I heard as a young man listening to Wagnerian music really had nothing to do with Wagner; that when I described Dionysian music I described what *I* had heard (*Ecce Homo*, *Birth* 4)

repeats the solipsism with which Nietzsche looked back on the *Untimely Meditations* but also lets him move into the place of *Birth*'s father that had been occupied by Wagner.

In still other passages, reproduction becomes so extravagantly impossible it is hard to derive any coherent statement from *Birth*'s words. Logical impossibility is implied by Nietzsche's "explanation" of the Oedipus story by means of the Persian superstition that "a wise magus can be born only from incest" (9). That hysteron-proteron explanation not only puts Oedipus's incest before his answer to the Sphinx, when his answer made the incest possible, but also turns him into the product of the incest he committed. To be born of incest and condemned for initiating *that same incest*: that is a fate fit for a god, for instance the kind of god who fathers himself.

Hysteron-proteron. Literally "latter-former": the latter presented as the former.

In rhetoric, a species of anastrophe or reversal of elements in which what follows temporally is put in the place of what precedes it. The Christian words of institution "Take, eat, this is my body" (Mt 26.26; Mk 14.22) are traditionally considered an example of hysteron-proteron. More broadly speaking, a hysteron-proteron is any arrangement of ideas in the opposite of their natural or temporal order.

The birth of tragedy. Nietzsche hides a sleight of hand behind his title. The real news about tragedy in *Birth* is the news not of its beginnings but of its death and incipient rebirth.

The gods may have brought tragedy to life, but the wisdom of Silenus teaches that the best fate for a thing already born is "to die soon" (3).

If tragedy was the first poetic genre to be tried and put to death, and if its trial was prosecuted by a historical figure called Socrates, then you'd have to say that Nietzsche makes the death of tragedy a historical event.

Its rebirth becomes historical too, because the rebirth of tragedy will bear some relationship to Wagner. And whatever historical reality Socrates may have, Wagner has incomparably more of: he lives not in the absent past but in Switzerland. Tragedy's resurrection will be an event as much as its death was, an event belonging in history and in a causal sequence.

In other words, the causal narrative that Nietzsche has to offer begins *in medias res* with tragedy, watches tragedy die, and anticipates its return. "We have sought to make clear," at *Birth*'s turning point, "how just as tragedy perishes with the evanescence of the spirit of music, it is only from this spirit that it can be reborn" (16).

The manner of news that Nietzsche's bringing about the birth of tragedy is therefore very different from his news of its death and rebirth. He accepts on Aristotle's authority that tragedy began with the chorus (7) but denies that anyone understands this obscure fact. He offers his own reading of the chorus as a transfigured crowd that sees Dionysus (8). This bewitched transformation of the chorus, a "metamorphosis" into another metaphysical status, describes no events that Nietzsche has unearthed.

In short, *Nietzsche has nothing to say about when and where tragedy came into being.* His claim to philosophical authority rests on having discovered a new interpretation of the known facts. That interpretation claims a new ground or condition for the possibility of tragedy.

But where the ground for tragedy is a mythic ground, tragedy's "birth" does not mean any historical event.

Out of the spirit of music.   In 1886, Nietzsche presents his first book a second time, covering the unsold copies with the "Attempt at a Self-Criticism" but also with a new title page:

The Birth of Tragedy
or
Hellenism and Pessimism

replacing the original

The Birth of Tragedy
Out of the Spirit of Music.

Ecce Homo calls the new subtitle "less ambiguous." "Hellenism and Pessimism" would even have made a better title for the book (*Ecce Homo, Birth* 1). People kept misremembering the old title as saying not "birth" but "re-birth." Is that because being born of the Spirit suggests being reborn (Jn. 3.5)—which Nietzsche seems to have been contemplating in section 16?

Or is the problem that, spirits being the kinds of things they are, the spirit of music is the same now as it ever was? In that case a spirit that gave birth to tragedy once should always be prepared to do so again. Spirit becomes an eternal origin for tragedy, as much the cause of rebirth as of birth.

(Perhaps spirit's suggestion of the abstract and changeless explains Nietzsche's eruption to Lou Salomé: "What is *Geist* to me? . . . I value nothing but impulses": Middleton 189. If impulses are causes of motion, what he wants to shake off about the spirit is its immobility.)

Ecce Homo thinks the new subtitle will draw the reader to learn "how the Greeks got over their pessimism, how they *overcame* it" (*Ecce Homo, Birth* 1). The Greek nature embattled against an aspect of itself: a tangle of two natures out of which tragic culture emerges: this sedentary "and" that you might use in describing a married couple, therefore an abbreviation for the Greeks' struggle to live with their pessimism.

But the coupling of ponderous abstractions is not likely to read that way. However Nietzsche parses "Hellenism and Pessimism," it seems to denote a static condition of Greek antiquity. Nietzsche wants to specify a time for the birth of tragedy but it keeps sliding back into eternity.

The move to mythic activity.   To establish his philosophical credentials, Nietzsche speaks from both inside and outside Schopenhauer's metaphysics. He takes over the dualism but also mythologizes it into agents of poetic creation. In this mythologizing, both aspects of the disappointing double movement happen at once.

Temporalization. Rather than speak of art in the conceptual language of will and appearance Nietzsche recounts a species of art history in the language of Dionysus and Apollo. Myth makes natural principles actors in a story.

Temporizing. As soon as Nietzsche raises the question of tragedy's parentage he begins to blur his answer. The gods brought movement to the discussion of art, but their marvelousness makes it a sudden movement, not the type covered by causal explanation. And no wonder: miracles violate the laws of nature.

Gods move, so there are sequence and order in Nietzsche's account; they move in mysterious ways, so the order can't be explained.

Supernatural birth resembles a natural process governed by causal principles, but only in the sense that a drunken rant resembles closely reasoned argument (the resemblance of caricature).

So Nietzsche withdraws his explanations in the act of demanding them. Where does tragedy come from? Tell the story in a way that makes its origin a mythic event. Answer: Tragedy is a miracle.

Not an objection to Nietzsche.   The mythic order of things that Nietzsche imports into tragedy's history is intentionally an order uncongenial to causal coherence.

The gods' metaphysical remove from nature is an emblem of their remove from the nature of the present. A past in which tragedy could live cannot be explained by, or explained to, an untragic present.

"So there's no double movement in this book and no disappointment?"

But *Birth* is a book about more than tragedy. The time to see what *Birth* did not say and *should have said* will be after the book elucidates its conception of causality.

Philosophy without causality.   Kant posited the causal relation as one of twelve categories of the understanding (*Critique of Pure Reason* A80/B106). Abandoning the other eleven, Schopenhauer retained only causation as a principle by which reason organizes phenomena.

In Kant the causal connection almost immediately showed up a contradiction between his attempt to find order among phenomena and his transcendental attempt to differentiate those phenomena from things in themselves. If causation only makes sense within human experience, it cannot explain how a thing-in-itself stands outside that same experience and yet gives rise to it. Jacobi (*David Hume über den Glauben*) and Schulze (*Aenesidemus*) pointed out that contradiction in Kant's lifetime.

Translating Schopenhauer's metaphysics into mythical language may have been Nietzsche's strategy for telling a story of tragedy without causality. But this is not to say that Nietzsche has no justification for his omission of causal explanation, not even to say that he leaves his reasons unstated.

In the first place a denial of causality lies at the heart of Nietzsche's critique of Aristotle, the first author of a philosophical work on tragedy.

More fundamentally, the quest for causal sequences is un-Dionysian. As the first tragic philosopher Nietzsche wants to reintroduce the Dionysian spirit into a philosophical tradition that began by expunging it.

Above all Nietzsche insists on the fissure that separates the tragic age from the present. No ordinary nativity story of tragedy will be possible in a time that lacks tragedy. Causal accounts given today can only encourage the nostalgic fantasy of a continuum between tragic past and Socratic present.

Nietzsche criticizes the Aristotelian conception of tragedy.   *Birth* mentions Aristotle rarely but every reference is negative. Nietzsche either rejects every Aristotelian teaching about tragedy or twists it beyond recognition.

Mimesis, for instance: Nietzsche acknowledges that tragedy contained an element corresponding to what ancient aesthetics called its "imitation of nature" (2); he only denies that that element consists in representing objects. His denial sounds self-contradictory. The definition of mimesis has always implied some tie between the object being depicted and its depiction. But that definition, common to Aristotle and Plato, already degrades the artistic image. Even on the most favorable accounts, mimesis offers the image the left-handed compliment that it reminds the viewer of something else.

For Nietzsche, the image does not represent an artist's intent to duplicate something outside the art, but a blind compulsion to go on dreaming.

> If we conceive of our empirical reality . . . as a . . . representation of the primal unity, we shall then have to look upon the dream as a *mere appearance of mere appearance*, hence as a still higher appeasement of the primordial desire for mere appearance. And that is why the innermost heart of nature feels that ineffable joy in the naive artist and the naive work of art, which is likewise only "mere appearance of mere appearance." (4)

That phrase that Nietzsche emphasizes, "appearance of appearance," misstates the Platonic "imitation of appearance" (*Republic* 598b), a phrase usually misstated the opposite way as the imitation of imitation.

Nietzsche's version hails as a virtue every value that Plato had made an insult. For Nietzsche an image brings delight regardless of what it refers to, in the same way that the joy of dreams derives not from their relationship to the objects of dreams but from their sufficiency in gratifying the dreamer. The "mimetic" image is something easy on the eyes—not because it's true but because it is not, inasmuch as real objects have their murky parts and complexities.

Aristotle takes the pleasure of images to inhere in someone's reaction that "this is so-and-so" (*Poetics* 1448b17). This really looks like that dog in your yard.

Nietzsche imagines an audience for images more like the man in the joke who is looking for his keys under a streetlight. Asked where he dropped them, he points to the gloom across the street. "So why are you looking for them here?" "The light is better."

Nietzsche may settle for distorting the idea of mimesis. He has no use at all for Aristotle's claim of a moral dimension to tragedy. He reports incredulously that

> the serious events are supposed to prompt pity and fear to discharge themselves in a way that relieves us [zu einer eleichternden Entladung, literally to a relieving explosion or unloading]; now we are supposed to feel elevated and inspired by the triumph of good and noble principles, at the sacrifice of the hero in the interest of a moral vision of the universe. (22)

Which strikes Nietzsche as not only false but also a distraction from tragedy's artistry, and for that reason pernicious.

Thanks to Aristotle's influence, no descriptions of the tragic effect do justice to "aesthetic states" or to "an aesthetic activity of the listener" (22). Instead philologists debate whether catharsis ("the pathological discharge") "should be included among medical or moral phenomena." Nietzsche's comment:

> I am sure that for countless men precisely this, and only this, is the effect of tragedy, but it plainly follows that all these men, together with their interpreting aestheticians, have had no experience of tragedy as a supreme *art*. (22)

Treating tragedy as an art brings the revelation that its outcome is not catharsis, whose power assumes that the tragedy resolves itself in misery, but the "metaphysical comfort" of the message that life is eternal, "indestructibly powerful and pleasurable," "flows on indestructibly" (7, 8, 18).

In common language, treating a subject *as an art* can mean removing it from the realm of ordinary desires—desexualizing it, even. Nietzsche never endorses a doctrine of aesthetic disinterest, and yet something like disinterest, some prudishness, enters *Birth* when he opposes art to catharsis. A "pathological discharge [pathologische Entladung]" (22), an explosion, unloading, that some experts treat medically and others moralize about—this is what no one acknowledges the art of. He could be talking about orgasm—more to the point, orgasm looks like Nietzsche's only way of talking about catharsis.

Aristotle may have bequeathed his readers the true story of tragedy's origins, but his biologist's imagination only knows one way of picturing reproduction and birth.

(It should be noted here that other interpreters have worked out much different contexts for understanding Nietzsche's opposition to Aristotle—e.g., Peter Yates, who sees "the arch-propositionalist" in Aristotle as Nietzsche's paramount target: Yates 76–77.)

Aristotle and Euripides.   The scientific imagination enters tragedy at an even deeper level and does more harm than you might think.

The greatest trouble begins with Euripides. But what's funny is that the *Poetics* treats him disapprovingly too, almost every time that his name comes up, often for the same qualities that Nietzsche condemns:

Plot. Nietzsche scorns the Euripidean *deus ex machina* (17, 18); Aristotle takes Euripides to task for trafficking in plot contrivances (1454b1, 1454b31).

Character. Nietzsche thinks that in Euripides's hands the hero sinks to the level of the everyday (11) and tragedy portrays "only prominent individual traits of character" (17). Aristotle finds something unsatisfying in several of the characters that Euripides draws, namely that they are improbably dominated by a single trait (1454a28, 1454a32, 1461b20).

Chorus. Aristotle criticizes Euripides for reducing the role of the chorus in tragedy, below the appropriate point it had attained in Sophocles (1456a27). That criticism is too tepid for Nietzsche—he finds the decay of the chorus beginning in Sophocles, "even if Aristotle favors precisely [Sophocles's use] of the chorus" (14). Still Aristotle stands closer to Nietzsche than to Euripides.

And yet; and yet; "even if Euripides does everything else wrong," Aristotle says, "he is the most tragic of all the dramatic poets" (1453a26–30). When it comes to achieving the tragic effect, all Euripides's sins of composition are forgiven him.

Aristotle will never redeem himself with quibbles about plot contrivances or caricatured heroes, not when he turns around and hands Euripides the highest praise Nietzsche can imagine for any poet (for any philosopher either). What does it mean to call Euripides the most tragic poet? Aristotle delivers that judgment in *Poetics* 13, after deciding that the best tragic plot must take its hero from good luck into bad. Even Euripides's detractors will agree that he ends many of his plays this way, "tragically" in the slackest, headline-language sense of the word.

For his part Nietzsche almost denies the existence of tragedy's plot. Certainly his synopsis of the Oedipus story betrays a casualness about plot. The Apollinian eye sees a moral order in the life of Oedipus, but that Apollinian transfiguration of the man needs to be blinked away to expose the dark illumination below the after-image: that violence against nature in the form of incest produced this bearer of "prophetic and magical powers." The sequentially ordered plot inverts what its Dionysian audience understands the tragedy to reveal.

When Nietzsche boils down the story latent in every Greek tragedy, seeking the plot line of tragedy as such, he arrives at something like an inversion of all possible plots and therefore a rejection of all plots' general statements. Considered ritualistically every plot has a mystery beneath it whose hero is Dionysus. This "one truly real Dionysus appears in a variety of forms, in the mask of a fighting hero, and entangled, as it were, in the net of the individual will" (10).

Symbolic names like Swell-foot, Quarrel-much, and Stand-firm only mask the mysterious Dionysus (*his* name's etymology "a conundrum": Burkert 1985, 162), who is "experiencing in himself the agonies of individuation" (*Birth* 10). The more individuation that Oedipus, Polyneices, and Agamemnon enjoy—the higher they stand above the everyday run of humans—the greater the agony for the god. Their worldly success and royalty are his suffering.

So Nietzsche speaks of the secret Dionysian conception of art "as the joyous hope that the spell of individuation may be broken in augury of a restored oneness." The hero's defeat and death signal the end of that agonizing partition of Zagreus.

If every tragedy murmurs the story of Dionysus, those with the ears to hear that story ought to do their mourning at the beginning of the play, when the actors appear differentiated into several *dramatic parts* symbolizing the god's severed *body parts*. When the heroes brought down to everyone else's level dissolve into a primal unity, the reveler sees Zagreus reconstituted. The sad ending becomes relief that life flows on indestructibly.

Nietzsche consistently conjures up the delight that tragedy brings—in the late books *Twilight* and *Ecce Homo* he will speak of tragic joy—but without wishing for happy endings. Indeed *Ecce Homo* says that the tragic joy "includes even joy [Lust] in destroying" (*Ecce Homo, Birth* 3). Nietzsche finds tragic conclusions desirable for the same reasons that they are commonly called *unhappy*.

It follows that the right audience could find Euripidean tragedy as tragical as Aristotle does, provided that audience can read the slide into misfortune as its opposite. So it is not the arc of the Euripidean story that goes awry but the interpretation Aristotle gives to that arc. Aristotle calls Euripides the most tragic author only because he does not see what really makes a tragedy tragic.

For Aristotle it is a pitiable and terrifying matter that someone who began in the place of a king comes to a lowly end. His obsession with plot blinds him to the disappearance of myth, music, rapture, everything both Dionysian and Apollinian, from the tragedies of Euripides. He declares that hearing the plot of a good tragedy can produce the tragic pleasure with no need for a trip to the theater (*Poetics* 1453b1–11); Nietzsche would read that line as proof that Aristotle long ago forgot what the tragic pleasure was.

You might expect Aristotle of all people to see that Euripides marks a decline in the tragic tradition, given his overview of its history and his special admiration for Sophocles. But his obsession with plot brings him to award the prize of "most tragic" to the dramatist who least deserves it. Aristotle goes wrong by reading tragedy as a plot, which is to say by reading it as a causal statement.

Nietzsche's sarcasm about catharsis felt like a misfire. Why that fussy distaste ("don't talk to me about discharge") for Aristotle? But suppose it is not catharsis that really riles Nietzsche, it is Aristotle's attachment to the causal statement in tragedy. Aristotle insists on finding continuous causal stories in tragedy and for that reason calls Euripides, with his sure touch for the tale of woe, the most tragic tragedian. Nietzsche insists on denying that title to Euripides and therefore denies that tragedy is a matter of causes and effects.

The quest for causal sequences is un-Dionysian.   What Nietzsche calls the Dionysian spirit in tragedy is the spirit in which cause and effect lose their significance. Overvaluing tragedy's plots as Aristotle does will occlude your vision of that spirit.

Nietzsche's new Dionysian readings contain "the *mystery doctrine of tragedy*: the fundamental knowledge of the oneness of everything existent" (10). To arrive at this mystery doctrine he has to retell the Oedipus and

Prometheus stories and the story behind all tragedy, either neglecting causal order or defying it. The "blending and duality in the emotions of the Dionysian revelers remind us . . . of the phenomenon that pain begets joy, that ecstasy may wring sounds of agony from us," more generally that ordinary causal sequences belong outside the Dionysian realm (2).

The Dionysian impulse appears in the terror that strikes when in Schopenhauer's language "the principle of sufficient reason . . . seems to suffer an exception" (1). That principle expresses itself in the form of space, time, and causality. The Dionysian impulse has no truck with those categories.

The Dionysian artist therefore also works oblivious to the causal order. Nietzsche's modern example is Schiller, who set himself to work not thinking of "any series of images in a causal arrangement [geordneter Kausalität: ordered causality]," but under the influence of "a musical mood" (5). A musical mood, something Dionysian, stands opposed to ordered causality.

By the way, that opposition is Nietzsche's own. He quotes the words of Schiller's that support his point, and you can see where he put his thumb on the scales. "With me" says Schiller

> the perception has at first no clear and definite object [bestimmten und klaren Gegenstand]; this is formed later. A certain musical mood comes first, and the poetical idea only follows later.

The musical mood is present as in Nietzsche's summary, but what Schiller contrasts that mood to is an "object." It is Nietzsche who imports the idea of causal arrangement as opposite to Dionysian music. He seizes upon the Dionysian to license his rejection of causality, even if he has to torture the testimony before Dionysus serves that purpose.

The critique of causation becomes explicit when Nietzsche elevates myth above history. Every myth is fated to degrade into "some alleged historical reality, and to be treated by some later generation as a unique fact with historical claims" (10). The myth loses its Dionysian life. In the hands of dogmatism, "the mythical premises of a religion are systematized as a sum total of historical events"; *Birth* will later say it is the historical sense, not mythic insight, that "insists on strict psychological causality [psychologische Kausalität]" (23). Myth dies and leaves a causal account for a corpse.

Even this slender agreement between Nietzsche and Aristotle, their disdain for history, attests to the gulf between them. The *Poetics* ranks poetry above history because well-made tragic stories express statements of cause and effect and history does not (1451a37–b9). History presents particulars

(1451b8): Aristotle has Herodotus in mind (1451b2), probably also Choer-
ilus of Samos, whose epic translated Herodotus into verse (Janko 1987, 91;
Poetics 1451b3). Significantly, Aristotle does *not* name Thucydides, who
looked for the general principles that explain the Peloponnesian War. A history founded on causal principles would have to be poetry's equal.

By Nietzsche's time history has changed so completely that he attacks it
exactly for trying to uncover causal principles. *Birth* classes history below
myth and implicitly below poetry because the Dionysian element in poetry
eschews causal claims.

Ultimately the Socratic impulse is to blame for this drive toward causal
coherence. Socrates finds tragedy objectionable because he finds it "full of
causes [Ursachen] apparently without effects [Wirkungen] and effects apparently without causes" (14). The Socratic type trusts that "thought, using the
thread of causality, can penetrate the deepest abysses of being" (15).

Euripides watching his predecessors' tragedies keeps losing the thread of
causal connection. As an exemplar of the theoretical type, he thereby feels
compelled to write those tell-all prologues to his own plays: "any missing
link, any gap in the texture of the background story" is bound to distract the
audience (12). If the spectator has to figure out "the presuppositions of this
or that conflict . . . he cannot become completely absorbed in the actualities
and sufferings of the chief characters"—not if it's a spectator like Euripides,
who values the veridicality of a plot's assertions so highly he often has gods
deliver the prologue, "to remove every doubt as to the reality of the myth—
somewhat as Descartes could prove the reality of the empirical world only by
appealing to the truthfulness of God."

Descartes argues for the truthfulness of God in the brief second paragraph
of *Meditation* IV. Every instance of fraud is an imperfection. Because every deception in ordinary life implies imperfection, a deception by God must imply
the same thing and contradict *His* perfection.

The suppressed premise—that deception means in the divine order what
it means in experience—betrays a theology in the tradition of Thales. No
gulf separates the human from the divine. Euripides enlists himself in that
same tradition when he calls upon his prologue-gods to uphold the causal
order.

The Dionysus who takes his initiates out of organized causality was never
the type to guarantee the reality of a myth.

Nietzsche insists on the discontinuity between past and present.   Nietzsche's decisive reason for resisting causal explanations draws more specifically
on his portrayal of the Dionysian impulse.

Dionysians give up causality because the trance they're in dissolves any normal order. Nietzsche despises the dimwitted assumption of continuity in history (the conception of history that *Genealogy* ridicules in English psychologists), according to which nothing has ever really happened: Greece and its glorious tragedies wait ever-readily to be revived, relived, reworked, and replayed in the present, their "universality" making them a constantly available possibility for later generations.

One of the things that nostalgia assumes in its fantasy of return is a continuous causal nexus extending from right now back to the dawn of time. If nostalgia possesses the saving grace of its *algos*, the pain of loss that acknowledges the fact of loss, it is damned by the *nostos* and its talk of going home.

Nietzsche's critique of nostalgia comes when he mocks simple-minded modern attempts to continue tragedy. Modern opera for instance presupposes a classical paradise shaped by natural forces that are still available today. The inventors of the recitative "could abandon themselves to the dream of having descended once more [wieder] into the paradisiacal beginnings of mankind" (19). This "faith in the primordial existence of the artistic and good man" (19) refuses to recognize that all things are not possible at all times. It

> supposes that there was a primitive age of man when he lay close to the heart of nature, and, owing to this naturalness, had at once attained the ideal of mankind in a paradisiacal goodness and artistry; (19)

and if that ideal had a purely natural origin then natural forces can revive it.

With equal contempt, Nietzsche dismisses the idea of a naïve artist, as Homer is imagined to have been. The greatest trick that Apollinian art achieves may be the illusion that it comes out of nowhere, when in fact it presupposes and arrives after the Dionysian (2, 3, 25).

> Where we encounter the "naïve" in art, we should recognize the highest effect of Apollinian culture—which always must first overthrow an empire of Titans and slay monsters. (3)

Art's union with nature must be read as an achievement, "not a condition that, like a terrestrial paradise, *must* necessarily be found at the gate of every culture" (3).

Greek tragedy lies across a second gulf from modernity too, a literal separation that symbolizes spiritual distance. Nietzsche admits when beginning to elucidate the Apollinian impulse that he lacks essential data:

In spite of all the dream literature and the numerous dream anecdotes of the Greeks, we can speak of their *dreams* only conjecturally, though with reasonable [ziemlicher: fair, middling] assurance. (2)

The Greek Apollinian must dwell most completely in Greek dreams; but those dreams though crucial evidence of the Apollinian can be spoken of only conjecturally.

Not to worry, Nietzsche says in half-consolation: the *fruit* of that dreaming impulse remains in classical art. The Apollinian is detectable to anyone who reflects on "the incredibly precise and unerring plastic power of their eyes, together with their vivid, frank delight in colors" (2). Too bad the colors are also gone. Modern Europe has discovered the ancient Apollinian spirit in marble statues washed and bleached to suggest an abstemiousness they never possessed. The right vivid colors may explain the Apollinian impulse, but the right vivid colors don't exist.

As for the Dionysian, Nietzsche remarks that ancient tragedy "of course presents itself to us only as word-drama" (17)—"of course" he says, for it's a passing remark. But given Nietzsche's identification of the Dionysian with tragic music, his truism amounts to the announcement that *the lost essence of tragedy that his book rediscovered lies beyond modern experience.* Music lies at the heart of the Dionysian more or less in the way that dreams constitute the Apollinian; but the music is lost.

> We are almost forced to construct . . . by scholarly research the superior power of the musical effect in order to experience something of the incomparable comfort which must have been characteristic of true tragedy. Even this musical superiority, however, would only have been felt by us had we been Greeks. (17)

(See Porter, *Nietzsche and the Philology of the Future*, on a related point about Greek poetry. Nietzsche's insight that meter in antiquity was based on syllable length, not on the stress or volume of syllables, reflects his intuition that ancient verse *can no longer be heard*: Porter 2000b, 133–138.) Even if the musical notations of tragedy had not been so close to entirely lost; even if moderns knew how to reconstruct the sound of the music from those notations—even *going back in time and hearing tragedy's music* would not recover the heart of Greek tragedy, whose dislocation from the present age is merely represented by, and does not consist in, the empirical nonexistence of tragedy's music.

The dislocation amounts to the evanescence of tragic culture: the dislocation begins with that "one turning-point [Wendepunkt] and vortex of so-called world history" that is Socrates (15).

The chapter thus far, and main points ahead. Nietzsche's first book aims ambivalently at establishing him as a philosopher. He wants to join the ranks of his predecessors and yet not belong to philosophy as it has thus far been—to be that impossible thing, another first philosopher.

One token of Nietzsche's new philosophizing is his use of the labels "Apollinian" and "Dionysian" for the artistic impulses he discovers in Greece's pre-philosophical era. Philosophy founded itself on the abjuration of religious explanations, but "Apollinian" and "Dionysian" conjure up mythical beings. A mythical being is a being that acts, and Nietzsche courts the power myths have of imparting movement to what would otherwise be philosophy's immobility. Movement has reentered philosophy.

Things happen, or at least they used to.

Not only does Nietzsche give divine names to abstractions, he bestows new powers on the figures who bear those names. In particular the two gods boast *generative* powers that verge on the impossible.

Dionysus especially up-ends the causal principle. Under his spell Nietzsche runs tragedies backward, elevating hysteron-proteron into an organizational principle. He criticizes two general features of causal explanations (before-and-after ordering; continuity through change) and one famous application of causality to tragedy, which is Aristotle's claim that the plot of every good tragedy displays causal principles.

Nietzsche embraces one consequence of his view of causation, that despite its title his book cannot tell of tragedy's birth. He implies the incomprehensibility of that birth to the present when he calls tragedy the product of Apollo's coupling with Dionysus. Magically impossible divine fertility made tragedy happen—which is why tragedy is not automatically available to all ages.

You could say that Nietzsche yields to nostalgia. But at least nostalgia acknowledges the abrupt changes that have intervened between past and present. So tragedy remains in a time unlike the present, with a birth incomprehensible *to* the present.

Nietzsche's appeal to myth is only an advance warning of the movement he plans to reveal, that tragedy passed out of existence at one time and philosophy gave birth to itself. Tragedy and philosophy are not abstract nouns: they live (or lived) and die (or should). Thus *Nietzsche's appeal to religious tropes and structures signals the temporalization that Birth introduces into philosophy.*

If Nietzsche temporalizes he also temporizes. *Birth* is really about tragedy's death and disappearance and the birth of the Socratic philosophy that judged tragedy and found it wanting and commanded it to kill itself. This Nietzsche ought to account for; yet from the rush of movement that surrounds his myth-ical presentation of the tragic age he comes to speak of Socrates statically.

Neither the Dionysian nor the Apollinian will be able to explain Socrates. Nietzsche tries to squirm out of the problem by hypothesizing a Socratism be-fore and behind Socrates; his squirms only verify that he has no answer to give and knows that he needs one.

The Nietzsche disappointment of *Birth* consists in two intertwined pro-gressions: from the movement of myth to stasis (Apollo and Dionysus en-gendering tragedy; then Socrates' eternal presence); from insistence on the historical event that Socrates causes to erasing Socrates' origin from history. In the end Socrates seems to have come out of nowhere.

Nietzsche's word for a creature capable of such sudden appearances is "de-mon." Evocative of Eden's tempter and the Cartesian skeptical possibility, the demon also brings *Birth* into uncanny conversation with Plato's *Symposium*, which also tries and likewise fails to say where the demon Socrates comes from.

As the first tragic philosopher Nietzsche might seek to end the battle that Plato declared long ago, on philosophy's behalf, against tragedy. But his first book aims ambivalently at establishing him as a first philosopher. Nietzsche has to face his own conundrum of identifying with Socrates—of wanting to be Socrates but also wanting Socrates not to be—and so he blocks himself from accounting for Socrates' origins.

Temporalization.   The eternity that *Birth* challenges is that eternal ap-plicability of causal laws that is implicit in the continuous time with which Thales replaced mythic epochalism. Instead of betokening failure, Nietz-sche's appeal to the supernaturally fertile progenitors of tragedy reflects his respect for the difference between then and now. He promises not a nativity story about tragedy but a new *Apology* that depicts tragedy's trial and death at the hands of that first philosopher of human life called Socrates.

But if the birth of philosophy in the person of Socrates guarantees that the birth of tragedy remains ineffable, this new temporalization demands a story about Socrates.

"Something happened," Nietzsche tells the nostalgists and those untragic philosophers that he plans to supplant. Socrates happened and inspired the theoretical type, and the Platonism that continues to govern European thought. "*The dying Socrates* became the new ideal, never seen before, of no-ble Greek youths" (13) and especially of that quintessential youth Plato.

But anyone can retell the death of Socrates. Nietzsche's story, which no philosopher before him has told, has to account for his birth. Where does Socrates come from?

"All philosophers." "The lack of a historical sense is the hereditary de-fect of all philosophers" (*Human* I.2).

That tragedy had a beginning, every philosopher has asserted since the first one who theorized about tragedy. But that tragedy had a decisive end co-inciding with the decisive beginning of philosophy introduces more move-ment than the story of philosophy has thus far attributed to itself.

Socrates, Apollo, Dionysus. The more Socrates resembles either Apollo or Dionysus the easier the answer to where he comes from. If he represents ei-ther impulse in distorted form you will be able to call him the overgrowth of a natural drive, which after all is still a growth.

To make Nietzsche's mythology coherent, therefore, readers sometimes highlight the similarities between the Socratic and the Apollinian. Socrates carries on Apollinian cheerfulness; adheres to Delphic maxims about moder-ation and self-knowledge; and gets his first ordination from Apollo in the or-acle's declaration that no one in Greece is wiser than Socrates (*Apology* 21).

Even Socrates' restatement of the oracular phrase about him suggests Apollinian restraint. "How can the god say that I am the wisest?" (21b). But the Apollinian had already spoken in him when he first interpreted the ora-cle as implying that *someone* was wisest. The Dionysian would have embraced the oracle's message. No one is wiser than Socrates because people are equally wise. Nobody wiser than anyone else, nobody greater, everyone rep-resents that primal living unity.

Nietzsche himself cites an event from the life of Socrates as evidence for some alliance that remains possible between Socrates and art, and the art in question sounds Apollinian. In Plato's *Phaedo* Socrates confesses to having heard a dream-command all his life—"Make music!"—but ignoring it figur-ing that his philosophizing counted as musical. Near death he thinks again, what if "music" does mean poetry? So he composes a poem in praise of Apollo and starts setting Aesop's fables in verse (*Phaedo* 60e–61b).

> It was something akin to the demonic [dämonischen] warning voice that urged him to these practices; it was his Apollinian insight that [he] was in danger of sinning against a deity. (14)

A song to Apollo; a fable of cleared-away Apollinian form; the Apollinian insight to stay in your place and not reject the gods' commands: as Nietzsche retells the anecdote it almost turns Socrates into a wayward son of Apollo.

Not for nothing does Nietzsche say outright, "We may recognize in Socrates the opponent [Gegner: even adversary] of Dionysus" (12). The Socratic drive to knowledge even today "can express itself in hostility to art and must particularly detest Dionysian-tragic art" (15).

The Socratic and the Apollinian, both of them clear-eyed and disciplined, stand against the Dionysian side of culture as the drive to elucidate stands against what will not let itself become lucid.

Nietzsche almost unites the Socratic with the Apollinian entirely and casts Euripides as their intermediary when he relegates Euripidean drama to the "Apollinian domain of art" (12). Euripides aims at epic, which is Apollinian, and after all that is Socrates speaking through him.

But just when Nietzsche feels tempted to equate the Socratic with the Apollinian he recoils, as if he saw a misinterpretation coming and wanted to block it. One page after mentioning the Apollinian domain of art he corrects himself: "It is impossible for [Euripidean tragedy] to attain the Apollinian effect of the epos" (12). What seemed like the epic tradition speaking through Euripides turns out to have been a fraud. Euripidean tragedy "requires new stimulants, which can no longer lie within the sphere of the only two art-impulses [der beiden einzigen Kunsttriebe], the Apollinian and the Dionysian." They may be the only two impulses, but *neither of them* impels Euripides.

The following sentence speaks of those "cool, paradoxical thoughts, replacing Apollinian contemplation," that choke Euripides's plays (12). Nietzsche warns that this *is* a replacement, just because you might otherwise mistake Euripidean (Socratic) cogitation for Apollinian consciousness. The theorist's thoughts drive Apollo away. And similarly Nietzsche says that Socratic ethics does not continue but replaces the famed Apollinian restraint with a theoretical surrogate:

> Even the most sublime ethical deeds . . . were derived [abgeleitet] from the dialectic of knowledge by Socrates and his like-minded successors, down to the present, and accordingly designated as teachable. (15)

What Apollinian Greece had found the hardest achievement, to shape human nature into civilized form, Socrates demonstrates to be an automatic occurrence. "Ableiten" has the technical sense of drawing a mathematical inference. The magic of tautology ensures that no one voluntarily does anything wrong (because it wouldn't make sense to: you wouldn't be acting "voluntarily" then).

If common observation seems to deny the inevitability of virtue at every turn, then it is common sense, the surface wisdom that the Apollinian observes, that philosophers need to call into question. A new conception of virtue has taken over.

Respectful references to Apollo attributed to Socrates do not make Socratism Apollinian, any more than his prayers to Dionysus belie his anti-Dionysianism.

Boil Nietzsche's theology back down to claims about natural impulses and the contrast becomes even sharper. The Apollinian impulse reduces to delight with illusion. "Whenever the truth is uncovered, the artist will always cling with rapt gaze to what still remains covering even after such uncovering" (15). This gaze at the veil for its own sake does not come from the Dionysian artist who feels "the veil of mâyâ . . . torn aside" (1) but from the Apollinian whom Nietzsche has already lined up against the philosopher:

> the aesthetically sensitive man stands in the same relation to the reality of dreams as the philosopher does to the reality of existence. (1)

Being is philosophy's subject and dreaming is Apollo's.

In this respect, the anti-Apollinianism of Socrates shows in every Platonic reference to images, beginning with the *Republic*'s divided line and allegory of the cave (509d–521c). Those "images" that the Apollinian love—vivid things as opposed to objects of thought, pluralities rather than unities—go into the lowest epistemic category (510a). And the opposition between appearance and philosophical reality begins with Socrates' use of the sun as an "offspring" and lower manifestation of the Good (506e, 508b). Considered as the sun, with which he was often identified, Apollo remains the inferior child of philosophy's unbegotten master principle.

Take the Apollinian impulse any way you like. As image adoration it suffers every Platonic and Socratic demotion of the visual in favor of the intelligible. Taken physiologically as nature's dream instinct it comes in for abuse when Socrates calls himself the gadfly waking Athens from her slumber (*Apology* 30e; cf. 40d in praise of "dreamless sleep"), also in *Republic* 5, where Socrates demeans visual experience and dreams together (476c). Taken as the drive to make images, the Apollinian receives as much criticism as Socrates knows how to give. Plato's treatments of mimesis in *Republic* 10, in the *Sophist*, in the *Phaedrus*, consistently assign the most dubious status of all to artistic images.

The main problem with assimilating the Socratic to the Apollinian is that being Apollinian does not exactly consist in *opposing* Dionysus, so opposing Dionysus does not make you Apollo. The Apollinian impulse *reacts* to the Dionysian, always waiting for it to move first. Nietzsche pictures

Greek cultural history as an oscillation between eruptions by the Dionysian and the Apollinian reimposition of limit (4). "The truly existent primal unity . . . also needs the rapturous vision . . . for its continuous redemption [Erlösung]" (4). The Dionysian *calls for* its Apollinian relief—which suggests that denying the Dionysian, as Socrates does, will have to mean undoing the Apollinian too.

One might even reduce the Apollinian to the Dionysian, as Robert John Ackermann does: "The Apollinian is a mode of representation of the Dionysian" (Ackermann 15); for the Apollinian never *argued against* the Dionysian, never "denied" its brother-impulse or "objected" to it, any more than courtship denies sexual desire simply by evolving out of that desire. Courtship can distract from sexual desire, which makes it look like self-discipline, but when the desire goes the courtship will be gone too. When Socrates brings down the Dionysian in tragedy he will finish off the Apollinian. Because he objects to Dionysus he doesn't belong with either god.

In mythic language: Diogenes Laertius may pass along the testimony that Plato was born "on the seventh of Thargelion, the same day that the Delians say Apollo was born" (III.2), but that is as far as their birth relation goes. Nietzsche's Apollo did not give birth either to Socrates or to Plato's Socrates.

The Apollinian and the Dionysian collectively exhaustive. When Nietzsche follows Spinoza in keeping his divinities naturalistic, the Apollinian impulse becomes the orientation toward phenomena and the Dionysian is the orientation toward noumena, things in themselves—as Schopenhauer would have it *the* thing in itself, the will. *Birth* never suggests that Schopenhauer has interpreted being too narrowly, that some other domain exists besides those two. So the Apollinian and the Dionysian together exhaust all orientations toward the world.

But then, being a manifestation of neither Apollo nor Dionysus, Socrates cannot exist.

Objection: The art impulses as nature. Doesn't this argument miss the point? The Apollinian and the Dionysian exhaust all natural orientations toward experience and knowledge. They do not account for Socrates because *nature* fails to account for him.

Nietzsche presents Socrates' unnaturalness as deviance. This "utterly abnormal [abnormen] nature" in Socrates in which instinct becomes censorious; Socrates "a monstrosity *per defectum*" (13). In Socrates' mouth the words "only by instinct" are an accusation, because in him the natural instincts perform none of their usual functions. The "logical urge [Trieb: drive, bent]" that powers this man dominates him as the great instincts dominate more natural people. And where other people have natures to guide them he has the denial of nature.

The mythology, the miracles, the divine births—none of these really denies *Birth*'s allegiance to nature, as long as "nature" is taken the right way. If following Thales you take nature as the condition that remains the same at all times, then Nietzsche does want to emphasize the mythic elements in his story. Tragedy was natural once, but *its nature is no longer natural*.

The incommensurability between Socrates and the Apollinian-Dionysian order therefore means: Socrates did not arise naturally but as an alienation from nature. In the person of the theoretical type he made that alienation permanent, so that nature as the Greeks once knew it has become an object of nostalgia and the subject of myth.

But this line of interpretation makes the explanatory failure stand out worse than before. What could be the purpose of equating art impulses with nature, if not to show that philosophy can do without special human powers—genius, reason—in explaining cultural effects? The human supervenes on the natural, adding nothing to the story. And then Nietzsche comes to speak of Socrates who does *not* supervene on the natural and who adds everything there is to add to the story of tragedy, namely an ending.

Can Socrates be neither different nor same? Translate the impulses into human psychology and they still belong in the natural domain but only more starkly make a mystery of Socrates.

In psychological terms the Apollinian represents the impulse to ward off an experience, to declare a thing *different*. Intoxication says, One for all and all are one. The Dionysian impulse is the drive to recognize an experience as one's own, in short to absorb the experience declaring it *same*.

The logic is crude but effective. You can treat your experience as identical to you or as something other, but there won't be a third alternative.

Socratism before Socrates. It still might feel as though some undetected explanation of how Socrates arose out of pre-Socratic nature lurks in *Birth*. Interesting that Nietzsche himself exhibits the fear that he won't find one. For at least twice he tries to account for Socrates by positing a pre-Socratic Socratism. For example:

> Anyone who, through the Platonic writings, has experienced even a breath of the divine naïveté and sureness of the Socratic way of life, will also feel how the enormous driving-wheel [Triebrad] of logical Socratism is in motion, as it

were [gleichsam], *behind* Socrates, and that it must be viewed through Socrates as through a shadow. (13)

"As it were," eh? That's convenient. If you can't account for Socrates you invent Socratism and slip it in as it were behind the man.

The multiplication of entities to include Socratism only intensifies the problem of evil. Instead of a surprising new man who violates the laws of nature Nietzsche now has to account for a new instinct, still something beyond the Apollinian and the Dionysian and therefore still (if it moves Socrates in his particularly Socratic ways) unnatural. Socratism needs an origin.

Besides, if the movement that ends tragedy comes from a Socratism in motion behind Socrates, what justifies calling Socrates the turning point of history? Why heap blame on Socrates?

Nietzsche does not linger on logical Socratism long enough to let these worries speak. But in the section after introducing that drive (14), he winds back around to much the same thing. Socrates (he says) brings tragedy to an end. Certainly its chorus has to go. "Optimistic dialectic drives *music* out of tragedy with the scourge of its syllogisms" (14).

Couldn't someone object here? The choral part had begun to dwindle earlier. Already with Sophocles, "the Dionysian basis of tragedy is beginning [beginnt] to break down." Yes, Nietzsche concedes that "we must thus assume an anti-Dionysian tendency [Tendenz] operating even prior to Socrates, which merely [nur] received in him an unprecedentedly [unerhört] magnificent expression."

There is no word but "ambivalent" for a sentence like that. The "merely" denies that anything new happens with Socrates, the "unprecedentedly" insists that something does. If the anti-Dionysian tendency existed before Socrates then at least Nietzsche would not have to attribute impossible powers to the man; but then the inevitable and continuous dissolution of tragedy means that no great event came along in Socrates to separate the ancient art from modern eyes and ears.

An altogether newborn demon. Nietzsche will look back on the younger Nietzsche who wrote *Birth* as "a memory bursting with questions . . . after which the name of Dionysus was added as one more question mark [Fragezeichen]" (AS 3)—a memory so fertile that it spun the divine name out of itself. He came upon a doctrine opposed to Christianity.

What to call it? As a philologist and man of words I baptized [taufte] it, not without taking some liberty . . . in the name of a Greek god: I called it Dionysian. (AS 5)

Nietzsche can take that liberty because Dionysus belongs to him. Dionysus only appeared in *Birth* to begin with because of Nietzsche's choice of labels for a certain ancient drive.

Socrates appears under different circumstances. At the time of *Bacchae*,

> Dionysus had already been scared from the tragic stage, by a demonic power [dämonische Macht] speaking through Euripides . . . the deity [Gottheit] that spoke through him was neither Dionysus nor Apollo, but an altogether new-born demon [ein ganz neugeborner Dämon], called *Socrates*. (12)

That demon *called* Socrates, but not named by Nietzsche. Nietzsche might baptize the Dionysian, but Socrates already has a name and an existence beyond his reach.

Then too Socrates is altogether newly born. He makes his first appearance in *Birth* as he appeared in tragic Athens, a formerly unseen phenomenon:

> all alone [der einzelne: the only one], . . . as the precursor [Vorläufer: forerunner, as John Baptist is called] of an altogether different culture, art, and morality, he enters a world, to touch whose very hem would give us the greatest happiness. (13)

A forerunner of an entirely different culture, Socrates *enters* his world, as if having been born and cultivated somewhere else.

Socrates' singularity needs to be distinguished from the strangeness of tragic Greece to modern eyes. Nietzsche's biblical metaphor makes the pre-Socratic epoch a godly time with miracle-working powers. Moderns trust that one reach back to touch Greek antiquity could bring the life back to an age it keeps ebbing from, as the woman in Mt. 9.20 reaches for the hem of Jesus' garment to heal her endless hemorrhage. (Her "issue" may be a flow of blood mimicking permanent menstruation, like a hypertrophy of fertility that signals sterility and death.) Socrates walks in this world without recognizing that divinity of it that Nietzsche in nineteenth-century Switzerland will get nostalgic for the minute he lets his guard down.

But Nietzsche called Socrates the godhead that spoke through Euripides; he names the "divine [göttlichen] naïveté and sureness" of Socrates' life. Does Socrates become another god on a par with Apollo and Dionysus? Is *that* all that comes of being "this most questionable [fragwürdigsten] phenomenon of antiquity" (13), somehow akin to the question mark that is Dionysus?

As soon as he has put Socrates into that questionable single-membered category, Nietzsche says three more things about him to amplify the word that he introduced Socrates with, "demon."

What demonic power [dämonische Kraft] is this . . . ?
What demigod [Halbgott] is this . . . ? (13)

And in the subsequent paragraph:

We are offered a key to the character of Socrates by the wonderful [wunderbare] phenomenon known as "the *daimonion* [Dämonion] of Socrates." (13)

Plato's dialogues repeatedly attribute a "sign" or "voice" to Socrates that he calls his *daimonion* (*Apology* 31d, *Euthydemus* 272e, *Euthyphro* 3b, *Republic* 496c, *Theaetetus* 151a). If that little *daimôn* tells Socrates what to do then maybe he does represent demonic power—which might make him a demigod.

(Even if Socrates is merely the type of man who'd be called *daimonie*, that address still suggests that a person is incomprehensible to other humans: see Brunius-Nilsson.)

Dämon.   Calling Socrates a demon makes him the serpent in tragedy's garden.

Nietzsche calls Euripides "frevelnder," sacrilegious, for his outrages against tragedy (10). He has just applauded the Aryan myth of the fall, the Prometheus story, which dignifies sacrilege (9). But its Semitic sister story associates sacrilege with curiosity and deception, traits that *Birth* might associate with the un-Promethean Euripides, and through him with Socrates. Hence this sacrilege is the serpentine kind.

"Demon" also hints at a paralysis of will reminiscent of the paralysis that the demon of modern skepticism brings to Descartes. Philosophy's quest for truth to the contrary, the Socratic demon promises lies.

Is the resolve to be so scientific about everything perhaps a . . . last resort against—*truth* [die *Wahrheit*]? And, morally speaking, a sort of cowardice and falseness [*Falschheit*]? (AS 1)

Whether he is a serpentine demon or a skeptical one, Socrates joins the ranks of unaccountable creatures. Where did that talking snake come from when only Adam and Eve had the power of speech, and how could it have been a snake if God only subsequently took its legs away (Genesis 3.14)?

The Greek *daimôn* as such was no demon. The word at first carried no special meaning distinguishing it from *theos*, "god" (Burkert 1985, 179–182). But in Plato's dialogues, a *daimôn* stood below a god in the divine hierarchy and the word is therefore translated "spirit." This *daimôn* is a god's assistant, intermediary between gods and humans (*Statesman* 271d, *Timaeus* 41a; cf. *Laws* 717b, 738d, 801e, 848d).

In the *Symposium*, the hunch that a *daimôn* might be *not fully* a god elides into the *denial* that it is a god. Because Eros cannot be a god, says Diotima, he must be classified as a *daimôn* (202d). A *daimôn*

> interprets and transports human things to gods and divine things to humans. . . . A god does not mix with a human, rather it's through a *daimôn* that all speech and dialogue happens between gods and humans. (202e–203a)

The *Symposium*'s readers notice that Diotima's description of love describes someone much like Socrates himself (Santas 15). This dialogue, more than casual references to the *daimonion* elsewhere, is where Socrates himself becomes a *daimôn*.

When Nietzsche calls Socrates a newborn demon he is following Plato's lead and with special reference to this dialogue, a shadow or counterpoint to *Birth* in its valedictory summing up of Athenian culture. (By happy coincidence, James Porter's *Invention of Dionysus*, which arrived too late to leave the mark on this chapter that it ought to, very similarly calls the *Symposium* a "virtual leitmotif" for *Birth*: Porter 2000a, 111.)

Nietzsche mentions the *Symposium* in *Birth* (13), seeming to take it to represent the essential Socrates (see McNeill 260). So what is it that the *Symposium* reveals?

Diotima says that Eros lives in poverty and that poverty makes him tough and brave. He walks barefoot, maneuvers to gain whatever is beautiful, pursues the wisdom he loves (203c–e). A wisdom lover is by definition a philosopher, but the *Symposium* also matches Love's other qualities with Socrates, who is said in this dialogue to go barefoot (174a, 220b), to scheme to sit near handsome men (213c), to exhibit tough courage in wartime (219e–221b). No wonder he says that love is one thing he understands (177d, 199b).

Alcibiades supplies a lot of the details that add up to make Socrates resemble Diotima's Eros. He also makes the point head-on, calling Socrates *daimonion* (219c) or saying that the man looks like a satyr (215a–b), that is, a half-divine creature. (See Nussbaum 165–199, on the *Symposium*'s attribution of divine qualities to Socrates.) No man yet born has resembled Socrates, Alcibiades says (221c–d), as if because Socrates is not human, and forcing the question of who could have given birth to Socrates.

Where could *any* middling creature have come from? The *daimôn*'s intermediate status makes Socrates a demigod; but in Plato's cosmology gods and humans never mix. If the in-between entities must first exist to make the crossover possible, the in-betweens could not have been born of any such crossing.

Moreover Socrates is not just any demon, he is Love, the desirous, procreative kind. He must owe his origins to an even more peculiar process than other gods and spirits do. Who would have bothered with the effort of siring Love, or the pain and strain of bearing him, in that time so archaic that it lacked the erotic motive to sexual intercourse?

The *Symposium* keeps returning to the question of Eros's birth. The first speaker, Phaedrus, echoes the tradition that Love has no parents any human can know of. He quotes Parmenides who called Love the first-created god, also lines 116–120, more or less, of Hesiod's *Theogony* (178b).

The longer *Theogony* passage (lines 116–134) that contains the lines quoted makes it clear that Eros appears after Chaos, Earth, and Tartarus—not *because* of any of them though; the world's first four beings simply come into existence. The births after Love's arrival, however, are products of erotic couplings, like the ones between Night and Erebus or Earth and Heaven. Once Eros is here everyone else can be accounted for.

Without the rigor of a philosopher's cosmogony that would specify which cause preceded all the rest, but still marking the divide as myths can do between the world before there was love and a world with love in it, the *Theogony* makes Eros an unmoved mover.

Platonic procreation.   In Diotima's fable, Poverty and Resourcefulness give birth to Eros (203b). That tale personifies the mixed traits that go into Love, but it doesn't address the question Phaedrus put into play, of how Love could have been conceived in an unerotic world. It does not even address the questions implied by its own setting. Poverty and Resourcefulness couple at the feast of Aphrodite's birth—but how did *her* birth happen? Again without love? If Aphrodite and the other gods and spirits owe their existence to a reproduction that does not presuppose love, then Socrates' birth must have a cause radically unlike the births of humans. That is still no answer but rather moves any possible answer into another and mythic era.

Indeed Diotima's way of linking procreation to love renders any fuller answer impossible. This point needs to be emphasized, because the *Symposium*'s readers routinely observe that its all-male oratory about lust neglects to mention pregnancy and birth, that it takes a woman's entry into the conversation to reconnect sex and childbirth. That is an observation worth making, but it's not worth being blinded by. You have to take Socrates' word for it that Diotima taught him this theory about love, and Plato's word for it that Socrates turned around and reported the theory. And if their interpolations

between Diotima and the reader leave the story open to distortions, the result may be something less like a woman's attentiveness to her own body's
powers and more like a man's fantasy of what women might say.

For what Diotima says is that everyone is pregnant "in body and in soul"
(206c). Because they want to give birth to something beautiful—*en kalôi*, "in
the midst of beauty" (206b)—they look for beautiful mating partners. A
man's bodily pregnancy makes him pursue physically beautiful women as the
right environs for the children he is carrying (208e). His soul-pregnancy
makes him crave another kind of company, though still a beautiful one: the
agile mind, the well-shaped character, in addition to the comely body, will
present the man's "inner pregnancy" with the occasion to produce virtue and
wise conversation (209a–c).

Myles Burnyeat has drawn attention to the causal hysteron-proteron in
Diotima's metaphor. Pregnancy causes love (Burnyeat 54).

What Diotima calls higher love reverses the causal order more remarkably.
In this meeting of minds the soul's pregnancy begins before the boy reaches
manhood, which is to say in his virginity (209b).

Plato may portray Socrates as an Eros come down to earth, but the Platonic Eros no longer performs the task normally associated with his name.
Nothing takes his place, either; so the newborn demon called Socrates,
whether as an individual delivered out of a pregnancy or as an abstraction,
always presupposes some unnamable first origin.

When Diotima begins her analysis of reproduction with the bodily version
common to humans and animals, she says:

> It's from this that the thrill [*ptoêsis*] comes about beauty for those who are preg-
> nant and already swollen full [*spargônti*], because beauty relieves [*apoluein*]
> them from their pains. (206d–e)

If this is a man's attempt to imagine how it feels to carry a swelling heavy burden and to crave relief from its turgidity, it easily slides into a masculine image of sex. The fantasy implies that the man's seed already contains the new
child: intercourse with a woman merely delivers the man of his baby.

The sexualized details in Diotima's story should not distract from its central asexuality. When it comes to telling where babies come from, the Platonic account posits an already-existent being only in need of delivery. Sex
enlivens the tale of the birth; Socrates still arrives out of nowhere.

Aristophanic procreation. Aristophanes talks about reproduction in his
speech too, the myth of double humans cut in half to form the bipeds who

now call themselves men and women and wander searching for their missing pieces (189d–193d).

According to the story, the happy first humans reproduce asexually (191c). In the initial phase of bisected existence they continue casting their seed on the ground; meanwhile they might happen to find their lost other halves and embrace until they die of hunger (191b). Zeus relocates their genitals so that the embrace leads to sexual intercourse, which provides for procreation among the heterosexual couples and relief for homosexuals. Life goes on (191b–c).

Here love becomes accidentally conjoined with birth. You might call Aristophanes' picture of reproduction a parody though not a subversive one inasmuch as love still leads to intercourse and intercourse leads to birth. If anything, it is an old joke: Zeus created genital intercourse so people would know when to stop embracing.

But the story's digression to explain where babies come from masks its other image of procreation. Plato puts a manifest account of birth into the mouth of Aristophanes to distract from the latent image against which Diotima's backward love story is a reaction. *The transition from happy mythical quadrupedal humans to miserable historical bipeds is itself an image of the transition that is birth.*

Prôton, "first of all," is how Aristophanes begins; he will speak of "our long-ago nature [*palai phusis*]" (189d). In that distinctly different time the one you now perceive as your object of love was part of your own body.

When Aristophanes details the features of those double humans, he could be describing a pregnant woman: the round shape, the contentment, the four hands and four legs and two sets of genitals, the faces that look so much alike, as a woman and the baby in her do (189e–190a). In his story the navel is the scar left over from the bisection of the original humans (190e–191a), and this reinterpretation of the navel resonates poignantly enough to make Plato's readers almost forget that it is not a metaphor. The navel really is a scar, it really does mark where a creature was torn in two, and when you look at your own navel you do see the slash that ended your primal spherical happy existence.

The metaphor is romantic only as long as it's a metaphor. "Romantic" might mean "imperfectly perceived as sexual," because other romantic "truths" in this story lose their sentimental charm when they sound like plainer truths. Every human life is premised on the traumatic separation of one of those happy first creatures (193a). Erotic love is the attempt to reconstitute this murkily remembered unity (191d). If you feel tempted to call these claims "Freudian," that might be because they are grim and sexually direct, which is to say unromantic.

Aristophanes says that the human species would become happy if each person chanced on his own *paidikos* and returned to his ancient nature (193c). This noun *paidikos* means a sweetheart, though the identical adjective means "like a child"—youthful, but also: like a son or daughter. Aristophanes concludes that although finding that special child would bless all humanity, under present circumstances the closest alternative would be for each person to get lucky with a *paidikos* who is like-*minded* to him (*kata noun*).

Why settle for someone of similar mind when that falls short of the real blessed union? Why does the nostalgic story insist on the pain of loss but finally shy away from the return home?

Aristophanes might mean that finding the true other half, coming back to the child who'd been torn from you, unleashes new dangers. Those lucky lovers who find their other halves are craving an inexpressible something that isn't sex: "that each one's soul wants something else is clear, something it can't speak of, instead telling what it wants oracularly and in riddles [*manteuetai ho bouletai kai ainittetai*]" (192c–d). But the one who deals in oracles and riddles—the one who left home because of an oracle and found his new wife when he answered a riddle—is Oedipus; and his desires were unspeakable.

In Aristophanes' cover story, the critical claim about birth and love was that they're accidentally connected. The two had nothing to do with each other before Zeus joined the embrace to reproduction. But in the theory of love *implicit* in the myth, birth and love belong together because Eros implies a mother.

Aristophanes keeps his mouth shut about Socrates in this dialogue, although *Clouds* shows what temperature his anti-Socratic invective can reach. Imagine this slander of Eros to be the *Symposium*'s urbane substitute for that invective. Seen as Eros, Socrates represents desires whose beginning is loss and whose end will never come, no matter how sternly those desires are judged and condemned.

As an erotic man Socrates must have had a mother, must have experienced a very bodily relationship with her, and must long for more very bodily relations with her in the future.

Socrates versus Aristophanes. What matters most for the Socratic love story is that it not collapse into the Aristophanic one (Nussbaum).

Socrates tries to keep up the illusion that the ideas he is presenting are Diotima's, but at one point he gives away the fiction. He quotes her having spoken of a false theory that lovers seek their other halves (205d–e). Odd that she should have interrupted herself when teaching Socrates to rebut an idiosyncratic claim that someone will first present years later. What a coincidence for Diotima to have been discussing exactly what *you* said, Aristophanes (Nehamas and Woodruff, 52n77).

Plato's recklessness with his own fictional construction has the look of panic. He needs to ward off Aristophanes' view of love. You're not in love with your mother, you're in love with what is good.

None of the other speakers saw the loss behind love as Aristophanes did. But to make philosophy out of that loss, Plato needs to begin by repressing Aristophanes.

If Nietzsche calls Socrates a demon because Plato does, Plato makes him a demon because the real *daimôn* is Eros, and Eros comes from a masculine pregnancy that has no cause. Having a cause, coming from a mother, is the intolerable alternative.

The Platonic interpretation of Socrates reappears in Nietzsche. Nietzsche leaves a hole in the middle of his story when he takes up Plato's conception of the demonic Socrates. It's one thing to say that because philosophy came to be there can be no tale of tragedy; something else to turn around and say there is no tale of philosophy either.

The first omission comes of awe. Unlearn the temporal continuity that philosophy taught you, acknowledge that a holy time once existed. The second omission cannot claim to be a respectful silence. Socrates created the present, so he can't belong to the godly past age. But now he doesn't belong to the godless present either: the present cannot understand him.

Not only can gods and mortals not communicate with each other, neither one can communicate with the demon between them either.

That Plato shrank from thinking of the circumstances of his old friend's birth makes sense. Why should Nietzsche take over the same nervous avoidance?

A Socrates who practices music. *Birth* asks "whether the birth of an 'artistic Socrates' is altogether a contradiction in terms" (14). In an obvious way the answer must be Yes. An artistic Socrates would be a second Socrates, which is to say a second figure with effects on history comparable to Socrates' effects. But Socrates' overriding effect, which is the death of tragedy and tragic culture, has left him in a solitary position at history's vortex. Maybe not the first by every reckoning, still as a philosopher who practices dialectics on human existence he is first.

In a trivial sense there is no contradiction in being "another first." If Dad is the first doctor in town and Son becomes the first to set up a law practice,

there's another first in the family. But if "first" has to mean something decisive, then the next first can only become a first at all by eclipsing the original first, as it were retroactively rendering that first no longer a first. Then
there is no call to speak of *another* first. The original is as if it had never been.
And obviously if the newcomer fails to eclipse the first he won't be a first
himself, therefore again not another first.

The artistic Socrates of *Birth* 14 seems to be the "Socrates who practices
music" (15), and he in turn may be the person Nietzsche is thinking of in
1886, when he wishes the new soul that wrote *Birth* had sung and not spoken
(AS 1). He wants *Birth* to make him not only a philosopher but the first in
some new lineage.

The rebirth of philosophy out of the spirit of music.   In the last ten
sections of *Birth*, Nietzsche claims that he has accounted for the tragic chorus as never before, seen the musical basis of myth as no one else had, and
explained—again for the first time—the audience's response to tragedy (see
Pletsch 136). Looking back in *Ecce Homo* he packs six claims to *Birth's* singularity into six pages:

- for the first time, a psychological analysis of [the Dionysian phenomenon] is
  offered. (*Ecce Homo*, *Birth* 1)
- Socrates is recognized for the first time [zum ersten Male] as an instrument
  of Greek disintegration. (1)
- [Nietzsche] became the first to comprehend the wonderful phenomenon of
  the Dionysian. (2)
- I was the first to see [Ich sah zuerst] the real opposition. (2)
- I have the right to understand myself as the first [den ersten] *tragic philosopher.* (3)
- Before me this transposition of the Dionysian into a philosophical pathos
  did not exist. (3)

To earn the right to these claims, Nietzsche needs a status equal to Socrates'—
however contradictory the idea of equals may be in this context, where Nietzsche must either make himself the first philosopher or let Socrates keep the
title.

Nietzsche therefore needs Socrates to exist, and also not to exist, as a separate being. His motives are the motives of one who identifies himself with
Socrates. He makes Socrates someone utterly different from himself and simultaneously tries to absorb him as the same.

Identification.   Not many years after *Birth* first appears, its author writes perplexingly to an old friend: "Did I wish you a happy birthday? No. But I have wished myself happy on your birthday" (Middleton 175), as if that were the same thing really, as if a good way to observe the date of someone else's birth were by treating it as your own.

Birth celebrates itself when it should be observing Socrates' birth. What if Nietzsche celebrated Socrates' absence of birth by treating it as an absence of his own birth? So that he doesn't need an origin either.

Nietzsche, Socrates, Zarathustra.   Can Nietzsche identify with Socrates when he *opposes* him? (Nehamas 1985, 24–41, looks deeply into the relationship between them; see Allison 2001, 57–69, Sallis 111–145.) Consider Nietzsche's orientation toward Zarathustra, whom he transfigures into his own mouthpiece on the grounds of no more similarity between himself and the historical Zarathustra than exists between him and Socrates. He can absorb opponents.

Ecce Homo points the way from Zarathustra to Socrates. "Why I am a Destiny" (3) is instructive. "I have not been asked," Nietzsche begins,

> what the name of Zarathustra means in my mouth, the mouth of the first immoralist: for what constitutes the tremendous historical uniqueness of that Persian is just the opposite of this.

Nietzsche establishes his own uniqueness in the gesture of acknowledging the uniqueness of the historical Zarathustra, as if there were no contradiction in a double uniqueness. Zarathustra's distinctiveness is "just the opposite" of Nietzsche's, which consists in being the first immoralist—but then Socrates is unique too, the first untragic philosopher where Nietzsche is the first tragic one.

> Zarathustra was the first to consider the fight of good and evil the very wheel in the machinery of things: the transposition of morality into the metaphysical realm, as a force, cause, and end in itself, is *his* work.

Now it's Zarathustra who is the first of the moralistic breed that includes Socrates.

(Diogenes Laertius rejected the possibility that philosophy originated with the Magi, "beginning with Zoroaster": I.2. Nietzsche moves away from his training in philology when he takes Zarathustra as a philosophical original— but then he had already moved away in his early studies of Diogenes [1869,

1870], when he called his author a sleepyhead, stupid, careless, pretentious. See Barnes 20.)

Anyway *Birth* attributes something like Zarathustra's projection of morality into the universe to the Socratic maxims, under whose influence "there must be a necessary, visible connection between virtue and knowledge, faith and morality" in Euripides's tragedies, and "poetic justice" (14).

> Zarathustra created this most calamitous error, morality; consequently, he must also be the first to recognize it.

But "consequently" means something tricky here, evoking two principles of development both of which Nietzsche wants to endorse.

> Not only has he more experience in this matter, for a longer time, than any other thinker . . .

Let enough time go by and any idea's shortcomings will show themselves, let alone an idea as misguided as that of "morality." (Compare *Birth* on the theoretical culture that Socrates bequeathed to Europe: science "speeds irresistibly toward its limits where its optimism . . . suffers shipwreck": 15.)

> . . . what is more important is that Zarathustra is more truthful than any other thinker.

Again the ancient Zarathustra stands apart from everyone else. The zeal of his truthfulness distinguishes him, much as Socrates had been said to express a "new and unprecedented value set on knowledge and insight" (13).

And if Zarathustra bequeathed truthfulness to morality, Socrates made his dialectic so appealing that after him "the hunger for knowledge reached a never-suspected universality" (15).

> The self-overcoming of morality, out of truthfulness; the self-overcoming of the moralist, into his opposite—into me—that is what the name of Zarathustra means in my mouth. (*Ecce Homo*, "Destiny" 3)

"Into me" drops all pretexts about a Zarathustra distinct from Nietzsche. The ancient moralist becomes his opposite, and one name for a moralist's opposite is "Nietzsche."

This will do as a nativity story for Nietzsche. It is unimaginable that he should come from anyone like him. Somehow, he arises from this one parent who is opposite to him, without any causal account of the transformation, therefore both spontaneous in his origin and (given that the moralist who changed into him has been around so long) continuously present already, in need of no origins.

And if the ancient moralist Zarathustra could grow up into the future's immoralist Zarathustra/Nietzsche, then the Socrates who thought to write poetry just before his death might go on living as the first philosopher of a new type, call him the Socrates who practices music (Nietzsche).

ᔕ

Initial Objections

One imaginable response.   "Who needs this bothering with Nietzsche's metaphors of fatherhood and from there to his anxieties over having been born and his wish to have been a first philosopher?

"Biographical interpretations are very well in their place but they *have* a place, which you reach after other explanations have failed. It makes sense to give up on other interpretations in cases of pathology. But there is nothing pathological here, nothing peculiar to Nietzsche and nothing excessive. The disappointment two-step that Nietzsche dances up to the reader and away again hardly distinguishes him from Socrates or any other initiator of philosophical inquiries. Why examine Nietzsche and not the whole tradition?

"Even supposing that Nietzsche is uniquely incomplete and disappointing—that his books invite questions that have no answer—still he can take the blame for that as a thinker, not as a person.

"Finally there is the possibility that Nietzsche leaves his questions unanswered on purpose. Why theorize about Nietzsche's involuntary acts of omission when they might be voluntary?"

Synopsis of the objections.   The reaction as imagined contains four challenges to the argument thus far. There is some justice to each one:

1. Nietzsche's putative incompleteness might only reflect an aborted reading. There are other books he wrote and posthumous notes. It could be

that a more extensive survey of what he has written collects up the dangling questions.
2. Nietzsche resembles plenty of other philosophers in asking questions
he does not answer. Therefore, he does not stand in need of an explanation unless Socrates does as well, or unless "philosophy as such" does.
3. If Nietzsche's books are doomed to incompleteness as other books are
not, that incompleteness may be a regrettable fact about his project but
only reflects on the impossibility of his particular subject matter, not on
any disorder within his soul.
4. Nietzsche may be purposely refusing to answer his own questions, for
reasons the hasty reader has not understood yet.

The testimony of other writings.   *Birth* and "History" are only two
pieces and they date from Nietzsche's earliest period. A statement about the
corpus requires more than two examples.

Objection (1) is the reason for turning to *Genealogy* next. As Nietzsche's
premier "historical" work, *Genealogy* makes its own promises about explanatory mechanisms and then does or does not keep them. Methodologically
more self-conscious than *Birth*, it opens its own paths into the past, whether
it sets foot on those paths or not.

Beyond is not historical: orienting itself toward the future, it makes something new out of temporality and temporalization. The question regarding
Beyond will be whether talk of the future goes any smoother for Nietzsche
than his talk about the past did.

The result of considering these two books may not be a complete look at
Nietzsche, but it will be a representative look. It will not silence objection
(1) though, which could say: even if a structure of disappointment about
Nietzsche's histories and prophecies emerged out of reading *all* his published
books, such a disappointment could not mean enough. Behind those published writings are masses of unpublished ones—the notes collected in *Will*;
variants of passages he published; interpretations of his own books and even
repudiations of them; plans for future books and the paragraphs or pages
Nietzsche wrote for those books.

"It's not fair to look for Nietzsche's historical explanations within such a
limited field and then complain about his limited answers."

What does this complaint want, exactly?

Suppose the Nietzsche disappointment concerns the origin of Socrates.
Nietzsche fired you up to find out where Socrates came from and led you
down neglected roads into very old history but clutched himself and stopped
short just before reaching Socrates.

At that point you might say that Nietzsche halted because of his own un-utterable identification with Socrates. If Nietzsche were Socrates then an ori-gin for Socrates would mean an origin for Nietzsche. An origin for Nietzsche would locate him in a time after Socrates, and then he'd be no Socrates.

You could say all that about why he stops, or say nothing. But *that* he stops is not a speculation. Nietzsche does stride off looking for where Socrates comes from and then does stop. And given that he does, what would more information contribute to the sense that *Birth* resists the subject of Socrates' birth (but also seeks the subject out)? The issue is not what Nietzsche knows about Socrates, it's what he is willing to say publicly.

A note about Socrates. Make the example more specific. Sarah Kofman and John Sallis both mull over a note in which Nietzsche says Socrates is si-multaneously Prometheus and Oedipus—"Prometheus before his theft of fire and Oedipus before he solved the riddle of the Sphinx" (Kofman 1989, 21; Sallis 1991, 129).

They are right to mull it over. Nietzsche's comment on the identifications within *Birth* breathes new interpretations into existence—Kofman's reading, for example, that Socrates exhibits Dionysian excess (Kofman 1989, 303–304). Or the reading that Socrates would have been a hero except for his failure to take his own decisive action against nature, and hence follow-ing the traditional loser's strategy translates "true heroic action" into the realm of dialectic; hence that Socrates exists in a domain outside action in which his origin cannot be told.

Then too Nietzsche's remark exposes that machinery of identification that operates in "History" and *Birth* (and *Genealogy*). This seems to be a pattern of Nietzsche's thought, to combine apparently opposed individuals.

Given all these uses you could put a single sentence to, you might ask why not bring all the rest of Nietzsche's unpublished writings into the picture.

But *what* picture? This one is a picture of certain books in which Nietzsche uses history and prophecy in ways that philosophy had denied itself; books in which he stakes his investigations on causal questions that philosophy had never let itself ask, then drops the questions or represses them. And at least two things follow from the form this picture takes.

First it follows that the disappointment is built into these books' narrative order. These books in particular drop the causal and temporalizing questions they press, it is these books that disappoint. How they light a fire and then smother it you can only see by reading *them*.

It is not that Nietzsche can never form a thought about the origin of Socrates. It's that he cannot form that thought when his argument demands it of him: when he is ready to pin the blame for all subsequent culture on Socrates and sneer at misguided moderns who do not get it, just then Nietzsche cannot account for what he says needs accounting for. And this phenomenon, the Nietzsche disappointment, is a feature of Nietzsche's books almost regardless of what he could have written somewhere else.

Second it follows from the rhythm in these books (question / no answer) that the omissions being examined are no easygoing matter of oversight. Nietzsche does not leave a question suspended to be answered somewhere else. He leaves the question unanswerable. It *is* not answered and it shall not be.

"Is this a prescription not to read the notebooks? But no one can deny the relevance or the suggestiveness of their contents in advance." There are good reasons to read Nietzsche's notebooks and there will always be good purposes they're put to. But defanging the disappointment of his published books can't be one of them.

(There is much more on methodology in the conclusion. Publishers' readers have pressed criticisms that led to improvements in these discussions.)

Heidegger. The conception of Nietzsche's published work as incomplete, with his posthumous writings the means to completing it, dates back to Elisabeth Förster-Nietzsche's decision to turn some of those writings into *Will.* But as a philosophically credible project it begins with Heidegger.

Heidegger does not mine *Will* for insights about Nietzsche's most secret thoughts, even if he sometimes reads that way:

> Nietzsche himself in his published work scarcely spoke of will to power. This must be taken as a sign that he wanted to protect as long as possible what was most intrinsic to his recognition of the truth concerning beings. (Heidegger 194)

Put that way, it does sound like a furtive plan and an author's trickery. But for Heidegger *wanting to protect a thought* does not mean keeping an experience secret, any more than *what is most intrinsic* means what is personally most significant and emotionally strongest. When he tries to pursue Nietzsche's thought to its deepest source, he understands that source as an orientation toward beings and not as an event in the mind of the man whom Heidegger with his tight smile calls "Herr Nietzsche."

Philosophy in the psychological sense is "a matter of utter indifference" (Heidegger 8). The book called *Will* is enough to bring Nietzsche's reader "to think Nietzsche's sole thought" (Heidegger 13). The enterprise of pawing over the published works *instead* of reconstructing this "thought" condemns

Nietzsche's readers to remaining in the "foreground" of his thought (Heidegger 46–47).

For all his dismissal of the published works, still Heidegger agrees at crucial points with the strategy of unearthing the Nietzsche disappointment.

First of all he agrees that *a disappointment exists*, though he characterizes it as Nietzsche's revelation of the meaninglessness in Western metaphysics joined with his inability to release himself from that very metaphysics (Behler 314). Because Nietzsche begins the essential movement of departure but does not complete it, finding him unfinished as a philosophical writer is a necessary stage in any confrontation with his thought.

Heidegger would agree second that the disappointment *will not be resolved by the discovery of new information*. What Nietzsche wrote stands in need of being reimagined and reassessed. *Then* his "sole thought" can be rethought, and not upon the receipt of additional clues.

Finally, Heidegger would agree that *there can be no completed book* that solves the problem of Nietzsche's incompleteness or that could have been written to solve it. He does not lament Nietzsche's failure to write the book he had envisioned as *The Will to Power*.

All these points of agreement are critical. So is the disagreement, which may be described as Heidegger's instruction to the reader not to feel disappointed, to set aside the published works as foreground once their capacity to disappoint becomes clear. One who tries to assess Nietzsche's biologism, for instance,

> always gets stuck in the foreground of his thinking. The predilection for this state of affairs is supported by the form of Nietzsche's own publications. His words and sentences provoke, fascinate, penetrate, and stimulate (Heidegger 47)—

which Heidegger says not to praise those words and sentences but censoriously. Readers ought to resist being fascinated, ideally by not reading Nietzsche's publications. They should resolve the problem of the publications by thinking about something else.

But if the pattern of proselytism and frustration acts itself out in the narratives of Nietzsche's published books there won't be anything else to think about. Nietzsche's publications have posed a problem and the problem will have to be understood by reading those publications.

Heidegger assumes that Nietzsche does not disappoint until you abandon the foreground of his thought. He would do well to look closer at that foreground instead of considering it the easy part of Nietzsche to read.

The problem of Socrates.   Objection (2) turns this discussion of a single philosopher to confront the philosophical tradition. Isn't the Nietzsche disappointment a warmed-over version of the Socrates disappointment? Therefore not in need of special explanation?

The first move of the Socratic sting imagines a paradigm of knowledge compared to which earlier claims of knowledge amount to nothing. Laches merely acts from something like courage; a Socratic Laches will know what courage is. The old morality tumbles before the onslaught of philosophy because it possesses no Socratic definitions for its most prized terms: virtue, wisdom, justice, friendship.

Then the second movement: Socrates does not know the Socratic definition either. One dialogue after another ends inconclusively. *Aporia* is the name for an irresolution about the meanings of ethical terms, irresolution out of which Socrates himself cannot lead his interlocutors, even though he started them on these expeditions in the first place.

When Nietzsche inspires an unsatisfiable curiosity he is only doing what Socrates did. Why pathologize him and not Socrates?

The best reason might be that the Socrates disappointment is not only visible but *made* visible. It is announced within the disappointing conversation. "We call ourselves friends and we don't know what a friend is!"—the conversation's failure is thematized within Plato's dialogues. Plato gives the failure a meaning: it shows how unwise Socrates' contemporaries are (*Apology* 21c–d), or it tames the arrogant adherence to falsehood (*Sophist* 230a–d).

Because Plato thematizes the *aporia* it dominates subsequent accounts of Socrates, until describing the Socrates disappointment almost is how one tries to understand Socrates. His enemies say that his requests for definition go unsatisfied because they are nonsense. His friends might read the failed inquiries as signs of the open prospects for philosophy. The interlocutors' inability to give Socrates any tolerable definition only betokens the prospect of better interlocutors in the years ahead, and longer conversations.

Nietzsche's friends and enemies may end up reading his explanatory failures oppositely too. But there is no corresponding sense of their beginning with interpretations of his failure. Unlike the Platonic dialogue, the Nietzsche book does not thematize its incompleteness. Nietzsche's reader feels the disappointment as a sting but feels that sting obscurely and even has to work to find its location.

Not only the incompleteness of Nietzsche's books but his inclination to hide that incompleteness also calls for explanation. Socrates advertises his failures, and you might wonder why, but there will be no concealment to account for where nothing has been spirited out of sight.

The unanswerable metaphysical question. Another form of metaphysical failure does not get thematized within metaphysics.

Take "Socrates" synecdochally to name not only the man that Plato wrote about but *the philosopher*. In that case a larger version of objection (2) will contain the Platonic Socrates but also a lot of other philosophers, and therefore might exonerate Nietzsche.

If Nietzsche remains guilty of pathology, it could be pathology he shares with all metaphysicians, no longer an idiosyncrasy. For on one view of philosophy the metaphysical theory goes astray not in the fine points of how it answers a question but in the form of the question itself. (This version of a Wittgensteinian portrayal of metaphysics is thoroughly indebted to Burton Dreben's seminars, Harvard University, 1981–1987.)

When the metaphysical question gets asked, *and*—this is the crucial part—before the one who asked it delivers an answer, it is not clear what form the answer will take. In *Grundlagen der Arithmetik*, Frege asks "What is the number one?" and rejects all other answers before basing his own on the sizes of sets.

Frege's question and its open prefatory "What is" do not lead to the answer (however useful that answer has proved to be to mathematics). The question introduces the answer accidentally, you might say, the answer more like someone bumped into on a street than like someone you go calling on with a letter of introduction. The question gives no indication that an adequate accounting of "1" will refer to the sizes of sets.

A scientific question by comparison assumes a great deal about where to look for its answer. "What is water?" has come to mean, "What elements combine to make water, and in what proportions?" Indeed, until the form of the answer can be taken for granted in the forming of the question, science does not know how to work.

It is not that "What is water?" or the meanings of the words logically contain the constraints on its answer. But it becomes a scientific question by virtue of arising within the science of the day, and that science does constrain answers to the question.

(Here Dreben's picture of metaphysics squares with the Kuhnian description of science in its first stages. Treatises on optics bog down in definitions and sallies against rival theories, until Newton shows how to study light and optics accepts limits on its questions and the science moves forward: Kuhn 13.)

The confusion that strikes Socrates' interlocutors is a sign that he asked questions like Frege's. What is courage? The real reason that every answer feels wrong is not the interlocutors' unwisdom or carelessness. Rather Socrates' question does not show what a right answer ought to look like.

Go beyond definitions. "How do I know I'm not dreaming?" "How are *a priori* synthetic judgments possible?" The metaphysical question betrays itself by its vertiginous openness to answers in advance of being answered, followed by stabilization as soon as the questioner supplies an answer.

The question cues the answer only in the way that a cliffhanger victim's hand-wringing "How will I ever get out of *this?*" cues the *deus ex machina*.

If metaphysics builds on questions that only the questioners can answer, disappointment is apt to be endemic to the enterprise. The double movement of question and answer promises a wide field of inquiry and then immediately narrows the field down to a single path.

When Nietzsche rifles through the past to find transformations in those practices that once looked stable, he may similarly be looking for accounts that are not there to be found. Temporalization might be a metaphysical demand, doomed to be disappointed by every answer.

In short, there is nothing wrong with Nietzsche except that he's a philosopher.

This objection has some truth in it, as the comparison to Socrates also does. Still it should be observed that on this picture of metaphysics the philosopher disappoints by giving an answer. Nietzsche is being accused of disappointing his reader by *not* giving answers.

The difference amounts to more than it might seem to. Take one of the problems with *Birth*'s introduction of Socrates. First, all orientations toward experience are divided into the Apollinian and the Dionysian. Then Socrates appears from an unnatural domain beyond the reach of those forces. This is not in any ordinary sense a disappointing answer: the disappointment does not come up until the reader wonders how Socrates ever could have appeared in the pre-Socratic world that Nietzsche imagines—and Nietzsche gives no answer.

Questions and riddles. Moreover, Nietzsche's questions about causation and the past differ from philosophical questions in a way that demands not just an answer to the query but an answer that he has up his sleeve. Nietzsche presents his questions as *riddles*, he queries his readers with the suggestion that he knows the trick of answering.

The questions he posed in *Birth* were riddles. In "Attempt at a Self-Criticism" Nietzsche calls his younger self a "riddle-friend [Rätselfreund]." He says he was "bemused and beriddled [verrätselt]" (AS 1).

Genealogy III is a riddle in its own way. Lately John T. Wilcox has described how that essay unpacks its own first section (Wilcox 1997, 1998); and this structure—a cryptic statement followed by its elaborated solution—is the structure of a riddle.

You might say that a riddle is a manufactured question. A philosophical question stakes its integrity on not having been manufactured. This is why the accusation of raising merely academic questions is such a serious one in philosophy. It is the charge that there is no real issue living inside a debate, only the generation of an automatic question in the absence of anything that needs to be known.

The philosophical question cannot become a riddle and still understand itself.

The Socratic question might even be said to exist as an *antidote* to riddles, if riddles trade in the ambiguities that Socratic questioning wants to undo. For at *Republic* 479 the objects of the world are themselves seen as riddles. They are ambiguous with respect to certain predicates, they go by the name "large" but also "small," "double" but also "half." Glaucon says they're like

> the children's riddle [*ainigma*] about the eunuch, about his hitting the bat—with what and on what he struck it. For the manys are also ambiguous, and it's not possible to think of them fixedly as either being or not being, or as both or neither. (Allan Bloom translation, 479b–c)

Plato seems to be thinking of an old riddle:

> There is a story that a man and not a man saw and did not see a bird and not a bird perched on a branch and not a branch and hit him and did not hit him with a rock and not a rock (Bloom 461n40)

—that had the solution, "A eunuch who did not see well saw a bat perched on a reed and threw a pumice stone at him which missed."

In ordinary life, that solution resolves the riddle's nonsense. But the riddling "bird and not a bird on a branch and not a branch" and the rest is also Plato's way of describing *a man who saw a bird on a branch that he then hit with a rock*. If you want to be precise about it, every particular object or event needs to be described with that phrasing: the quality of both being P and not being P characterizes every particular thing that the world has to offer. If every act of hitting also partly misses, then to hit is always also *not* to hit, and it should be more accurately described by "hit and not hit," as every bird should be called "a bird and not a bird."

The recurrent is-and-is-not phrase shows that the "many" things cannot be talked about philosophically. Talk about particular objects is not clear talk, because their properties apply equivocally to them, univocally only to the Forms. They are riddles whose solution has not yet been guessed.

Faced with such a world, philosophy aims at a domain in which riddling is impossible. The riddle's solution about the eunuch and the bat only celebrates the ambiguity that dialectics was created to undo. When Socrates hears about "a man and not a man" and the rest of that sentence, *he* looks for a solution that would let him say, "A man saw a bird on a branch and hit it with a rock."

Because a riddle announces itself as a contrivance, the solution consists in reaching an intended answer. God gives Ezekiel a riddle to tell in the form of a story:

> a great eagle with great wings, longwinged, full of feathers, which had divers colours, came unto Lebanon, and took the highest branch of the cedar: he cropped off the top of his young twigs, and carried it into a land of traffick; he set it in a city of merchants,

and more in that spirit. The story allegorically foretells the restoration of Israel (Ezekiel 17.1–10). If the allegory seems open to other interpretations it is too bad for those interpretations: God's intention fixes its meaning.

One last example of the distance between riddles and philosophical questions. The Sphinx's riddle asks, "What goes on four legs" etc., and the answer is, "Man." If the philosopher asks what man is, a wide range of answers may be possible, but *not* "that which goes on four legs in the morning" etc.

Why doesn't the riddle work in reverse? Other questions and their answers do. ("Who was Thales?" "The first philosopher." "Who was the first philosopher?") But a reversible riddle is a poor sort of riddle, much too easily guessed. The riddle chooses one among many ways of describing the thing it is asking about. Its manufactured quality follows from this advance process of selection. And the process of selection again shows that a riddle has an intended answer.

If Nietzsche is a riddler, then the Nietzsche disappointment is in fact a disappointment with his person. For where a question might have no answer it does not have to reflect badly on the questioner that no answer comes. When the questioner asks a riddle, as Nietzsche does, and *then* does not deliver the answer, the problem lies in the riddler.

The objection of an intentional lacuna. If objection (3) has to face the question of Nietzsche's intentions, objection (4) hardly considers anything else. It proposes that any gap or causal failure in Nietzsche's histories is there intentionally.

For even a first look at the objection (see conclusion for more), it is essential that all sides acknowledge what Heidegger considers a joke, namely that Herr Nietzsche is under discussion. Anxiety and repression appear "in his books" metaphorically: anxiety in *Birth* is Nietzsche's birth-anxiety. And if something not said in the books is intentionally left unsaid, it is Herr Nietzsche who intentionally isn't talking.

What does it come to, to call a problem in Nietzsche's books intentional, that the books not only fail to provide the causal explanation he has stirred his readers up to desire but fail on purpose? "Fail on purpose" threatens to trivialize the idea of "on purpose." Something can be intentional gibberish or intentionally false, but then it is still false or gibberish. Does "on purpose" modify failure into success?

(You can intentionally tell an unfunny joke. In that case you succeed when no one laughs. And you might have good reasons, which make you welcome the joke's unfunniness. Your host's quip just fell flat unintentionally and you want to deflect the embarrassment. But without a reason the success alone is not worth much.)

If "on purpose" merely reflected an author's sincerity then intentions would be as elusive and private as some readers take them to be. If it might turn out that in his heart Spinoza really saw thought and extension as two separate substances—*and if his secret made his writings a hoax*: if his secret thumbs-down invalidated his philosophy—then philosophy would depend on philosophers' sincerity.

But it is not clear that philosophical hoaxes (as opposed to forgeries) are possible. Announcing a hoax—"I didn't mean it"—sounds like trying to announce "I didn't really promise, because I never intended to meet you."

Sincerity—speaking on purpose, believing what you say—is a word for *seriousness*. Nor is it the best way to capture what matters about seriousness. The author's seriousness does not make the words true, but it does suggest a promise about the writings. If Nietzsche is serious, the claim that he left causal stories out on purpose means not just that he did not care about origins, but that his baffling changes of pace play a productive function in his writing. "Nietzsche is serious" means: there is a reason for the way he writes. That is his promise, and studying Nietzsche is a way of trusting that he will keep his promise.

But *then* the question of what Nietzsche might be doing on purpose becomes the question of what purpose the gaps in his books might serve. Nietzsche's books can be usefully said to fail on purpose if their failure serves a purpose, produces some effect.

The effect might be triumph over nostalgia, if nostalgia saw the past as a larger and bolder-colored version of the present; also if the past were the present day's encodement in a small and unsullied seed. Given a temptation to nostalgize, Nietzsche's writings get you to look into the past and see sharp breaks between its eras and thereby give up the wish to return.

Genealogy is widely cited (by Foucault for one) as the first inspiration for a historical inquiry that searches out discontinuities. If Nietzsche is serious then what looked like a failing is actually a successful revision of historical method.

In *Birth* Nietzsche already plays up the chasms between historical epochs. What he mainly does differently in *Genealogy* is to emphasize this interpretive practice and make it self-conscious. So *Genealogy* may be considered his best shot at deflecting the accusation that in neglecting certain causal accounts he fails at his own purpose and specifically because of some unknown motive.

Genealogy contains Nietzsche's reason for withholding certain causal explanations: the strategy behind his silence. If that strategy holds up there then the disappointment of books like *Birth* indicates only a stumble along the way. The serious purpose of telling a punctured story has been served. If the strategy falls in *Genealogy*, however, the Nietzsche disappointment begins to look like a persistent feature of Nietzsche readings.

⁓ꞔ

On the Genealogy of Morals: The Problem of "Evil"

Introduction.   *Genealogy* blazes through three sustained inquiries into morality barely pausing for the belittling attacks or the brilliant freestanding observations that Nietzsche is known for. This book finds him on a mission.

But how to describe *Genealogy*'s mission? Like other knotty books, it loosens up best at the tug of a single strand, in this case (no surprise) the theme of the past, past-causing-present, the sources of modern morality.

Is there a real life beyond morality?   Does moral language name something, or can it only pun on old words and their meanings?

And to answer that question, first tackle these:

Was there a truer human existence before morality, a reproach to the debasement that modern values represent? Or is humanity coeval with morality, so that anything you can call a human creature is a thing governed by what you must call morality?

Nietzsche's private anxieties play an obbligato to the philosophical questions. What existence can Nietzsche claim for himself apart from his writings? Can he say something new, something to *put his name to*, or is it too late for that, and must he only parody, quote, and translate other language, guessing at its oldest meanings?

Metaphorically speaking (as well as literally), is this priest who reigns over "morality" and its canny smarmy language, whose honorific is "Father"—is he Nietzsche's father and master of Nietzsche's vocabulary? Or is there a Nietzsche independent of the lexicon he was born into, who can grant himself authority apart from his moral inheritance?

The question of a truer former state, whether for the species or just for him, is really the question (of momentous philosophical *and* psychological interest to Nietzsche): Is there only the present?

Nietzsche begs goddesses he does not believe in to grant him a glimpse, "*one* glance," of some better human specimens than the ones standing in front of him (I.12). A doomed wish, given that there are no such deities? But listen to him plead, the man is practically singing, and when Orpheus sang even grim de-loved goddess Persephone gave him another chance.

"Yes but Orpheus peeked and the chance disappeared. Maybe alternatives to Christianity have been sucked down to the underworld forever too. Then the task for a philosopher of morality is not to scorn reactivity and weakness and the hospital's stink. What smells like rank garbage to you is candy in a fly's little nostrils, and even if you cling to the thought that you outrank the fly you still have to admit that it breeds and buzzes—it too is will to power— and the philosopher is the one who can see all valuations as signs of power."

Genealogy lives in the tension between these two conceptions of philosophy. Nietzsche dreams of a detached perspective that can see all acts as positive. But he also engages himself with the present, *moralizes*, he dreams of a past positivity that shows up the negativity of present decadence so that he can condemn the values he observes.

The detached perspective effaces oppositions between morality and any alternative, assessing all phenomena equanimously as signs of will to power. Dualism leaves Nietzsche spoiling for a fight; "the moral *as such*" is all wrong, the worst values anyone could have invented. "I could show you hills, in comparison with which you'd call that a valley."

My writings. "I am one thing [Das Eine bin ich: literally, The one is me], my writings are another matter [das Andre sind meine Schriften]" (*Ecce Homo*, "Books" 1).

Other passages likewise record Nietzsche's wish to separate himself from the words he's written. *Beyond* closes with a leave-taking from "my written and painted thoughts" that sets those thoughts a distance from Nietzsche's person (296). The distance does not mean that Nietzsche disavows his words (Schacht 1983, 530); it does reflect his need to insist on his own unwritten identity, as if something in his nature might dissolve away if Nietzsche were to turn out to be identical with those writings.

In the multifariousness that is a Nietzsche book it might be the unity of his nature that dissolves. "I am one thing"—he talks that way in other places too (e.g., *Ecce Homo*, "Clever" 9). He is the one, the same, he has no wish to be different (*Ecce Homo*, "Clever" 9: "I myself do not want to become different"), while his writings are "das Andre," the other or the different.

By comparison the ascetic priest in the third essay of *Genealogy* is "the incarnate wish to be different" (III.13). Does this make the priest the one person that Nietzsche is absolutely *not*?

But then Nietzsche fiddles with the question of who he is relative to *Genealogy's* priest. Writing of *Genealogy* in *Ecce Homo* he concludes: "I have been understood. . . . This book contains the first psychology of the priest"— on its face an aggressive proclamation. Here am I Nietzsche writing to you, and if you have figured anything out at all it's that I am the man who put the priest in his place.

Except that Nietzsche says *he's* been understood, not that *his book* has. Didn't he just distinguish himself from his writings? *Genealogy* saw to it that Nietzsche the man is understood; and if he has been understood *because* this book contains the psychology of the priest, then maybe Nietzsche is a priest after all.

Far-fetched? But the question of how he is related to the priest possesses Nietzsche all through *Genealogy*.

Moreover the question of Nietzsche and the priest is very nearly the question of how Nietzsche the man is related to his writings. Nietzsche's books have ties to other books (a genealogy) that he would not want for himself. Consider *Genealogy*, which while delivering such blasphemously different news from the Gospel of John still speaks in that book's language. You could say it is fated to be the Gospel's shadow lingering on the cave walls of Europe. *Genealogy* has to deliver the bad news it was born to tell in the good-news language that its audience will recognize: in this respect it is Christianity's book. Nietzsche the man, however, still registers the wish to live outside of this fate that his writings are subject to.

Never spoke man thus.   Do you want to read about conspiracies, the law, the mob? The Fourth Gospel contains all those elements and also (like *Genealogy*) priestly machinations in the service of a strategically organized religion.

The high priests in John 7 are the ones who say "mob." They send court officers to seize Jesus (the first time they try that). The officers come back without him, and the priests ask:

Why haven't you brought him?
The officers answered, Never spoke man thus, as this man does.

Then the Pharisees answered them, Are you deceived too? Have any of the rulers or the Pharisees believed in him? But this mob [ochlos] that does not know the law [nomos] is cursed. (Jn 7.45–49)

Parenthesis on the Gospel of John. Nietzsche sneers when he says "amorous-enthusiastic Gospel" (I.16) about the Gospel of John yet treats it as definitive of Christianity.

Genealogy calls the ascetic priest a shepherd (III.16) and—in quotation marks—"savior" (III.17). Nietzsche would have known that "Savior of the world" (Jn. 4.42) and "good shepherd" (10.11) are Christological titles specific to John. And Nietzsche describes Jesus as "the incarnate [leibhafte] gospel of love" (I.8). *The* gospel of love is John's (see I.16), so Jesus is that gospel or good word *in person* as you could also translate "leibhafte." That would make Jesus someone identical with the writing about him, certainly identical with that particular writing whose first sentence calls him a *logos* (among other things a word) and whose prefatory chapter says that this *logos* became flesh (1.14).

In the passage from John about the botched arrest, what gets Nietzsche's attention may be the officers' report: "Never spoke man thus." Morality arrives speaking a new language and the old law loses its purchase. Failed communication comes to receive a new diagnosis in John 8:

Why don't you understand my speech [lalian]?—because you cannot hear my word [logon],

or "because you cannot hear my thought, my reasoning, my collected ideas." The reason for that incomprehension, according to Jesus, is that

You are of your father the devil . . .

where "devil" transliterates *diabolos*, literally and etymologically and also as a matter of general Greek use before the New Testament, "slanderer";

there is no truth in him. (8.43–44)

The new language makes everyone who can't understand it a liar.

Like the Gospel of the Word, Genealogy will approach morality through the portals of language. Nietzsche's history becomes a history of linguistic innovation, or as he sometimes puts it *metaphor*.

My own language. Twenty years before Genealogy Nietzsche wrote to Carl von Gersdorff:

It would be a very sad state of affairs not to be able to write better and yet warmly to want to do so. (Middleton 22)

Nevertheless this young man devoted to the idea of writing shrinks from identifying himself with certain of the words he writes.

I have nothing "solid" or "real" to tell you, or whatever the current slogans of the shopkeepers are. (Middleton 24)

Nietzsche will take it upon himself to say something besides what slogans are built to deliver. He will not treat current slogans as his own words. This is what it will mean to write better.

Nietzsche obviously writes against the current in *Genealogy*, which as Eric Blondel observes

is interminably translation and transposition, as indicated by the quotation marks, equivalences, and phrases like "in my language," "I mean," "I under-stand," "that is to say," and "translated into German." (Blondel 1994, 314)

Nietzsche's translations move back and forth between German and a vocabulary that bears a previously unimagined relationship to German or to any other modern language.

The most noticeable signs of Nietzsche's foreignness to his own writing are the quotation marks that crown or wreathe almost every value term. "Unegoistic" (P.5), "the evil man" (P.6), "readable" (P.8), and then Essay I is studded with the marks: "utility" (I.2), "moral" (I.3), "aristocratic" (I.4)—but you don't have to drink the whole ocean to know that it's salty, a methodical list is beside the point when any section of the book could mention "sacredness of duty" (II.6) or "angel" (II.7) or "God" (III.1) or "virtues" (III.8).

Pace those interpretations that deny the possibility of general accounts of genealogy (e.g., Salim Kemal), the genealogies that Nietzsche writes share certain strategies, among them the exposure of the devious linguistic change that effected changes in metaphysics, morals, and human souls.

Nietzsche could spare himself the effort and talk trash the way everyone else does.

But why stroke the effeminate ears of our modern weaklings? . . . if a psychologist today has *good taste* (others might say, integrity) it consists in resistance to the shamefully *moralized* way of speaking which has gradually made all modern judgments of men and things slimy. (III.19)

This word "resistance" makes clear that the task of writing better will be negative and strategic. Nietzsche says he has his own "*a priori*" (P.3) and proposes to speak "in my own language" (I.2) not as if he came from another world but to express the peculiarity of his life in this one, always antagonistically engaged with its language. His own language takes the language that is in current use and diverts its meanings.

So Nietzsche claims the right to mean something idiosyncratic by his words. His integrity demands that he be able to say: "I employed the word 'state': it is obvious what is meant—some pack of blond beasts of prey" (II.17). Using "state" contrary to standard usage is his way of not accepting the denaturation that words have suffered. And "denaturation" is a nice way of saying what Nietzsche less nicely calls "tartuffery" (P.6, II.1, II.6), "counterfeiting" (e.g., I.14, III.14), "slandering" (II.24).

Nietzsche's own language will be a language to use among friends who set aside the slogans of moral shopkeepers. Meanwhile "I *know* of no friend" (III.27). Maybe there is no one to understand him—though Nietzsche does not blame himself. "If this book is incomprehensible to anyone and jars on his ears, the fault, it seems to me, is not necessarily mine" (P.8). The moral ideals of the present "slander the world" (II.24), so an adherent to modern morality belongs to the slanderer who has no truth in him. A devil-child like that will miss the point of Nietzsche's speech by not hearing his neologism.

The new language might not contain new words. The old words will have to do even if they no longer do anything. They need to be put to new work, first of all by being corrected—possibly the way Nietzsche says he corrected Paul Rée's speculations, "not in order to refute them" (and if you don't refute a theory then you really don't refute a word) but "to replace the improbable with the more probable, possibly one error with another" (P.4).

Epanorthosis.   A figure in which a word is used and then immediately withdrawn to be replaced (Quinn 68).

"Look, the hour is coming—it has come now—for you to be scattered . . . and leave me alone" (Jn 16.32): an example in which the correction moves from what the audience understands to news it is likely to choke on.

Nietzsche writes epanorthotically in *Genealogy* II speaking of "the delicacy and even more the tartuffery of tame domestic animals (which is to say modern men, which is to say us [will sagen moderner Menschen, will sagen uns])" (II.6).

An epanorthosis replaces the worse word with the better one, possibly one error with another. It is not a refutation. If you tell Nietzsche the ascetic priest's moralizing has improved human beings, "I shall not argue: only I should have to add what 'improved' signifies to me—the same thing as . . . 'weakened,'. . . 'made refined,' 'made effete,' 'emasculated' (thus almost the same thing as *harmed*)" (III.21).

Like aposiopesis and praeteritio, epanorthosis is a way of not saying *something else*. In his epanorthotic moments, Nietzsche does not want to speak within the possibilities that modern moral discourse allows.

Nietzsche on language.   Nietzsche differentiates two linguistic operations: literal naming, the direct ostension he calls "coining"; and metaphorical renaming, "counterfeiting." The former operation is innocent, the latter strategic. The first orients the human to the world; the second establishes a new orientation among words.

Nietzsche registers the temptation to let morality deflate itself into a language but also resists that temptation. If there had never been a time of ostension, if naming is renaming and always was, then there's never been any movement besides circulations inside an existent language; and a book like *Genealogy* becomes one more such circulation, and Nietzsche's place is inside language. If nothing ever happened between then and now, if there is no problem of evil, then first of all the priest is Nietzsche's father (being everybody's), and second the priest's language is the only language there is, and Nietzsche is nothing different from his writings.

Nietzsche is fighting for his life; hence the fighting words. He is speaking his own new language.

The wish to be different.   But if the insistence that he is something other than his writings grows out of Nietzsche's distaste for the words that have been set before him, and if he gives body to the wish for his otherness by gainsaying the words as he says them, his wish begins to look like the ascetic priest's perennial wish to be something different and to change the meanings of words.

What if Nietzsche *inherited* his wish from the ascetic priest?—in which case his act of differentiating himself from that nay-saying type actually becomes a point of resemblance between them. This is not a psychological matter about Nietzsche: it is a way of talking about the version of the Nietzsche disappointment that haunts *Genealogy*, which emerges as its reader tries to figure out who the book's priest is.

The degree of likeness that holds between Nietzsche and the priest—and the degree of unlikeness that Nietzsche insists on—translates into the question of what role the priest will play in Nietzsche's explanations of the present. Make the two of them too different from each other and the priest becomes identified with everything that Nietzsche wants to overcome: he is the source of that slimy moralizing against which Nietzsche writes every word he has to say. If the priest is Nietzsche's opposite, Nietzsche is seeing him as the one who corrupted the world. The priest turns into a devil figure.

A history that contains a devil tells the story of a world with a problem of evil. Did someone come along suddenly to ruin the human species? And how did *that* happen? If Nietzsche uses the priest to explain the decadence of the species he will have to account for the decadence of the priest.

Now in general one can settle the problem of evil by denying that evil exists. And Nietzsche can escape the trouble of accounting for the priest's magical corrupting effect on humanity if he resists the urge to speak of corruption, if his genealogical explanations do not depend on something's having gone wrong in history. At several points *Genealogy* lends itself to such a reading. No morality tale and no lost innocence, everything has always been as it is. What might have looked like decadence is at most the (decadent) misinterpretation of a natural condition.

The priest does not disappear and he continues to work his effects on morality's history; only now the values that he presides over are those that have always prevailed.

In Essay I the priest first appears as a cross between master morality and slave morality, but then it turns out that everyone else is too, and always has been. Only mixed types have ever existed. As the paradigmatic human the priest is now the one that everyone resembles; in which case Nietzsche resembles him too; in which case Nietzsche cannot only regret the priest's existence but also has to acknowledge that the priest has fathered him.

The alternative to an impossible explanatory puzzle is therefore a different way of denying the modern conception of history as steady progress toward the splendid present. *Genealogy* is famous for denying that error in one way especially, breaking history's motion into discrete episodes. But another possibility exists in the same book, namely the denial of progress on the grounds that everything has always been this way.

On this alternative Nietzsche becomes not the priest's polar opposite but his beloved son, less metaphorically the expected and even the inevitable child of Christianity.

"The priest has fathered him"?   If "History" raises and drops the question of where the first human comes from, and *Birth* follows a similar question about the first philosopher with a similar failure to answer, *Genealogy* brings the disappointment even closer to Nietzsche's own identity.

When "History" temporized about the root causes of inwardness, it identified historical existence or self-consciousness with the nature of the human. Maybe inwardness means the human philosopher, considering the essay's return to Cartesian matters, but if not that then still the philosophical human.

"Did the thoughtful human (me for instance) come to exist?" Nietzsche might be asking.

Birth narrows Nietzsche's subject down to the birth of Socrates; which includes the birth of that elusive new Socrates called Nietzsche. The original philosopher—a philosopher who can be original—how could such a thing be? Will natural forces even supernaturally personified ever account for a being like that?

By the time of *Genealogy* Nietzsche's defensiveness has toughened. There is still no talk of his being born but also something more exact and held to with more muscle, no question of his father's having given birth. The fear is not just that anyone fathered Nietzsche (though that would be bad enough) but that it had to be *this* father the bumbling country parson.

What justifies the move to psychology in readings of *Genealogy* is the book's ambivalence of purpose. If not the resistance to having been fathered, then some other powerful wish is needed to understand a project that calls itself genealogy and then shows no interest in finding the father figure that genealogies aim at.

Blondel touches on the ambivalence: "when he discusses life as a state of pregnancy . . . Nietzsche is not concerned with revealing a father" (Blondel 1977, 154). Graham Parkes likewise feels driven to remark

> that in all this talk of pregnancy there is no mention of an impregnator: the father, whether a figure in the world or in the thinker's own psyche, is neither named nor even alluded to. (Parkes 243)

Just as disappointment over causal accounts will mean something sharper and more poignant in *Genealogy* than it did in *Birth* or "History," so too will Nietzsche's resistance to the father of humanity, of philosophy, of the philosopher (Nietzsche).

But first a caution. To speak of *Genealogy* in terms of Nietzsche's resistance is to diagnose problems that seize that book's argument and make it seize up: problems of evil and bidirectional causation. Disagreeing with claims about Nietzsche's anxiety therefore means rejecting a *diagnosis* of these argumentative failures. But that is all the disagreement means. The symptoms, the argumentative failures, are another matter: the Nietzsche disappointment for *Genealogy*, that stories of the past are promised and left untold; that the crucial turns in history are both whipped up into high drama and also obliterated. The symptoms will persist apart from any given diagnosis.

So you may accept or reject an explanation for Nietzsche's writing. But rejecting the explanation will not ease the problems of reading him. And this chapter is dedicated to making those problems show.

Such a self-conscious book. *Genealogy* is a book of modernity in that it finds no form of writing ready to contain what it has to say. Nietzsche is out to speak as *man never spoke*, and there is no obvious way to do that. So *Genealogy* explores what genealogical writing is in the midst of writing genealogically.

Such a self-conscious book and yet it disappoints the enthusiast who would love it. Nietzsche watches what he says but still manages to talk himself into corners.

Psychologically speaking the disappointment with *Genealogy* begins with the powerful feelings it arouses, aggressivity and anger and regret that then cannot find an object to attach themselves to. *Genealogy* has the fervor and the effectiveness of a call to arms—but which way to the battlefield? whom to shoot? (See Higgins 1994, 49–50, on the pains of reading *Genealogy*.)

But the Nietzsche disappointment does not belong only to the realm of feeling. Nietzsche raises specific questions about where the moral order of the present has come from, and after fighting to get his readers to consider this incomprehensibly new kind of question he denies them a coherent answer.

For example: *Ecce Homo*'s summary of *Genealogy* refers to "disagreeable truths" that rumble in the distance and then more closely, as the book's essays charge toward their three resting points. These truths are intended to say precisely what is not said in "the world." Thus it should astonish Essay II's reader to hear that far from being God's voice in the soul, the guilty conscience is the human impulse to cruelty expressing itself inside the human interior. Don't ask what substance the inner life is but (unimaginable that someone should be asking this and yet Nietzsche does) where it came from and *what* it came from.

What makes this truth disagreeable is that you never would have asked such a question. Now you do. And Nietzsche never quite provides the causal account that would answer it.

Outline of the disappointment. Each of the three essays begins with human beings in an animal condition and follows their decline into angels.

The essays detail the pressures that come to bear on innocent humans. Social inequality is one kind (Essay I). A more generally applying pressure is social existence as such, meaning existence in a community that enforces its rules with punishment (II). The most pervasive pressure is the suffering inherent in existence as such (III).

Nietzsche sketches the history of human responses to these pressures in a three-part structure.

First the primitive human responds to the pressure with a rough system of valuation. Modern softlings don't want to admit it but that system is a morality in spite of its hardness and its unashamed unsubtlety.

In a second stage the original morality warps into a deviant system recognizably like the morality of the present. The new system's convolutions, and the self-hatred it contains, indict what modern civilization has unreflectively thought of as morality as such. Thus the tale of increasing deviance exposes the diseased quality of modern morality.

But—mind you, this third part of each story comes and goes quickly— while there is much to deplore in modern civilization, even its decadence points the way to hope for the future.

Given the arc of each essay's narrative, a problem of evil arises in each. Actually (though the ear won't hear the difference) it should be called a problem of "evil," because each story's turn for the worse comes with a twist in the moral lexicon. Concepts of wickedness and perversion enter moral discourse. Nietzsche has to explain how guilt-ridden interiority ever came into existence (Essay II), how the ascetic ideal could have become the only evaluative game in town (III), and also explain the most famous historical change he describes, how slave morality ever conquered master morality (I).

Nietzsche can present the stages of the past as temporally successive. In that case he has to show how innocence led to decadence. When he does try to show that change happening, a Lucifer figure emerges as the cause of the fall—the priest in the first and third essays, God in the second. *But that would-be explanation of human decadence itself remains unexplained.*

What's worse than a problem of evil is that exactly when the reader's aroused fury at the sorry state of the present prepares to attach itself to the priestly Jew or to the ancestor god that grew into Christianity's God or to the ascetic priest, the unsustainability of these narratives invites another reading: Nietzsche is not really describing historical changes that ever happened. This counter-reading appears in the essays to ward off the problem of "evil." The priest or god does not represent any sudden misfortune that spoiled the human animal but was always present, the cause of all values and not their undoing. He is God the creator, not Satan.

When *Genealogy*'s tale of decline gives way to this other reading, the account becomes more coherent. No inexplicable tempters are needed. But intellectual disappointment over causal lapses gives way to an affective disappointment: that fury that had aimed at the priest who *spoiled* things for everyone does not apply to the same figure now conceived as the one who *made* things for everyone.

Nietzsche as moralist. Henry Staten finds a split story in *Genealogy*, too. He speaks of two Nietzsches writing, one of them a vitalist committed to explanatory monism (taking will to power as undifferentiated force), the other a moralist who acts in accord with a dualism (taking will to power as bivalent, either active or reactive).

The first Nietzsche sees will to power everywhere. He dominates Essay III, as when that essay concedes a life-enhancing function to the ascetic priest it had been vilifying. He is the high-minded Nietzsche who surveys an "overall economy" of power.

The contrary impulse to blame belongs to that other hand that Nietzsche has, that writes such invective as his fable of the lambs and the bird of prey (Staten 105–106).

> On the one hand, there is an overall economy that includes both health and decay; on the other hand, Nietzsche cannot deny himself the satisfaction of sounding the note of strong ascendancy over the forces of decay. (Staten 30)

Alan Schrift discovers a similar division of loyalties in *Genealogy*:

> *quantitatively*, Nietzsche affirms all manifestations of power or force. But *qualitatively*, he affirms only active or affirmative force while criticizing those forces that he determines to be qualitatively *reactive*. (Schrift 1995, 43)

(See Simon May for a contemporary attempt to patch up this tension, also Bailey on May.)

The Nietzsche who distinguishes types of force is the one who makes his readers feel bad worrying that they are secretly reactive or slavish. The other Nietzsche can see even your most indirect passive-aggressive neurotic guilt as will to power at work and make you feel good about it.

Where there is room to champion one event over another, there is room to ask why things should have gone wrong. Then Nietzsche faces a problem of evil. The problem of "evil" arises for the moralizing Nietzsche who separates active will to power from the sheepishly merely reactive versions of it.

Then there is Nietzsche the monist. And when criticizing makes no sense because everything expresses will to power, the demand for an explanation falls away. Only then the vilified priest represents the greatest power around and must be raised out of the pandemonium of modern morality into a new kind of pantheon.

The long view and the shortsighted view. Considered as human actions the trial and execution of Jesus are evil: the betrayal by Judas, the machinations of Caiaphas and the other high priests behind Judas (Jn. 18.3), the machinations of Satan behind them all. Thus Jesus dips the Passover sop into his cup and gives it to Judas, "and after the sop Satan entered into him" (Jn. 13.27).

The priests have been scheming all along to have Jesus seized (e.g., Jn. 7.45), Caiaphas the high priest the most energetically (Jn. 11.49–50, 18.13–14, 18.19–28, 19.15). John outdoes the other gospel authors in pinning the blame on priests and Pharisees—not to put too fine a point on it, he blames the Jews. Their priests in particular act indistinguishably from Satan.

In this respect, however, one might say there are two evangelists John, for considered as a great plan for human salvation the same events issue from a contrary Cause. On the long view they are even events to be celebrated. Engaged and detached, the Gospel laments the Crucifixion as historical event and venerates its eternal meaning.

"It benefits [*sumpherei*] you that I go away," as Jesus says (Jn. 16.7). At the time of his arrest he rebukes Peter for slashing the high priest's servant. "The cup which my father has given me, shall I not drink it?" (18.11).

What was true of the blind man is true again (Jn. 9.1–9). The disciples in their moralistic myopia had wondered "who sinned, this man or his parents, that he should be born blind." But no one did anything wrong, Jesus says; the man was blind so that (as the long view would have it) the works of God would be manifested in him.

Intruding as an exegetical narrator and a monist, John calls the human explanation for the Passion the shortsighted account; first when Caiaphas lays out his plan (motivated by fear of the Romans):

It benefits [*sumpherei*] us that one man should die for the people, and the whole nation not perish (11.50)

Caiaphas says, which leads into this gloss:

And this he spoke not from himself [*aph'eautou*], but, being high priest that year he prophesied that Jesus would die for the nation—and in fact, not only for the nation, but so that all the scattered children of God would gather into one. (11.51–52)

John's epanorthosis shows what "for the nation" really means, how much more it means than Caiaphas can realize. That real meaning comes not from Caiaphas but in spite of him. A longer view than he is capable of speaks from his words.

Thanks to his position as high priest, Caiaphas's words get their true sense from a prior source.

Here is another appeal to the long view:

> You will be sorrowful, but your sorrow shall be turned into joy. A woman in labor has sorrow, because her hour is come: but as soon as she is delivered of the child, she no longer remembers the anguish for joy that a man is born into the world. (16.20–21)

Nietzsche will use the same analogy when he wants to raise his own histories above the pattern of innocence and deviance. He finds the prospect of a new birth harder to enjoy, but like John he needs to reconcile two incompatible perspectives and often alternates between short and long views to do it; and pregnancy makes a familiar image of suffering redeemed.

Is history possible? First the historian has to determine what the long view is and what it is trying to look at.

In part, *Genealogy* deserves the name "self-conscious" by virtue of its reflections on the nature and possibility of historical inquiry.

A few months before the book appeared (February 1887), Nietzsche wrote to Franz Overbeck about Renan's *Origins of Christianity*.

> At root, my distrust goes so far as to question if history is really *possible*. What is it that people want to establish—something which was not established at the moment when it occurred? (Middleton 261)

History has wanted to justify modern institutions by incorporating past events into a teleological account that runs smoothly to the present. Renan thinks he can look straight into the moment of Christianity's conception and spot its defining sentiments like birthmarks. But you can't even call it history when a scholar has gone digging for some weighty event that, back when it originally happened, had none of its present heft.

Nietzsche's corrective will consist not in ignoring the past but in presenting it as historians have not.

The historical spirit.   Someone ought to write a genealogy of morals, Nietzsche says. These English psychologists who have been *called* genealogists—"these [diese]" is the first word of Essay I, Nietzsche points with the demonstrative pronoun to mean the theorists of today and right in front of him—made a stab at looking for the origins of moral values but botched the job.

What Nietzsche charges these sorry predecessors with is lacking "the historical spirit" (I.2). These opening sections say three things about "unhistorical natures":

> (1) the English psychologists are only describing their own minds, "the idiosyncrasy of the English psychologists" (I.2)
>
> (2) they wrongly assume that the concept "good" must get its meaning from "those to whom 'goodness' was shown" (I.2)
>
> (3) they did not consider "the real etymological significance of the designations for 'good' coined in the various languages" (I.4)

They only know their own way of thinking and have not paid attention to the language of morals.

Possessing a historical nature therefore means leaving yourself open to the discovery that the past was radically different from the present. Nietzsche often expresses the differences between epochs in the form of paradoxes. From hatred comes the religion of love; from noble attributions of goodness come slavish ones. The story that moves from past to present leaps from a phenomenon to its opposite.

Assuming Nietzsche can tell just when a historical step stretches out into a leap, the genealogical conception of history promises to transform historical inquiry forever. But making that difference clear—the difference between historical continuity and the discontinuity that genealogy claims to find—is harder than it looks.

What will prove to be even harder is using the conception of interrupted history to combat self-satisfied moralism about human progress without slipping into another kind of moralism: how bad the present is, how far it's fallen—sentiments that bring the curious student of history to ask what *made* it fall.

The genealogical spirit.   A genealogy traces the pedigree of modern institutions and practices. Traditional histories take the steps for granted: they know too well what they are looking for. The pedigrees they produce paper over fissures in the past with tautologizing narratives that (for instance) make "good" a name for *The Good* and deserving its name by virtue of its goodness. The insufficiently historical history, because it refuses to look at jumps in the past, surveys an unruffled field of human behaviors and values as far back as the historian's eye can reach. Love today means what love meant to Jacob or Achilles. English psychologists take their moral discourse and assume that it describes something—not just anything either, what words of praise and blame describe and always did is the utility of people and their actions (I.1).

Nietzsche's genealogy of morals refuses to take this paternity as given. *Genealogy* will expose the illegitimacy of modern morality by illustrating the stages of descent that led to it—stages full of bastard children, monstrous births, and too many of the wrong people pairing off together. Don't be fooled by the persistence of certain names through the generations—"good" but also "justice," "forgiveness," "love"—when the modern phenomenon might have taken on an illustrious old title to hide the dishonorable circumstances of its own birth.

History as the true genealogist practices it is the only history that attends to the long view. Regardless of how many centuries the English psychologist studies, he will judge all the events in those centuries from the parochial viewpoint of the present.

Foucault.   Foucault reads *Genealogy* with emphasis on the dislocations between historical periods and also tries to say (more concretely than Nietzsche does) what dislocation amounts to.

To look for something very different in the past is to look for something *unpredictable* from a modern perspective, something you could study in detail without guessing at the later forms it takes. New phenomena and new discourses about old phenomena appear *by chance*, which in Foucault means that no final cause guides the progress of history. (Ansell Pearson 1991 supplies valuable sympathetic comments on Foucault's uses of Nietzsche.)

If *Genealogy* does not consistently invoke the "complete chance and fortuity of human events and human history" that some readers find in it (White 73), it does leave itself open to being read that way. Nietzsche does not shy away from casino language. After the development of a guilty conscience "man is included among the . . . lucky throws in the dice game of Heraclitus's 'great child'" (II.16). The bad conscience is not a new development of the conscience "but a break, a leap, a compulsion, an ineluctable disaster" (II.17). The same randomness characterizes the earliest human actions; the warrior nobles "come like fate, without reason, consideration, or pretext" (II.17).

Foucault's denial of final cause means that no explanations of history can be given in terms of a future that history approaches. "[Genealogy] must record the singularity of events outside of any monotonous finality" (Foucault 1984, 76). It may be worse than that, not only no future-directed reading of the past but no total account at all, only "the hazardous play of dominations" (83).

A total explanation would unearth the essence of a concept or institution. But when one period has nothing to say to another, genealogical inquiry demonstrates that there are no essences.

If punishment had an essence, that essence would stay the same as specific punishments came and went. The transition from hanging to guillotining or from flogging to imprisonment would only amount to the discovery of new paths toward the same goal. But there is no "same": state-sanctioned force in response to violations of law or contract has worked at different times, as Nietzsche observes, as compensation to victims or as isolation of the cause of harm; as a deterrent, an expulsion, and a festival (II.13). It *has been* all those things. Variant interpretations do not merely reveal disagreement in theory about something that remains stable in itself, because the interpretations (made by the people inflicting the punishment) shape the activity's real meaning.

By dissolving essences genealogy mocks the historian's quest for origins. Richard Schacht in similar spirit writes that an origin "settles nothing on either score."

> It is above all *by their fruits*—and not merely *by their roots*—that [Nietzsche] would have us "know them," whether it is morals or "the type *Mensch*" or ourselves as "men of knowledge." (Schacht 1994, 430)

To think otherwise is to expect modern phenomena to represent the fruition of what was there at the beginning. What the Athenians first did fumbling in their assembly, Americans enact in its full splendor and wide awake every time they enter the voting booth. If history is a flowering, its originary events must have made it happen as it did: history was guided. But in that case history is going somewhere. Making origins definitive therefore comes to teleologizing historical inquiry.

Nietzsche's critique of the quest for origins is now familiar, which means that readers can overstate the critique as both Schacht and Foucault threaten to do. Some cross the line into skepticism: "The past . . . is not accessible to us" (Ackermann 60; see Porter 2000b). It can seem as if Nietzsche's sarcasm about Renan ruled out all descriptions of historical origins.

It is true that origins appealed to as the foundations and legitimations of modern practice do not settle anything. But even discovering the *non*existence of essences requires that the genealogist first find the origins. You cannot describe the disconnect between root and fruit without starting at some idea of what the root was. To claim that things have changed from one species into another you have to have the two species to compare to each other.

Thus Michel Haar's deft analysis while asserting discontinuity avoids hyperbolizing it. He does write that Nietzsche's master/slave opposition "is based upon a rupture, a cleavage within humanity. Nietzsche does not want the moat between them to be filled in" (Haar 21); yet genealogy is not disruptive through and through. Nietzsche's method reveals continuities in the past: it reveals that "the initial direction in such-and-such evaluation persists through each and every derivation and transformation" (16)—not controlling those transformations but not disappearing beneath them either.

"A new truth."   Ecce Homo's thumbnailing of Genealogy identifies a structure common to its three essays. Each of the three has to be understood from an elevated perspective that amounts to a long view.

> Every time a beginning that is *calculated* to mislead. . . . Gradually more unrest; . . . disagreeable truths are heard grumbling in the distance—until eventually a *tempo feroce* is attained in which everything rushes ahead in a tremendous tension. In the end, in the midst of perfectly gruesome detonations, a *new* truth becomes visible. (*Ecce Homo, Genealogy*)

"Calculated to mislead" warns that what seems at first like an essay's bad news is the easy part to take. Readers need this warning, because from a shortsighted perspective the beginning of each essay looks disagreeable enough. Master morality's valorization of aggression; the brutality of primitive debt collection; the self-deception with which artists propagandize for chastity. And no doubt Nietzsche means these opening illustrations of moral phenomena to sound surprising. But the naivety that characterizes these phenomena, while it makes for coarse portraits of human existence, also moves the phenomena a safe distance away from the present.

In Essay I, master morality is mainly surprising for its difference from the morality of the present. It is surprising as ancient dining utensils and toilets can be, not because the morality's function is incomprehensible but the opposite, because its crudeness shows up the rococo of what had seemed simple. The engineering in a fork stands out next to the knife's prehistoric matter-of-factness; modern morality looks indirect, courtieristic, compared to master morality.

Slave morality astonishes in the opposite way, not because it is foreign but because it is not. Likewise the bad conscience of Essay II, a filigree of torment compared to honest excisions of indebted flesh (II.5). And in general neurotic misery ("*one* painful night of a single hysterical bluestocking") far exceeds both the pains of prehistory and "the combined suffering of all the animals ever subjected to the knife for scientific ends" (II.7).

The second surprise is the hard one to hear. The passage from a phenomenon's naïve version to its developed form releases the disagreeable truth of each essay.

Nietzsche speaks of the "detonations" that accompany his revelations of new truths. An explosion is not the sound that a gradual transformation makes. The contrast between simple and convoluted phenomena that shows up previously invisible complications also reflects, as a matter of history, the jumps from one time to the next.

A lost time. A straightforward reading of *Genealogy* sees it as the polemic that its own subtitle promises. Morality today has something wrong with it: look back to an earlier time and you will see what that is.

An inquiry into *Genealogy* (like this one) has to begin by puzzling over the idea of an earlier, now lost time. The polemic requires the changes between then and now to be absolute. Nothing but catastrophe can account for the difference between antiquity and modernity. So *Genealogy* looks for great divides in history.

But how can the present know a past so different from itself? The past begins to resemble a metaphysical posit, as needless as Berkeley said that matter was.

Nietzsche will sometimes appeal to etymology to escort him past skeptical obstacles. An etymology brings traces of the past into the present—isn't that evidence that things were once very different? But a fantasy of lost literality animates the Nietzschean etymology, namely the fantasy that once there were only solid things (real life) and sounds that transparently reflected those things' natures.

Nietzsche's linguistic nostalgia sets up another roadblock between present and past.

In the beginning there are humans and the words they sometimes use. As afterthoughts for the masters and for the primitive guiltless types, words are something distinct from action. But when people decline they come to use their words strategically. Moralizing decadence consists in linguistic subversion. It reduces human beings to their moral vocabularies, until they are nothing above and beyond the words they speak.

Morality now lives within language. So Nietzsche is identical with the words he writes: he is a child of the present. And yet he calls on his readers to speak of another kind of speech that draws its significance from another and truer source.

Moreover Nietzsche rests his pivotal claim about genealogy on an allegation of linguistic change. To silence the desire for causal explanations he traces that desire to a transformation from one grammatical form to another. The original form (A) became (B) and that has made all the difference—or rather he says that the trouble with causes began when form (A) became form (B), but also when form (B) turned into (A). He falls into bidirectional causality as if a diagnosis of language's changes could not be asserted in language.

A language whose words get their meanings by toying with other words tries to speak—but really, how can it?—of a language whose words brush up against reality.

Whether the gaps that Nietzsche announces are mainly gaps in morals or in language, they divide past from present so deeply as to invite the question: How can you know what came before this divide? And behind the epistemological question a metaphysical question arrives: How could such a radical change have happened?

In this respect the appeal to language only relocates the problem of evil. One asks not how the world went wicked but where that word "wicked" came from—and chokes on the answer quick as ever. How could the slaves have overthrown those masters? Where did the "soul" come from? or that shady guilt that is somehow more than soul and conscience combined?

Nietzsche solves his quandary with the figure of the priest. The priest does the dirty work of making the bad thing happen, even if another dirty work remains of accounting for *him*. The *deus ex machina* might arrive to effect the triumph of slave morality, but then Nietzsche has to say where the machine came from that his demon-god rode onto the stage of history.

The simple origins of morality.   The trouble begins with master morality. Or rather there is master morality and then the trouble comes; for if you had to characterize the valuations of the masters with one word you could hardly do better than "untroubled." Nothing could be more agreeable than master simplicity. "What is goodness? Whatever we are like"—which might translate into truthfulness or beauty or battlefield valor (I.4). It's as simple as the gangster slang "goodfellas."

Nietzsche's achievement in this part of Essay I is to show the masters' childlike attractiveness with an account of morality that could sound cynical in another historian's hands. "You're just calling that good because you like it" or "because it's like you." Nietzsche sees no reason to be cynical about the masters' self-regard. What do you *want* them to call "good"—what they are *not*?

Essays II and III start with the same joyful directness. Cruelty sounds innocent. Nietzsche catalogues the torments available to earlier peoples—stoning, quartering, the list goes on (II.3)—and reveals why those bloody means were first used for enforcing contracts: "to *make* suffer was in the highest degree pleasurable" (II.6). Cruelty provided "the great festival pleasure of more primitive men," and "in punishment there is much that is *festive*." (II.6)—Nietzsche recounting the torments with no lip-smack, only relief at such straightness of the primeval human spirit. In those old times "when mankind was not yet ashamed of its cruelty, life on earth was more cheerful than it is now that pessimists exist" (II.7).

Pain is only pain. If it comes from an external source at least it will stop when the external source has been sated.

The innocence is harder to locate in Essay III, whose mockery of Wagner might imply that he did something wrong in flirting with the ascetic ideal (III.2, III.3). (Ridley worries this topic productively.) But ultimately ascetic ideals mean nothing when artists adopt them, or "so many things it amounts to nothing" (III.5; cf. III.1). Artists have no independence. As "all-too-pliable courtiers of their own followers and patrons, and cunning flatterers of ancient or newly arrived powers" (III.5), they say whatever they think people want to hear.

Do the words "courtier" and "flatterer" belie the artist's innocence? Not at all—which is why Nietzsche circles back later to uphold art as the great alternative to the ascetic ideal: "art, in which precisely the *lie* is sanctified and the *will to deception* has a good conscience" (III.25), acquits itself in the act of parroting words of self-sacrifice without meaning them.

The naïve origins of moral language. The psychological simplicity that Nietzsche finds among barely moral first humans is reflected in the simplicity of the language they speak.

Language reflects psychology so limpidly in fact that it contains Nietzsche's main evidence for his psychological claims. Occasionally the evidence comes down to which words one uses ("bad," "evil"). More often it is a matter of whether one created one's own moral vocabulary, and if not then what one did with inherited words in order to put them to new use.

Nietzsche apparently believes that a plain and straightforward word can only come from a plain and straightforward man. So when he thinks he has discovered an elementary concept he posits an elementary soul that conceived it. At their most innocent, human beings coin words by ostension, pointing innocently, as Wittgenstein imagines primitive builders doing when they tell each other "slab" (*Philosophical Investigations* §2).

Wittgenstein may only be pretending to imagine such a thing. By the time he finishes looking at simple names, the idea that they can serve as the foundation for a complex sentence begins to seem like a fantasy, and not one that Wittgenstein himself subscribes to (Cavell 1979, 78). But *Genealogy* does speak as though unmediated naming took place in the minting of first moral values, and disappeared when human moral innocence did to be replaced by maneuvers within already existing language.

In a happier time, words only betokened sterner stuff—actions, promises, works of force. Nietzsche does not tell how the world changed so that lexical innovations could do the work once done by horseback marauders, but it did. The present's morality is governed by words that came along to correct other words.

Political power made the creation of those first elemental terms possible, the ostension being performed by

the noble, powerful, high-stationed and high-minded, who felt and established themselves and their actions as good, that is, of the first rank [als ersten Ranges],

(first by the nobles' count, but then they were the ones who counted)

in contradistinction to all the low, low-minded, common and plebeian. It was out of this *pathos of distance* that they first [erst] seized the right to create values and to coin names for values. (I.2)

The second essay's "responsible man" differs from the master but like him gives birth to fresh and directly meaningful moral terms. For instance:

What will he call this dominating instinct, supposing he feels the need to give it a name? . . . this sovereign man calls it his *conscience*. (II.2)

When he calls it that, the name sticks; such are the power and the obviousness of the language deployed by simplest moral beings.

Nietzsche finds original moral word making only among the strong and arrogant. "This self-overcoming of justice: one knows the beautiful name it has given itself—*mercy*; it goes without saying that mercy remains the privilege of the most powerful man" (II.10). Nor is it just a pun, it's a deep truth about ostension, that makes those same name-bequeathing creatures the ones who enjoy the right to promise ("versprechen," from "sprechen," to speak). Nietzsche defines the sovereign individual as the one who "gives his word [sein Wort gibt]" and his opposite as "the liar who breaks his word even at the moment he utters it" (II.2). The responsible man's ability to name extends into the future: he names the action he's going to perform and then he performs it.

Promises therefore share in the innocence of ostension. If you are a reliable promiser, you describe this future action of yours hardly caring or even noticing that it lies (as yet nonexistent) in the future: you call it into existence as plainspoken as God when the words "light" and "day" and "let the dry land appear" suffice to light the day and dry the land.

The spontaneity of stipulative definitions of moral terms in one way makes the words empty. Any word feels like an *afterthought*: "supposing [gesetzt] he feels the need to give it a name," Nietzsche almost wondering why the man would bother. Bergmann perceiving that afterthought quality writes that the masters' "good"

> did not transform or alter anything. The word "good" itself did not perform an *action*: it represented a mere summing up, a bracketing together. It was no more than a . . . *summative* term for the amplitude of attributes in which the masters took delight. (Bergmann 80)

The masters don't do anything with their term of praise because there is nothing to be done. (Mafiosi say *cosa nostra*, "our thing," never needing to be more specific.) Thanks to its uninformativeness the moral term matches the actuality it was coined to describe.

By definition, master morality does not make its moral ideal unreachable. If "good" is the name you tag onto yourself, "Am I truly good?" is simply a confused question. You can't assign a name to a thing *and* wonder if the thing lives up to that name, any more than you either deny or assert that the stipulated standard meter in Paris is one meter long (*Philosophical Investigations* §50).

For all these reasons, the naming that masters do is not the creation of metaphors.

The masters' and the sovereign individuals' moral terms do not take words out of some other domain and reassign them to new work. Nor do their new words invite exploration. If they are figures of speech at all they are similes. Complete explications are available for the name "conscience" or "good" when it first appears.

Consider "My love is like a red, red rose." Schoolbooks aside, that is a metaphor. "My love" and "rose" are such incomparable things that the very idea of calling one of them *like* the other is metaphorical. "My cooking is like a red, red rose" is different. It may be followed by "It looks all right but you won't enjoy eating it" or some other explication; but it better be followed by something, because this is a simile and that means it stands ready to be cashed out.

A metaphor might change the language. A simile requires that the language remain fixed while someone explains the comparison.

The difference matters because commentators like Sarah Kofman have thought they could deny the difference between the kinds of moral naming Nietzsche speaks of. Influenced by his early essay "On Truth and Lies in a Nonmoral Sense," Kofman presses the view that he consistently calls all language and every utterance metaphorical (Kofman 1993, 82) even when that reading does not apply; as it does not apply here. (See The Etymological Method later.)

Words as afterthoughts in master morality. The great speaker in Greek antiquity is Pericles. *Genealogy* quotes him approvingly as evidence for how master morality saw itself (I.11). And throughout his best-known speech, the funeral oration reported by Thucydides (*History of the Peloponnesian War* 2.35–46), Pericles disclaims the work of speech. Fine words at a funeral either do nothing to honor fallen soldiers' bravery, or they do the sordid work of inspiring envy (2.35.1–3). Athens does not even need Homer: it memorializes itself in the cities it builds and destroys (2.40).

Speech (*logos*) and action (*ergon*) belong to separate economies. The former adds nothing to what the latter does.

Nietzsche might appear to be contradicting Pericles in his outburst about modern weaklings and their beloved euphemisms (the section My Own Language earlier). He says he refuses to play nice and lie and speak of "enthusiasm" instead of ascetic "orgies."

> Why should *we* give way . . . to their tartuffery of words [Tartüfferie der Worte]? For us psychologists this would constitute a tartuffery in *deed* [der Tat]. (III.19)

Doesn't the word rise to the status of action in that passage? Yes, but only because the action has been debased. For a psychologist the right or wrong word about the soul is a right or wrong deed: this means that words are the psychologist's actions, or more correctly that in the domain of the soul a word means as much as an action does normally. But that in turn only shows that souls circulate in the economy of words, likewise the writer who would give a *logos* of the *psychê*. (His only hope is to remain something different from his writings.)

Instead of endorsing the language he finds himself in, Nietzsche resists it in a way that Faust does.

Goethe sets Faust in his study reading the Bible for "revelation" but not liking the revelation he sees; opening the Gospel of John to translate into his own language. "In the beginning was the *logos*." Faust considers "Im Anfang war das Wort," how Luther rendered the sentence (1224). A *word*, before everything else? He replaces "word" with "mind" (1229).

So far Faust is observing scholarly proprieties. Even on conservative grounds the plentiful senses of *logos* can be grouped into two categories, language and thought. But Faust cannot imagine the world's being made by mind, or by "energy [Kraft]" (1233), and he proceeds to the one word that *logos* could *not* mean: "action." Call "Im Anfang war die Tat" (1237) the devil quoting Scripture, because as soon as Faust says "Action," Mephistopheles appears.

Cynicism, logos, money.   Within ancient philosophy the mistrust of *logos* found its bluntest expression among the Cynics (Branham 1996, 83). (A conversation with Michael Lamb inspired this discussion.) They arrived too late to ignore the word completely, but the first Cynic, Antisthenes, insisted that virtue was a matter of *erga* not *logoi* (Diogenes Laertius VI.11). Aristotle says Antisthenes even denied predication, i.e., denied that any *logos* could be applied to an object (*Metaphysics* 1024b32; Navia on Antisthenes; Branham 2004 on the critique of *logos*).

Looking back over his books in *Ecce Homo*, Nietzsche says that sometimes they attained the heights of Cynicism (*Ecce Homo*, "Books," 3). He exploits the Cynical legacy as a way of living but also as a way of writing; its scurrilous argumentativeness too (Niehues-Pröbsting 353–363). He mocks the metaphrastic impulse as that exemplary Cynic Diogenes of Sinope did.

Nietzsche's source, especially regarding Diogenes, must be Diogenes Laertius. Although many of the anecdotes about Diogenes that Laertius relates could count as attacks on *logos*, the first is the most startling. Diogenes came from Sinope, says Laertius, where his father was a banker entrusted with the city's currency. Maybe both of them, father and son, were subsequently exiled from Sinope when the father defaced its coins (VI.20).

"Defacing"—you could also speak of falsifying, marking falsely—translates *paracharassô*, literally to engrave an object (with a *charaktêr* or impress, a character) in a wrong manner or at cross-purposes.

Maybe they were exiled for the defacement: Laertius records divergent versions of the story. In one variant this philosopher that Plato called "a Socrates gone mad" (VI.54) consulted an oracle. In mad counterpoint to the life of Socrates this oracle gives Diogenes permission "to change the political currency." Misunderstanding the advice, as Laertius says, Diogenes took a chisel to the actual coins (VI.20).

Apollo meant "currency" as a metaphor, which makes Diogenes' attack on Sinopean money an attack on the oracle's metaphorical way of speaking. The Cynics "employed the technique of displacing or transposing a rule from a domain where the rule was accepted to a domain where it was not in order to show how arbitrary the rule was" (Foucault 2001, 121), for example, from the metaphorical domain back into the literal. Thus defacing the currency became the Cynics' metaphor for everything they did (Branham 1996, 93). They resisted the stamp of the social. If you think you can fix the value of gold by inscribing it then they can write over your inscription.

It is worth pointing out in the interests of treating Diogenes justly, also in indirect defense of Nietzsche, that a debate persists about whether Diogenes defaced Sinope's sound currency or only the counterfeit coins that had been corrupting the city's economy (Branham 1996, 90n30). Chopping counterfeit coins until they were worthless would have protected the value of the genuine currency.

New meanings for words.   In the first innocent active stage of morality the values are active and innocent too. But the reactive spirit counterfeits the values that the innocent spirit had coined. Its actions are fantasy deeds stitched together out of old words.

In the simplest case, slave morality retains the referent of the nobles' "good" and calls it "evil" (I.7). This opposition is deliberate and strategic: slaves do not evolve a moral system that happens to censure what their masters praise but rather set out to censure their masters' praise. Slave morality does not name but renames.

As a result, it may turn out that slavish goodness has no content. The good for slave morality possesses a hortatory function of which master morality is ignorant. Goodness in slave morality, not being ostensively defined, is capable of having a nonexistent referent. It becomes possible to deny that anyone is good (see Romans 3:10; also Mt. 19.17, Mk. 10.18) and to make the pursuit of goodness a struggle that it never had been among the masters.

If "good" has different referents in the two systems and also different rhetorical functions, you can hardly call it the same word (I.11). And if masters and slaves hardly understood each other to begin with (I.10), now they can't communicate at all. Their words speak of incommensurable realities and perform incompatible tasks.

Nietzsche's word for these new terms at odds with the old ones is "lies." He takes the slaves' inversion of values for a mismatch between moral terms and the traits they purport to refer to. His interlocutor finally admits:

> "Weakness is being lied into something *meritorious*. . . . The inoffensiveness of the weak man, even the cowardice . . . here acquire flattering names, such as 'patience.' . . . They are miserable . . . these . . . counterfeiters." (I.14)

Parasitic renaming seems to be what makes them counterfeiters. Forcing old terms of praise where they were not made to fit gives their moral talk its labored sound. ("'They also speak of "loving one's enemies"—and sweat as they do so'": I.14.)

"No longer do I call you slaves."   "No longer do I call [*legô*] you slaves [*doulous*]; for the slave does not know what his master [*kyrios*] does. But you I have called friends [*philous*]" (Jn. 15.15).

Renaming without resentment.   Name changes bespeak power at work but it is not invariably resentful power and it does not have to invert the values it changes. Consider the ascetic priest:

> he required hardly more than a little ingenuity in name-changing and rebaptizing to make [slaves and prisoners] see benefits and a relative happiness in things they formerly hated. (III.18)

He is not fomenting a revolt: "the slave's discontent with his lot was . . . *not* invented by the priest." Drudgery becomes "the blessing of work," that's all; it doesn't become a thrill and it's not the noble's fault. Minor shows of power take on new names ("love of the neighbor") that make them look like acts of humility and altruism.

No wonder those sick men and women who follow the ascetic priest admire "the forger's skill with which the stamp of virtue . . . is here counterfeited" (III.14).

The ascetic priest performs his "chief trick" without resentment either. The trick of manipulating guilty feelings "was employed *with a good conscience*"; it too was a christening. "Sin," Nietzsche puts the word in quotation marks, "this is the priestly name for the animal's 'bad conscience'" (III.20).

Punishment has lent itself to the most iridescent display of new names. In an atypically long comment on his own method Nietzsche calls the history of any practice

> a continuous sign-chain of ever new interpretations and adaptations whose causes do not even have to be related to one another but, on the contrary, in some cases succeed and alternate with one another in a purely chance fashion. (II.12)

Not even slave morality's inversion of master morality here, not even the ascetic priest's tool-kit of euphemisms, but new names for no reason. Every new power that sculpts punishment into a new image treats the existent practice as a collagist treats a found object.

When naïve genealogists of morals presume that punishment originated in order to serve its present purpose, their error traces back to insensitivity about history's repeated rechristenings (II.12). History moves at random and ends up in a jumble. Practices like punishment antedate all meanings because they originate for no particular reason or none that Nietzsche is going to look for: "whatever exists, having somehow [irgendwie] come into existence, is again and again reinterpreted to new ends" (II.12).

If a thing only *somehow* came into existence it had no original name. Every interpretation fits as well as any other.

The blankness of subsequently interpreted practices explains why every time a fresh interpretation takes over, "any previous 'meaning' and 'purpose' are necessarily obscured or even obliterated" (II.12). Those last four words are worth weighing. Nietzsche's syntax puts the stress on the first effect: old names are more commonly obscured, as in a palimpsest, than obliterated. The old words will not disappear entirely but fade into a barely discernible background. Then history has at least a perverse form of progress to offer, if not movement toward superior values then at least more names and meanings for something that once had no name at all. (See Seitz 21 for a related comment on Foucault's method.)

The incomprehensibility of new meanings.   A regular effect of the new minting of values is that even using the same old words one says something unintelligible.

Pilate quizzes Jesus about being "king of the Jews" but "my kingdom is not of this world," not literal. There can be no proper interrogation when the words mean such different things (Jn. 18.33–36).

An anagram mystically symbolizes Pilate's incomprehension. He asks his famous "What is truth?" (18.38), *Quid est veritas?* in his language. No answer; but a canny shuffle of the words yields *Est vir qui adest*, "It is the man in front of you" (*that's* what truth is Mister). Pilate can no more hear this scrambled answer in his question than he can grasp what another world's kingdom would be.

In the final exchange between Peter and Jesus, even Peter can't bear the new vocabulary in mind (21.15–17). Three times Jesus asks "Do you love me?" and Peter answers, "I love you"—except that the first two versions of the question say *agapas me*, using the new term for Christian love, but Peter's reply is *philô se*, the older word for affection.

The third time Jesus finally asks him *phileis me*. Peter gives the same answer, *philô se*, and his answer finally matches the question. The exchange seems designed to diminish him. Peter stands as close as anyone could to the historical beginning of Christianity and yet cannot use its one essential new word.

Genealogists in the presence of linguistic innovation.   These English psychologists have not realized that they don't know what they are talking about. After millennia of counterfeiting you cannot assess a word by looking at it. Value-language does not circulate freely between ancient and modern moral economies.

Nietzsche complains that "modern man"—his words, his quotation marks—fails as a reader because he has lost the capacity to ruminate (P.8). Ruminative readers turn words over in their mouths in more than one form. So reading ruminatively means performing a genealogy on words. The "entire long hieroglyphic record [Hieroglyphenschrift], so hard to decipher, of the moral past of mankind" (P.7) is a set of marks about the holy made in a forgotten language, and it is time to work out what they once said.

Only a "free spirit" would say, "what do the words matter" (I.9). The free spirit is a "democrat," all words are equal in his eyes and any word will do; but Nietzsche wants to see what it is the words have been doing. The point is that they've had more than one kind of work, while those who purport to investigate morality's vocabulary treat terms of praise and blame as if they simply denoted things, or denoted things simply.

If you assume that "good" has the same job as "bird," to denote a set of objects, you will flop into the conclusion that the actions called good today and in prehistory are acts of benevolence or social utility.

If, however, you should suspect that "good" could behave thoughtlessly coming out of a master's mouth but strategically in a slave's, or that the ascetic ideal expresses different manifestations of power depending on whether an artist or a philosopher or a priest advocates it, you will already have begun to mistrust the look of smooth uniformity that the persistence of phonemes suggests.

Temporalization and causation. In *Birth*, temporalization had already meant not only change over time but changes so complete that no element persisted. Nietzsche brought gods into ancient history to tell where tragedy came from.

Recounting tragedy's *disappearance*, Nietzsche posited the birth of Socrates. Temporalization in *Birth* meant a complete and sudden change in his case too, but Nietzsche could not blame this change on the gods he loved and his story foundered.

Genealogical temporalization more programmatically sees radical changes in the past as the only ones a historically minded person could speak of. *Genealogy* rebukes bad genealogists for relying on a "brief span of experience that is merely one's own" when speculating about the past (II.4). The temporalizing genealogist will find sharp turns along the path of time. Hence the shifts in meaning that "punishment" undergoes, the metamorphoses of the ascetic ideal. To speak of history any other way is to speak as if nothing had ever happened.

If sudden transformations imply anything about historical inquiry it is the inaccessibility of causal explanations. What is abrupt enough is unpredictable, and where there is no predictability there can be no causal account. Just because of the gaps it finds between the before and after, genealogy calls for a new relationship toward causal explanations.

In that case, what stops the reader from finding genealogies unbelievable? It is implausible to speak of inexplicable sudden events. So Nietzsche has to discredit the expectation of a causal story. *Genealogy does not constitute a critique of causality, it requires one.*

Perhaps for this reason Nietzsche sometimes speaks of producing such a critique. Around the time of his letter about Renan he wrote to "Peter Gast" (the non-Jewish name he'd given Heinrich Köselitz) about a "full-scale attack on the whole idea of causality in philosophy till now" that he was planning (Middleton 259).

At the time of the letter, Nietzsche was probably working on Book V of *Gay Science*, in which a few sections address causal explanations (360, 373, 374); but there is no full-scale attack, no whole idea of causality.

A few months later Nietzsche began *Genealogy*. *Genealogy* speaks of causality on the fly, "Today it is impossible to say for certain *why* people are really punished" (II.13). Nietzsche glances back at those "unfortunates" who were first forcibly socialized and "reduced to thinking, inferring, reckoning, co-ordinating cause and effect [Ursachen und Wirkungen]" (II.16). There is a critique in that last line: the search for causes is undesirable even if possible, you can align causes with their effects if you must but there are better ways to use human talents. Still the comment flits by.

More potently Nietzsche's preface proposes investigating "morality as consequence [Folge], as symptom . . . but also morality as cause [Ursache], as remedy, as stimulant" (P.6). Morality as cause *and* as effect? Nietzsche might be pressing for systematic bidirectionality in causal accounts. Against the grain of traditional cause-mongering he might want to see A as the cause of B in one way but B as A's cause too. But it is hard to tell. When Nietzsche simply announces that he is going to look at morality every which way, the passage can't be called a program of research. He had better have more than that to say about causation.

The fable about lambs and a bird of prey inspires an observation from Nietzsche that comes closest to being the argument he needs, because it diagnoses trust in causation as a lazy extrapolation from syntax, therefore a disposable fiction (I.13).

The lambs in the fable believe in "the subject." Blame their belief on linguistic habit. Scientists say "Force moves" and regular people say that lightning flashes. They might start out describing events that way because their language parses their descriptions into a subject (force; lightning) and the action it performs. But habits of mind are hard to break. Dividing the first part of a sentence from the second part brings people and scientists to divide the causative subject from its effects. Nonsense about free wills is sure to follow from what is only a grammatical category.

Nietzsche says "'the doer' is merely a fiction added to the deed." If anything that translation is not snide enough: "'der Täter' ist zum Tun bloß hinzugedichtet," this "hinzugedichtet" combining the prefix "in addition to" with "dichten," to write as a poet does. "The doer" is merely poetized onto the deed.

What's done is done but then done over in a so-called explanation that fails to recognize that it consists in nothing but words.

The trick in this section's analysis takes extra effort to expose—and it is not *trickery*, as if Nietzsche were performing legerdemain, more like a trick argument as one has a trick knee that suddenly gives way. Causal bidirectionality unjoints this argument. Nietzsche says that the structure of a sentence leads you to expect a structure in reality, one end of which is the cause and the other end the effect. But when he has to say which linguistic habit is doing this particular dirty work, Nietzsche first blames the practice of turning verbs into nouns and then that of putting verbs where the nouns should be.

Nietzsche's examples about lightning and the common mind are not his argument. He made his real point a few sentences earlier, when the lambs wish that the bird of prey would control its violence. Impossible, says Nietzsche, the bird *is* its violence.

> A quantum of force is equivalent to a quantum of drive, will, effect—more, it is nothing other than precisely this very driving, willing, effecting,

— the epanorthosis consisting in his conversion of a noun like "drive [Trieb]" into the gerund "driving [Trieben]" (grammatically the infinitive: in German it is the infinitive that functions syntactically as a gerund, as the participle does in English); as if to say that the alleged nouns had always been verbs twisted into acting nominally—

> and only owing to the seduction of language . . . which conceives and misconceives all effects as conditioned by something that causes effects, by a "subject," can it appear otherwise. (I.13)

Not even a habit of thinking this time and not the popular or the scientific mind: language has got something wrong.

More precisely language's *way* of getting something wrong leads to the belief that everything has a cause. Language erroneously sees "all effects as conditioned by something that causes effects [alles Wirken als bedingt durch ein Wirkendes]."

This phrase is hard to Anglicize. Kaufmann captures the punch of the German translating "alles Wirken" into "all effects"; if it sounds circumlocutious to make "ein Wirkendes" into "something that causes effects," still that rendering is accurate; moreover one "effect" repeats the other "effect" more or less as "Wirkendes" echoes "Wirken" and the echolalia evokes the emptiness of this causal prejudice that Nietzsche ascribes to language.

Where Kaufmann does *not* translate literally, he misses a grammatical link between the echoing words. "Alles Wirken" can be all effects or all activity, maybe all work. The associated verb is "wirken," to work and sometimes to effect; and "ein Wirkendes," the verb's gerund, refers to a working or an effecting. A literal translation might speak of "all activity as conditional upon an activating" or "all effects as conditional upon an effecting." Alternatively: language erroneously sees all work as conditional upon a working, i.e., conditional on that which works upon it, a *cause*.

While it is not false to say that whenever there's activity there is an acting, to call it true would be curious. Compare: whenever there is a walk there
is a walking. You would not announce that claim but not fight to denounce
it either.

Calling one thing *conditional on* the other makes the sentence worse than
not exactly false. "Whenever there is a walk there is a walking" may sound
awkward. "Every walk is *conditional upon* a walking" is out to prove something, as if the walk needed the walking to be happening—as if, which is
Nietzsche's point, the walking had to happen *before* the walk. Every effect is
conditional upon that which effects: the tautology has become a metaphysical principle as soon as it suggests that something else must have happened
first, the cause. Now the sight of activity implies the antecedent existence of
the activating thing.

What is erroneous about saying that all effects are conditioned by an effecting? Just that the word "conditioned" has misunderstood the relationship
between work and the working of it. Language reads too much into itself. Yes,
there is working wherever there is work—but tautologically, not because of
any *a priori* causal principle. You have only moved grammatical forms around,
swapping a noun for the gerundive of its associated verb and calling the
gerund the cause.

Tautologies go without saying; but then a lot of things go without saying
and still get said, and sometimes a tautology makes good conversation. Business is business and boys will be boys. "When you've got to go you've got to
go"; why *not* "Every effect has an effecting"?

A tautology might be language's sea level. Left to itself it flows there. But
the tautological ease with which a work becomes a working distracts from the
significance of that change. You began by seeing a thing in the world represented by that foursquare decent noun "effect" and you inferred a process behind it, the cause. Unsatisfied with the world's empirical presentation you
went imagining unseen forces.

Language lets a noun become a form of verb so easily that it makes
causes—the gerund "Wirkendes" is the cause—look like natural accompani-
ments to all events. That is the seduction of language into causal thinking.

Or rather that is *one picture* of language and causation. The same sentence
in *Genealogy* also contains a different picture. When the sentence began ("A
quantum of force" etc.) Nietzsche replaced "drive, will, effect" with "driving,
willing, effecting." The move was epanorthotic. Don't use the nouns, they
will only confuse you: they are a *façon de parler* become jargon. Nietzsche
translates the nouns back into gerundive verbs to correct language's misleading bad habit. A "drive"! Don't bother with that word when it is no more

than driving. Force is forcing: pardon the expression (Nietzsche would not put it this way), but force is "force in action."

Nietzsche's parenthesis at the start of the sentence reflects a sound instinct. Saying "a willing" instead of "the will" blocks the insidious implication that a power lurks within the soul. Instead there is a movement, *willing*. Stick with such events, don't go hunting for entities, and you will resist the metaphysical gaffe that has triggered so much ethical error. You will resist speaking of empty causation: for *the noun "Wille" is the cause.*

In short, this lone sentence vacillates between two directly opposite linguistic transformations trying to make both of them language's path to seduction. Too bad language lets its gerunds harden into names of objects, this turns the mind to thoughts of causes; also too bad that language will not content itself with a noun but dolls it up as a gerund, this is where the idea of the cause comes from.

Nietzsche wants to point a finger at the seductress language but he can't keep his finger steady.

The etymological method.   The word, combining *logos* with *etymos*—real, actual—names a search for the originally coined words whose copies (metaphors, reinterpretations) circulate in current moral discourse. The true *logos* shows Nietzsche the way to "the right road" to genealogy as soon as he asks, "what was the real etymological significance of the designations for 'good' coined in the various languages?" (I.4), and finds master morality at the end of that road (where the road began).

In the gray past of moral language etymology discovers social status, frank talk of contracts. Etymology cannot help making such discoveries: it is not a neutral method. Any etymology worth its salt will yield up earthy literal senses of the words that later became high-flown metaphors. And if you find the modern human a weakened specimen and modern talk too nice, you will persistently look for traces of a cruder past life and find etymology telling you just what you want to hear. The movement toward older meanings is movement toward the literal.

If as Nietzsche believes two very different operations are at work in language, etymology keeps an eye out for both. For what the first and strongest humans did, pointing at things and labeling them, has nothing in common with the later innovations that riffed off those old words. Etymology begins with the improvisations and tracks down the non-linguistic objects.

Kofman writes: "Genealogical etymology does not aim to find the originary, true, and accurate meaning" (Kofman 1993, 87). Exactly what she is claiming in a sentence like that is worth getting clear about and also worth rejecting. If she means that Nietzsche's etymologies are not supposed to justify linguistic usage she is right but will not surprise Nietzsche's readers. His amused look at innocent humans' casual, even careless way with language implies the opposite. *True* language? When language is an afterthought it's never attended closely enough to be true.

But Kofman wants to say more. She does not merely speak of etymology's not *grounding* a meaning, she speaks of its *not even finding* that meaning. She considers this Nietzsche's thesis, that if you keep tracking etymologies you will always see metaphors. Genealogical etymology does not move toward a first coinage but perpetually from metaphor to metaphor.

Kofman supports her claim about Nietzsche and etymology with only a reference to Plato's *Cratylus* (Kofman 1993, 174n8)—maybe a sign that her attachment to her assertions exceeds her justification for them. Again, she appears set on using "Truth and Lies" as a master key to Nietzsche's subsequent works. Etymology can't go in the direction of the literal if everything is metaphor.

Nietzschean philosophy "deliberately uses metaphors" (17), and that word "deliberately" gives Kofman away. Above all, she insists on paying Nietzsche a compliment. But to pay him that compliment she has to deny the force with which Nietzsche speaks of lost literality and goes searching for it: like a Cynic hacking coins to show that he doesn't want to hear any more metaphorical oracles, Nietzsche roughens up the received modern language with etymology.

In the first place etymology cannot help highlighting the transformations that Nietzsche calls counterfeitings, for etymology sounds trivial where no such transformation happened. (The modern English "honor" derives from the Latin *honorem* meaning honor.) But where new moral systems took over earlier vocabularies a word's past will stand out against its present usage.

Moreover an etymology does not merely track any changes in word use but explains the later symbolic use by means of the earlier. It follows from the method that "the concepts of ancient man were . . . at first incredibly uncouth, coarse, external, narrow, straightforward, and altogether *unsymbolical* in meaning" (I.6), different types of words altogether from those of the present.

How the mighty words have fallen! Look at "gentle," which used to speak of status and parentage; see it now sunk in "the psychological." That is how Nietzsche sees the transformations in moral language. "Surly" meant "masterful" before slave morality gave imperiousness its negative overtones.

In one respect Kofman is right. If metaphorical is related to literal as Aristotle had alleged them to be, then a word and its genealogical etymology cannot stand in the relationship of metaphor to literal sign.

Aristotle emphasized the likeness of a word to the metaphor it becomes. Metaphors compare two like things (*Rhetoric* 1405a10–11). The *Poetics* elaborates: the metaphor connects to the literal meaning either by analogy (1457b26) or through the genus-species relation (1457b6–9). Thus if a word today were the metaphor built on yesterday's literal meaning, then etymology would go from one meaning to a similar one. A word's history would follow a continuous path.

Nietzsche etymologizes with no such expectation. He refuses to see continuity or similarity in the transformation that took "good" from meaning "godlike" to describing the meek inoffensiveness of today's nicest people (or in the transformations that "nice" has undergone). He seems to think of a metaphor as divorced from the word's earlier use and potentially opposed to it.

Nietzsche sneers at his predecessors' inability to spot etymologies.

> Have these genealogists of morals had even the remotest suspicion that, for example, the major moral concept *Schuld* [guilt] has its origin in the very material concept *Schulden* [debts]? (II.4; square brackets Kaufmann's)

That might be an extreme case—how does one pretend to *miss* the "Schuld" in "Schulden"?—but the other origins he traces are almost as obvious once he points them out. To demonstrate that "bad" and "low" grew up together he cites as his "most convincing example"

> the German word *schlecht* [bad] itself: which is identical with *schlicht* [plain, simple] . . . and originally designated the plain, the common man. (I.4; square brackets in Kaufmann's translation)

At most his "identical" overstates things only a little.

The same identity or near identity is at work when Nietzsche traces the Latin *bonus* (good) back to *bellum* (war), or the German "gut" to "Gott" (God): "does it not signify 'the godlike,' the man of 'godlike race'?" (I.5). He sees the *manas* in "man" that points to a self-definition "as the creature that measures values, evaluates and measures" (II.8). Why couldn't the other genealogists see it too?

Here is a suggestion. Other genealogists expected a modern word to link back to its literal origin through a chain of intelligible similarities of meaning. They assumed the likeness relation that Aristotle posits between the metaphorical and the literal. Their assumption about words runs parallel to the genealogists' unhistorical assumption about the past, that values have always looked pretty much the way they look now. These so-called historians can no more detect the hard unsymbolical indebtedness that lies behind guilt than they can see the morality that guided ancient warriors.

If you try to trace the present meaning of a word through old meanings that resemble it you will shut yourself off from the astonishing changes that the word underwent. Give up the Aristotelian expectation of metaphorical likeness and you free yourself to notice phonemic likeness. Nietzsche stays with the sight and sound of words and finds their uses and their overtones all susceptible to takeovers as unexpected as a palace coup.

The problem of "evil."   Far from celebrating the move into metaphor *Genealogy* sees it as the source of morality's falseness. Where words once got their meanings "on their own," they have become allusions to older words.

But in finding this route to the fissure between master and slave morality, Nietzsche sets up another version of his problem of evil. Something new and very bad is alleged to have happened—so new that calling the slaves' word "good" a metaphorical application of the masters' word amounts to saying that nothing links the two, Aristotle's theory of metaphor notwithstanding.

The newness is not just a matter of new words. Even if slave morality begins as an inversion of terms, that inversion only marks a first step toward establishing slave morality as the right morality for everyone. The slave *revolt*, which is the movement by slave morality to dominance, calls for abilities that the slaves do not have. And yet the slave revolt has succeeded.

In other words, the new concept of evil in itself is not the problem, only its widespread dissemination. A word that does not come into general use is something like a code; and Nietzsche's complaint about slave morality is that it did not remain a moral code. But just as *Birth* invites the question of how Socratism could have come into existence in a culture that knew only Apollinian and Dionysian impulses, *Genealogy* I makes you wonder how an antiquity that lived by master morality could have succumbed to an ideology of the powerless.

Like the religious problem of evil this one can be schematized as a set of incompatible claims. For Essay I asserts three theses:

(1) Master morality came first.
(2) Every morality reflects the circumstances of its creation.
(3) Slave morality has defeated master morality.

If (1) is true then slave morality could not always have been around but needed to win at a confrontation. (3) says it did win; but according to (2), slave morality grows out of a powerlessness that ought to mean it *can't* win.

(After all, master morality reflects the status, bellicosity, and physical prowess of its masters, while its young rival morality expresses the slaves' incapacitation.)

Nietzsche's understanding of power is at stake too. Every reader is now sophisticated enough to declare that "power" or "strength" does not have to mean pure dumb brawn. It can mean emotional domination; if that is still too ugly it can mean self-activation. But taking power so broadly that it means the propensity to lose takes more than sophistication, it sounds a lot like nonsense. How does weakness triumph and still deserve the name?

One sign that Nietzsche won't give a straight answer to the causal question is the way he glides over thesis (3):

> I recall the proposition I arrived at on a previous occasion . . .—that with the Jews there begins *the slave revolt in morality*: that revolt which has a history of two thousand years behind it and which we no longer see because it—has been victorious. (I.7)

He proved this already, no point going over it. If the world seems to deny what he says, that only proves his point.

Again:

> Which of them has won *for the present*, Rome or Judea? But there can be no doubt: consider to whom one bows down in Rome itself today, as if they were the epitome of all the highest values. (I.16)

John's Gospel on the triumph of Christianity.   It is a different testimonial but asserts the same victory:

> And there are many other things that Jesus did, which, if each one were written, I suppose the world itself could not fit the books that would be written. (Jn 21.25)

Nietzsche would accept this description, if only as a sign that Christianity has come to do all the writing. He might ask what battlefield victories are hinted at in 12.20–21:

> There were certain Greeks among those who came up to worship at the feast; so these approached Philip . . . and asked him, saying, Sir, we want to see Jesus.

The Jewish plot.   Nietzsche's proclamations of the slave revolt's success come across as embarrassed substitutes for explanations when they insistently answer the question "*Did* the Jews win?" to avoid the question that claims (1)–(3) invite: "*How* did the Jews win?"

Nietzsche says one thing that might work as an explanation: Christianity is a Jewish plot. Israel's plan for spreading slave morality required that it "deny the real instrument of its revenge before all the world as a mortal enemy and nail it to the cross, so that 'all the world,' namely all the opponents of Israel, could unhesitatingly swallow just this bait" (I.8).

Nietzsche's secret history fits a recognizable explanatory pattern. Though it is a mocking correction of Christianity still it chooses a venerable tradition to lampoon, inasmuch as the Patristics had accounted for the Crucifixion's effect with the same metaphor of bait and swallowing.

Inspired by one of God's questions to Job ("Canst thou draw out Leviathan with an hook?": Job 41.1), the Patristics reimagined the cross as a fishhook and Christ as the bait whose humanity blinded Satan to his divinity (Aulén 51–55). Gregory of Nyssa amended the language to make the Crucifixion a divine ruse in which "the hook of the deity might be gulped down along with the bait of flesh" (*Oratio catechetica* 24.4: see Pelikan 272). On both accounts, the devil is greedy for another human soul, draws God into Hell, and thereby ends the dominion of death over humanity.

Nietzsche translates the allegory into his own language (as he might say). Where God had gone fishing to snare the great Evil One, Jews fish for "the world" understood as one great evil. On both interpretations the bait and the hook are the two views of Jesus. As superficially no more than human he is bait, as secretly divine the hook: so the church fathers read his double nature.

Nietzsche doubles the reading too. As superficially the enemy of the Jews, Christ is the world's bait. As their secret representative he hooks the world.

Both the sacred and the sacrilegious metaphors make causal sense up to this point. The next step in the Patristic account would strike Christianity's opponents as invoking a dubious causation. Satan's power has remained so fearsome that God needs to enter Hell surreptitiously. And yet Satan did not detect the divinity on the cross: he must have been shut out of the supernatural realm already, which means that he had already lost the power that his reign depended on.

Whether or not the challenge stands up to a Patristic answer, it is an obvious first objection. The Patristics have begged the questions and imagined God's victory happening before the battle.

In Nietzsche's history, meanwhile, the world seized on an obscure revolutionary as soon as the Jews declared him their enemy. Embracing the one the Jews despise, the Roman world declares that he must be good. Isn't he the enemy of those horrible Jews? Then follow his commandments and take on his values; do whatever it takes to be the opposite of a Jew.

Only that reasoning on the Romans' part makes sense of Nietzsche's explanation of how slave morality conquered pagan antiquity. But *that reasoning repeats what was supposed to be peculiar to slave morality.* Its ultimate motive is not love or esteem or any of the other spontaneous drives at work when the masters say "good," but reactive spite and hatred. Its strategy is the inversion of values. In order to oppose the Jews, Romans will welcome the Christians.

The Jewish plot that is Christianity therefore brings slave morality to the world only on the condition that slave morality has already conquered.

Nietzsche's proposal is all the worse for being historically groundless. To the extent that facts survive about the Roman reception of Christianity they tell a profoundly different story. There is Suetonius in the second century mentioning a "Chrestus" who stirred up the Jews (*Life of Claudius* 25): if he means "Christos" he is lumping Jews and Christians together. A generation later Galen occasionally criticizes Christianity, likewise speaking without differentiation of the "followers of Moses and Christ" (Wilken 72).

The purported enmity between the religions could hardly be stirring Romans who did not even notice it.

Romans after Galen do distinguish Christianity from Judaism, but only in order *to attack it for not being Jewish.* Celsus (around 170) respects Judaism for the traditionalism that Christianity lacks; Porphyry honors it for hitting upon a monotheism that Christianity subverts (Wilken 112–117, 153–154). Not once does the difference between the religions become a Roman's motive for adopting Christianity.

Nietzsche's version is not even a saucy spin on ambiguous realities. It is sheer invention, begs the question, and begs that question exactly as Christian theology would.

The slave revolt never even began.   "Surely other accounts of how slave morality prevailed are possible."

But talk of other accounts is misleading if it suggests that Nietzsche needs some story where he so far has not provided one; as if the slave victory were explicable, merely *not yet explicated.* On the contrary, Nietzsche has to offer an explanation in the face of a positive argument against its possibility, meaning a powerful reason that he puts forward for considering even a meeting between the two moralities to be inconceivable (to say nothing of the weak side's prevailing).

Reflecting on the demand for lamb-like conduct from a lamb-eater Nietzsche says:

To demand of strength that it should *not* express itself as strength, that it should *not* be a desire to overcome, a desire to throw down, a desire to become master . . . is just as absurd as to demand of weakness that it should express itself as strength. (I.13)

It's not as though the confrontation between lamb and predator bird ended in failure, more as though it never began. The lambs may think there is a debate here, vegetarians against agnivores, but the two sides cannot debate when they have no words in common.

Look at the word "good." The lambs call themselves the good ones and the bird with a show of agreement says that he loves a good and tasty little lamb. It is like a joke. You almost hear the echo of Nietzsche's punch line in *Bringing Up Baby* (Howard Hawks, 1938), when Katharine Hepburn reads that the leopard she has been sent likes dogs and she wonders what that means, "that he eats dogs or is fond of them?"

That is *almost* the punch line though; the bird of prey is *almost* joking. The cases are different. There are dogs and leopards in *Bringing Up Baby* and they contribute to its comic action but they do not join in its comedy. It is a woman who wonders which way you would have someone you like for dinner. The joke is in her because liking can have both meanings to her. By comparison, one of the things that makes the *Genealogy* fable a fable, as opposed to either comedy or tragedy, is that its meaning lies outside it. (A fable's characters cannot learn from its moral. Hares do not learn to go slow and steady.) The bird's joke goes not only unheard but also unspoken, because there is no one in the fable for whom "good" might mean more than one thing.

Nietzsche and his readers can laugh, which shows that they are neither birds nor lambs. Inside the fable the two "good" words lie across a wide and permanent divide from one another. When the bird of prey says that he loves a good lamb his "good" does not reply to the lambs' demand but rather shows that he cannot hear it. No one hears it. Their demand is "absurd [widersinnig]."

But the absurdity of the lambs' demand cannot mean—Nietzsche can't mean when he says "absurd"—that the demand is doomed to fail. He is the one insisting that there can be no doubt of its success (I.16).

Still the demand is impossible. Fine; and what does "impossible" mean? Maybe that the lambs have fallen into a conceptual error. They don't see that moral imperatives assume power or leverage. The weak *have* no leverage, so how could they tell the strong to act differently? What do they know about commanding?

But speaking that way of impossible demands amounts to asking rhetorically: How can slave morality triumph?

The priest.   *Ecce Homo*'s look back at *Genealogy*—"This book contains the first psychology of the priest"—suggests where else to look for an explanation of the success of the slave revolt.

As a last word on *Genealogy* the remark captures something about the priests' irreplaceability in its narratives. In Essay I, the priest steps in where someone has to, to solve the problem of how slave morality could have carried the day. He is shoehorned into the story, Nietzsche straining his own conception of aristocracy to make it include a new caste.

> To this rule [Nietzsche's rule] that a concept denoting political superiority always resolves itself into a concept denoting superiority of soul it is not necessarily an exception (although it provides occasions for exceptions) when the highest caste is at the same time the *priestly* caste. (I.6)

He has just explained how the masters speak of themselves in a way that ought to rule out the possibility of priestly masters. Don't misunderstand, he is saying now, the nobles can be priests and the rule still holds.

Still the priestly caste provides occasions for exceptions. Although the nobles may well be priests, the priests will not always behave as nobles do.

In the first place the priests describe themselves not as truthful or brave—such predicates elaborate the masters' "good"—but as pure. They abstain from certain foods and the wrong kinds of women. They stay away from blood, they wash themselves. Priesthood therefore comes to mean "the habits ruling in [the priests] which turn them away from action" (I.6).

Purity suggests mixed modes of valuation. Aristocratic distaste colors the priests' aversion to "the dirty women of the lower strata"; on the other hand the imperative to purity is an inhibitory imperative, which is to say reactive, closer to slave morality.

In the second place, priesthood speaks with the vulgar. Only in the priests "did the human soul in a higher sense acquire *depth* and become evil" (I.6). The priests give that slave word "evil" a referent: if evil does not come into the world through them at least "evil" does. Before the priestly clan did its work there could have been no generally used disapprobative term that also connoted violence and mystery. It takes power to legislate new words so that they become part of a normal way of speaking.

Finally the priest is both healthy and sick. The purpose of ancient purity was bodily health. No dirty women who may be carrying diseases, no foods that lead to "skin ailments." But if the priest pursues good health that is because he runs a special risk of losing it. "There is from the first [von Anfang]," before any revolt, "something *unhealthy* in such priestly aristocracies . . . the intestinal morbidity and neurasthenia which has afflicted priests at all times" (I.6). Despite their abstinent regimens they have always been sick.

When Nietzsche says that the whole human species is "still ill with the effects of . . . priestly naïveté in medicine" he is simply mentioning one of the ways that the priest communed with the lower classes, seeking purity himself but also drawing his followers into the same pursuit. He is a sick man among the sick as well as a noble among nobles and he always was. Without his power the slave revolt never could have happened; without his built-in natural sickness he would never have been able to lead the sick.

Because the priest's intermediacy is written into the definition of him, merely pointing it out will not refute Nietzsche's history. Robert Solomon thinks he dissolves the magic of Nietzsche's persuasiveness by noting that

> moralities of resentment tend to be created by the comparatively well off. . . .
> Not slaves but freemen and scholars, not the martyrs but the Christian administrators, brought about the slave revolt in morals. (Solomon 115)

This objection only confirms what Nietzsche implied, that a revolution in the name of the poor cannot be led by them but needs someone of an in-between status. Given that Nietzsche speaks of the priest as someone in between, he is not leaving himself vulnerable to Solomon's observation but incorporating it into his story.

As a mixed type the priest achieves a strategic distance from morality that neither slave nor master is capable of. His own discipline eludes categorization as either clearly masterful or clearly slavish. And because slave morality is not his own code he can deploy it: he possesses the "discerning eye" that witnesses the effect of each morality. The masters barely notice what they say when they say "good," because if a word is an afterthought it can't have much thought behind it. The slaves' resentment blocks them from seeing the masters' "good" as a moral term. But the priest sees the sense of both sides and schemes to side with the slaves. Like the *daimôn* Eros in Plato he passes between worlds, or he's a fallen angel preferring to rule in hell than serve in heaven. That is how he would solve the problem of "evil," if his own nature did not create a new problem in the act of laying the old one to rest.

Caiaphas.   The Jewish high priest Caiaphas is a schemer:

> Caiaphas, the high priest that year, said to [the Pharisees], You know nothing at all,

(he belongs to an aristocratic caste as they do not and possesses knowledge that they lack),

> nor do you consider that it benefits us that one man should die for the people, so that the whole nation does not perish. (Jn. 11.49–50)

Pilate is no schemer. He

> wrote a title and put it on the cross. And the writing was, Jesus of Nazareth the King of the Jews . . . and it was written in Hebrew, Greek, and Latin. Then the chief priests of the Jews—

Caiaphas not named, but he was the chief of all the chief priests—

> said to Pilate, Do not write, The King of the Jews, but that he said, I am King of the Jews.

The priests distinguish acts of valuation from mere words, always noticing which words are in whose mouth. What matters is who is saying this and to whom. This is the priests' discerning eye. But this time their subtlety is wasted.

Pilate answered, I have written what I have written (Jn. 19.19–22): as bald a tautology as you could want, as empty of content as every other self-description that masters give. This is Pilate's way of calling himself truthful. The Romans "were the strong and noble, and nobody stronger and nobler has yet existed on earth or even been dreamed of" (I.16), and as a noble Pilate writes what he chooses to, and the deed of his word making remains fixed.

The triumph of slave morality and the soul. The priestly Lucifer does not revolutionize morality just by wishing it to be otherwise. He needs the stratagem that will let him convince all the world that only slave morality counts as legitimate morality. Assuming he can bring some message to the masters, what does the priest have to say?

Nietzsche's final explanation for the victory of slave morality, as well as its ultimate difficulty, emerges from *Genealogy* more indirectly than the other explanations do. Commentators like Haar have served Nietzsche and his readers well by identifying it. Haar presses the vital question "why and how did the weak man . . . come to be exclusively identified with the moral man?" (Haar 21), and answers that moral inwardness did the trick (21–22). The difference between masters and slaves that guaranteed the slaves' subservience in the material realm—physical subordination, social disenfranchisement—disappears when slave morality transposes the antagonism between the two to the domain of the soul.

Once the soul becomes part of the discussion one can say: maybe some people "act like" masters and others "act like" slaves but deep down inside everyone is the same and free to choose how they act. "By inventing moral inwardness" in short "the weak man has 'triumphed' over the strong, happy man" (21).

Identifying slave morality's success with the appearance of the soul brings the discussion into deeper waters than any Jewish-plot theory could enter. What is called morality today does plunge into hidden motives; and those Greek and Roman masters Nietzsche is talking about, don't they seem weirdly incurious about themselves?—remind you of boorish loud schoolyard toughs?—and doesn't Nietzsche deserve credit for acknowledging their superficiality?

How do you invent inwardness though? Is "invent" the word Haar wants to use? You wouldn't think so to judge from his next sentence: "Once moral inwardness was discovered, the strong man was driven to doubting the legitimacy of his actions" (22). Now moral inwardness has been not invented but discovered, meaning there already waiting to be found.

Haar does not change words on a whim; nor is he being slovenly. Each sentence needs the verb that is in it, even if Haar does not appear aware of having shifted from one to the other as one sentence went to the next. "Invention" preserves the sense of an abrupt transition between master and slave moralities. But "discovery" makes more sense of slave morality's triumph. The means to the victory lay there waiting for the practiced eye to see it. Moral inwardness existed but did not determine action—the strong heard the inner voice that Socrates heard and ignored it—until someone prodded the conscience of the strong.

What this explanation does for plausibility it achieves at the expense of discontinuity. This is no longer a story about sudden and complete shifts in history. Moral inwardness exists today and always did. In this sense history is continuous.

Moreover invention and discovery invoke oppositely directed causal sequences. If someone *invented* moral inwardness then slave morality plays the role of cause and inwardness becomes the effect. If someone merely *discovered* it then the inwardness (along with other things) causally produced slave morality.

This is not Haar's problem though, not his fault. The bidirectional causality he ends up in is present (only a little more hidden) in Nietzsche's own ways of linking morality and inwardness, as if Nietzsche felt compelled to act on his promise to know "morality as consequence . . . but also morality as cause" (P.6).

Go back to the lambs in I.13. It is a fable of course. These are animals talking. If every fable that humanizes animals also bestializes humans—if that slave Aesop's most fundamental lesson is, "You are simpler than you think"— then this story has a special reason for its form. Nietzsche is imagining a time before the appearance of the human. Humans have souls, lambs and birds do not, but these lambs wish for such a thing. The weak moral agent

> *needs* to believe in a neutral independent "subject," prompted by an instinct for self-preservation and self-affirmation in which every lie is sanctified. The subject (or, to use a more popular expression, the *soul*) has perhaps been believed in hitherto more firmly than anything else on earth because it makes possible to the majority of mortals, the weak and oppressed of every kind, the sublime self-deception that interprets weakness as freedom and their being thus-and-thus as a *merit*.

Given a free soul inside the body, the bird of prey has the *choice* to become a lamb and can be held "accountable [zuzurechnen]" for remaining a bird.

Power amounts to the expression of power in actions, so it is impossible for strength not to show itself in domination. Because slave morality wants to end that domination it differentiates between the action and the agent; and here is the subject, that in the person that does not act. Slave morality leads to the slaves' talk of the soul.

This account of the confrontation looks at the imperatives of slave morality from the slaves' point of view. The lambs need someone to bleat to. They posit a substratum beneath action to make logical sense of what they say. They create the fiction of the strong man's soul in order to pretend that their demands for weakness are made to some entity that can hear them, as a wizard invents demons to hear the spells he casts.

But a logical need for the subject as a posited entity is nowhere near enough to account for the success of the slave revolt. It explains why the slaves speak as they do, not why the masters hear them. And the masters *did* obey. That's the whole problem with "evil." Some soul must have been there to answer morality's call. The soul or subject or ego (Nietzsche criticizes it by every name: Schacht 1983, 130) is required not only logically but materially; otherwise the slave revolt would have remained absurd. The fiction of the subject devalues master morality's values by not remaining a fiction: slave morality leads not only to the slaves' talk of souls but to the soul's existence.

Meanwhile Essay I has been speaking of the soul along opposite lines. Because of the priests' powerlessness, "in them hatred grows to monstrous and uncanny proportions, to the most spiritual and poisonous kind of hatred" (I.7), spirituality following Nietzsche's law of a conservation of energy according to which force not consumed in action digs inward to produce the invisible actions of the soul (e.g., II.16).

Ressentiment belongs on the inside if anything does. The slave revolt begins with "the *ressentiment* of natures that are denied the true reaction, that of deeds [Tat], and compensate themselves with an imaginary revenge" (I.10), meaning a revenge within.

The interior space is the boot camp for the slave revolt (even if later it becomes the battlefield). While moral judgments belong in every morality they play a special role in slave morality. Assessing praise and blame is its work: in its starkest departure from master morality it goes so far as to praise and blame other modes of valuation. And that practice of giving every part of a story its proper weight goes on internally.

The effect of such passages is that when Nietzsche says the human animal "acquires *depth* and becomes *evil*" (I.6), the "and" functions causally. The human's ingrown soul gives it the ability to invert values; the slave revolt begins in the place of *ressentiment. The soul leads to slave morality.*

Which one is it? Does the soul bring slave morality about, or does slave morality force the creation of souls? In the tale of the slave revolt's success each one requires the other.

Judith Butler too complains of a bidirectional causality in *Genealogy*: "it will seem that there must first be a subject who turns back on itself," she writes, but at the same time "there is no subject except as a consequence of this very reflexivity." Butler does not say "bidirectional" but doesn't have to. "How can the subject be presumed at both ends of this process, especially when it is the very formation of the subject for which this process seeks to give an account?" (Butler 125).

Before the fall into guilt.   Leave Essay I there for now, where it is plain that the essay does not satisfy but without an outcome to the dissatisfaction. Because Essay I tells a more obviously temporal story than the others it slips more easily into a causal tangle and more clearly demands to have a devil at work in it; so it might prepare for a reading of Essays II and III.

Genealogy II may open in the prehistoric past and lurch toward a recent past, still it frustrates the reader who wants to take its episodes in chronological order. Nietzsche situates the brutal carefree punishment this essay speaks of in an era before the birth of guilt, when conscience existed but not the bad conscience. See II.7 and its time of punishment without shame; also II.14, according to which punishment "hindered" the growth of guilty feeling. But strict ordering cannot square with Nietzsche's claim that bad conscience begins in organized society (II.16). For all the elements of organized society already had to have existed for there to be creditors and debtors and the punishment-relation between them. Thus *the conditions for the possibility of guilt-free punishment are also conditions for the possibility of guilt*.

Nevertheless Nietzsche presses his material into narrative form. He has another story to tell about how things went wrong. From slave morality he has turned to guilty feeling, though the soul continues to play a pivotal role in the disagreeable new truth he has to divulge.

Linguistic changes also participate in this essay's movement to its own disagreeable truth. New metaphors mark the creation of new values. Go back far enough in time and even "guilt" was innocent. The German "Schuld" meant "debt" before it metaphorically signified a broader genus of obligation. (Likewise "ought" began life as the participle of "owe.") In the days before moralization "when mankind was not yet ashamed of its cruelty" (II.7), those outrageous punishments that Nietzsche catalogues (II.3) were business practices. Punishment began among "the fundamental forms of buying, selling, barter, trade, and traffic" (II.4) when business was only business.

Legal and moral thinking grows out of thoughts about money. *Genealogy* treats money as innocent, even a token of innocence (for instance in frequent contrasts between values as originally coined and their later counterfeits). The relationship between creditor and debtor comes before "the beginnings of any kind of social forms of organization and alliances" (II.8) and linguistically speaking lies "beneath" those social forms. "Exchange, the seeds of money, precedes 'the beginnings' of society . . . of people coming together in any sort of organized . . . fashion" (Hillard 44).

(In this respect Luther's complaint, that the church sells indulgences when forgiveness is free, feels like willful confusion about the literal and its metaphors. "Forgiveness of sins" is a monetary concept metaphorized into a moral one. Viewing indulgences as decline and inauthenticity amounts to inverting the metaphor-relation, resenting the literal as if the metaphorical existed in order to hide it.

(There is a lesson here about the sad condition of modern language. Once instituted the metaphor is taken to represent a reality truer than the literal one.)

The metaphorical movement that Essay II describes turned the slogans once current among shopkeepers into moral observations. The language of money "*transferred* itself" to the social domain (II.8); Nietzsche stresses that word "transferred [übertragen]," a commercial term. Money may be carried forward to a new budgetary period, property can be signed over to someone else, in both cases "übertragen." A shopkeeper might reach for the word as a metaphor for these first acts of metaphor making: "übertragen" breaks down etymologically to say "carry over"; and *metaphora*, which before Aristotle likewise referred to a transfer, is composed of *meta*, in some contexts "across" or "toward," plus the verb *pherô*, "to carry."

Metaphor. Nietzsche's etymologies dig into words for those primordial concepts that were "uncouth, coarse, external, narrow, straightforward" (I.6), and that adjective "external [äußerlich]" is essential. The priests' purity is later "internalized [verinnerlichen]" (I.6), presumably as other affects also are in "what I call the *internalization* of man [die *Verinnerlichung* des Menschen]" (II.16).

I.4 has seen "good" describe an external superiority long before it came to mean anything about "the soul." The step from literal to metaphorical meaning is a step from outer to inner.

It is a commonplace that language describing the inner life consists in metaphors drawn from the outer. *Genealogy* suggests that the converse also holds, that metaphor comes into existence for the purpose of describing the inner life. As Blondel writes, *Genealogy* makes internalization "*the* primal *meta-phor*, that which founds culture itself" (Blondel 1977, 152; emphases and hyphen in the original).

Nietzsche makes clear that the halting first step toward both metaphor and internalization happened when business deals (deals enforced by butchers—that is probably not a metaphor) were starting to bring consciousness to the human. The faculties of "reason, seriousness . . . the whole somber thing called reflection" arrive with the ability to remember and keep a promise (II.3). It was in the sphere of deals "that *promises* were made; it was here that a memory had to be *made* for those who promised" (II.5).

Metaphor and strangeness. "We can scarcely conceive [verstanden]" the literalness of ancient speech (I.6).

Aristotle's analysis had put things the other way. According to Aristotle people are struck by metaphors the way they're struck by strangers. Just as they notice a stranger in the street where they would walk past a neighbor, they notice metaphorical language (*Rhetoric* 1404b7–12). For metaphors are strange in the way that riddles are (*Rhetoric* 1405b4–6; *Poetics* 1458a24–30). Poets should "somehow mix" foreign or unfamiliar words (*xenika onomata*) among the dominant ones (*kyria onomata*) (*Poetics* 1458a31) to achieve the virtue proper to diction, namely that it be clear but not humble (*tapeinên*) (1458a18).

Kyrios refers to what rules or has mastery, the lord. So Jn. 13.13, "I the *kyrios* and teacher," and 20.28, "Thomas said, my *kyrios* and my God," in the religious sense of the word; but also in its ordinary meaning: 15.20, "the slave is not greater than his *kyrios*." (Each time Luther's translation renders *kyrios* as "Herr," Nietzsche's word for the master.)

Here is the oddity about Aristotle's account. Although diction made up "out of lordly names [*ek tôn kyriôn onomatôn*]" is the clearest or most truthful (*saphestatê*) way of speaking, it also turns out to be "lowly" (*Poetics* 1458a18–20).

Tapeinos, "low," might come from the word for "rug." Like the negative Greek words listed in I.10, it often connotes both inferiority—"humble," "mean": a doormat—and misery. And yet too many truthful masterful words together produce *tapeinos* diction! The master language is also the humble one, as if the base of language had always been a hybrid.

Hence Aristotle's counsel to combine plain and fancy language. Metaphors and exotic words "make for what is neither common [*idiôtikon*] nor low [*tapeinon*]," while the dominant words for things contribute clarity (*Poetics* 1458a31–34).

Both Nietzsche and Aristotle separate the *kyrion* name for a thing from the same word carried over to a new place. The dominant word is the literal word and the clearest. If Aristotle's Greek does not itself exemplify the lost language of the masters, that only shows how late a philosopher Aristotle was. Master morality and its first commands have receded into what even he considers prehistory. So it is understandable that Aristotle should find the *kyrios* to be *tapeinos*: the debasement of language has already happened. He only errs in assuming that literal words are as familiar as they seem and therefore at risk for being treated familiarly.

Suppose you could see the blunt and crude significations of extreme antiquity, those "straightforward [*geradezu*]" meanings (I.6), as the strangest words of all. You would understand that metaphor brings the pleasure of relief, not titillation over a new stimulus. Metaphor carries the thoughts away from home all right, only not with a sightseer's yen for curiosities, rather with the runaway slave's need to escape a tyranny. For the disagreeable truths about slave morality and bad conscience and asceticism disappear behind metaphors.

While the changes that language undergoes are not simply to be lamented—after all the appearance of the inner is not simply to be lamented—still Essay II makes it even clearer than the first essay did that the change takes words from literal to metaphorical meanings.

The fall into guilt.   Many readers have reconstructed the origin of guilt in Nietzsche's story (e.g., Risse 162–163), and such reconstructions are valuable. All those elements in the history, the resentment and conscience and guilt and religion, need a sorting and organizing that Nietzsche himself does not supply. But it's also worth bearing in mind that the difficulties trace back to more than Nietzsche's silence. There is plenty he does not say about where *ressentiment* comes from or the bad conscience comes from; but too much that Nietzsche does say proves to be inconsistent.

Take the two causes of bad conscience that watch for each other and leap into each other's arms and issue in this new kind of human "sunder[ed] from his animal past" (II.16).

First the state demands such tractability from its citizens that it inhibits them, and the drive to cruelty deprived of an external target turns back against its source (II.16). This twisting back is called internalization, becoming inward, acquiring a soul.

The state in turn owes its existence to warriors who forcibly collect all nomads under their apparatus of domination (II.17). So are they the ultimate cause of internalization?

But if Nietzsche says the bad conscience "would not have developed *without*" the blond beasts of prey (II.17), he also refuses to blame them: "one can see who has the invention of the 'bad conscience' on his conscience—the man of *ressentiment!*" (II.11). The newly founded state only explains bad conscience "as a piece of animal psychology, no more" (III.20). Something else accounts for its full development.

Internalization is a *prerequisite* for bad conscience. The inner is waiting to become something more. "Let us seek out the conditions under which this illness," bad conscience, "has reached its most terrible and most sublime height" (II.19), and Nietzsche's seeking leads him to prehistoric ancestor worship, the second source from which the bad conscience flows. Ancestors grow into gods and the community's debt to them compounds until religious rituals only pay back the interest on the debt, therefore stand in need of permanent repetition.

But notice: even here bad conscience has not become the neurotic fussbudgetry known to modern morality. The internalization is there, and also the religious interpretation of the internalization, but not true guilt.

Nietzsche admits to having put off his disagreeable truth about the really nasty thing that's entered the world. "I have up to now"—this is II.21, Essay II has 25 sections: he's nearing the end—"deliberately ignored the moralization of concepts like guilt and duty." He has spoken of the *inner* and of *religion*. What's left? Nietzsche says the transformation that makes this animal's pain the bad conscience as such begins with guilt's and duty's "pushing back into the conscience; more precisely"—and with this self-correction Nietzsche takes the human soul across the gap that separates past from present—"the involvement of the *bad* conscience with the concept of god."

Put the bad conscience together with religion and what had been mere inhibition turns into that sense of worthlessness that makes "modern man" such a nauseating sight.

Ancestors, religion in general, Christianity in particular. Religion predates the bad conscience.

If the creditor-debtor relationship "has been interpreted . . . into the relationship between the present generation and its ancestors" (II.19), that act of interpretation does not constitute the guilty conscience. The creditor-debtor relationship thus far only presumes rough-hewn community. Religion can hardly create guilt if Nietzsche says that the "man of the bad conscience has seized upon the presupposition of religion" (II.22). Religion merely becomes the occasion for a new twist.

But again, not just any religion will provide that occasion, not when ancestor worship merely reads as the repayment of debt. For then the external creditor serves as a barrier against the full internalization of the debt.

Ancestor worship lingers as polytheism and does not disappear until the ascendancy of Christianity.

When one polytheism defeated another one, the losers' gods became subordinate members of the new pantheon. Monotheism does not allow for such assimilation, so the gods became devils. Tertullian put "great Jove himself" into the "lowest darkness" (I.15); Milton coined "pandemonium" to reverse the set of all gods (pantheon) into that of all demons. This time, one religion's domination over another comes with a moralizing interpretation of the domination.

Nietzsche inverts the monotheistic inversion. The Greek gods lived by their shabby personal morals in order to take the guilt for human suffering on themselves, "precisely so as to ward off the 'bad conscience'" (II.23). They "served as the originators [Ursache, cause] of evil" so that even though internalization had occurred it did not attach itself to gods.

No wonder the gods went to hell when Christianity arrived. They had solved the traditional problem of evil by causing both good and evil, as Nietzsche at thirteen credited God with doing, in his essay calling God "the *father* of evil" (P.3). The Christian strategy quite different from Nietzsche's youthfully heretical proposal has God taking on the punishment and leaving humans with a bad conscience (II.21).

In this respect *Genealogy* perversely reiterates the solution that Nietzsche had found at thirteen. God becomes responsible for the real harm done to humanity. Far from being the father of what are called evil deeds, God is the father of "the most terrible sickness that has ever raged in man" (II.22).

Of course Nietzsche is not actually blaming God, that's just a metaphor, as Nietzsche himself is only metaphorically cleaving to the thirteen-year-old thought he calls his *a priori*.

Nevertheless an evil has entered the world and Nietzsche had better say how it got there. As *Ecce Homo* says, guilt is not "'the voice of God in man.'" Temporalization is supposed to show *that* it is not, that "the human" does not receive the divine word by a special faculty, but constructed the so-called voice of a so-called God until the so-called human of today can't stop hearing it.

But then the reader wants the whole story. If "God" does not explain guilt, then "God" will not provide the final account of how the bad conscience came to be moralized.

The challenge for Nietzsche mirrors the traditional problem of evil because he has set up his history of conscience in a way that calls for something extra. The *state* does not cause the moralized bad conscience, because in the primitive state things still follow a brute animal form. *Religion* doesn't cause the moralized bad conscience: religion merely projects indebtedness into the past and human beings can face indebtedness without internalizing it. *Religion after the advent of the bad conscience?* No, not that either, look at the Greeks. A fit of bad conscience now and then but nothing they couldn't handle by blaming the gods. All these phenomena remain to some degree innocent.

But now this creature with so many self-protective techniques has found itself hobbled by self-torment. Did something happen?

The blame for guilt.   Everything changes with the Crucifixion (II.21). As in Essay I, where it explains the triumph of slave morality, Jesus' execution becomes the work of Christianity. (Essay I calls it the work of Judaism; but then Essay I calls Christianity Judaism, so that is a distinction without a difference.)

But "Christianity" is an abstraction, and Nietzsche supplies no damning specifics comparable to his quotes from Tertullian and Aquinas (I.15). "A stroke of genius on the part of Christianity" is all he says by way of explanation (II.21), even if strokes of genius are names for what *can't* be explained, and even if they visit individual geniuses instead of institutions. For some reason still not specified the resentful inturned man of bad conscience took what had been there, which is to say religion—which maybe had even been there helping ward off the guilty feeling—and turned it into the version of debt and repayment that would most inflame the already existing sense of guilt.

That stroke of genius had to belong impossibly to a religion at large. Otherwise Nietzsche's explanation runs in circles, the moralized bad conscience both seizing on the presupposition of religion—not any religion at all mind you but this particular form of monotheism—and constructing it. Christianity and the guilty feeling cause each other.

Was there ever a human without bad conscience? This is really the question whether Essay II tells a story of guilt, which is in turn a story of ruined innocence. Was there a human without bad conscience followed by a completely different type?

What Nietzsche says about prehistory in this essay follows unclear chronology. How far back does the first economy go? Nietzsche looks into the dimmest past he can identify and discovers commerce; commerce means deals and deals need enforcing; so punishment you must have always had with you, therefore also the state and the internalization it bred. That much is clear in *Genealogy*. Where there was talk there was shop-talk, and where there was shop-talk there had to be memory. Memory makes people predictable. Primitive economies produce "the custom of comparing, measuring, and calculating power against power" (II.8). In every such system "man must first have learned . . . to think causally," and causal thinking transforms the one who practices it. "Man himself must first of all [vorerst] have become *calculable* [berechenbar], *regular*, necessary" (II.1).

If economy depends on promises, then it must "presuppose," as the breeding of promising animals also presupposes, "that one first [zuerst] *makes* man to a certain degree necessary, uniform, like among like, regular, and consequently calculable [berechenbar]" (II.2).

The calculability of the human came into existence. No harm done. The early torturers' consciences were clear; the ones they tortured probably didn't mind it so much either (II.7). Only after internalization were human beings "reduced to thinking, inferring, reckoning [Berechnen], co-ordinating cause and effect," and to the extent that he sees any point to pity Nietzsche pities "these unfortunate creatures [diese Unglücklichen]" (II.16)—"these" again, like the English psychologists they are right in front of him.

Nietzsche means to describe a turning point of history when he speaks of internalization. But once he lists the features of the newly broken man they sound like features of the well-built old one. Regularity, consistency: these happened before, in fact Nietzsche did such a thorough job of detailing the tortures that made them all happen, you'd expect the project to have been finished before internalization ever occurred.

The internalization, anyway, took place when warriors first founded their states—wild warriors, the unpredictable type. "One does not reckon [rechnen] with such natures" (II.17). So the conquerors never underwent even the training that produces a proud autonomous individual (Hamacher 34). Being so unpredictable the warriors belong outside any coherent story, which means there can be no account of the state's founding but only accounts of life since its founding. That stands to reason. If you are going to describe people who punish, you quickly come to an institution with judges and executions (II.14) and the power to restrain both criminals and victims (II.10). Legal codes represent a limit to the injured party's vengeance (II.11); but a political system that can control both sides is a *state*.

The punishments that a state administers may well reduce "the sting of conscience" (II.14), though not necessarily because they take place in a cheerful time before guilt and inwardness. Because punishment and the sense of guilt have nothing to do with each other they coexist, the one a cause of conscience and the other the effect of the bad conscience.

Given a state there must be internalization. Given an economy there is guilt. Put internalization and the economy together and you get metaphors of moral obligation. Given ancestors and an economy there will have been ancestor worship and then gods. What more could you want?: bad conscience and the words by which it moralizes, religion to provide the unredeemable debt to the past, *all the elements of the guilty feeling existed for as long as the state did.*

So: the ingredients needed to brew *ressentiment* were available in the earliest days of the state. And yet the "man of *ressentiment*" takes the blame for the present form of bad conscience. Therefore, the history of the state has always been a history of the bad conscience.

What about before the state? Before the state you had only unclassifiable nomads and indescribable masters. "Before the state" lies outside genealogies: there is only the state and the accompanying condition of bad conscience.

The history of guilt now follows a story line that has no need for special intercessions. The disappointment over Nietzsche's causal elusiveness ought to wither away. There is no demand for a new force to account for that familiar guilty feeling when that guilty feeling must have always been around. What looks at first like a history with an embarrassing rip across its middle ceases to be *that kind of story*—innocence and fall and maybe a hope for the future—once Essay II evades the very idea of explaining the transition into bad conscience. For what else is it but evasion when Nietzsche says the change into internalization "was not a gradual or voluntary one and did not represent an organic adaptation to new conditions but a break, a leap" (II.17)?

Don't dwell on how inwardness began because there is nothing to dwell on and no moment capable of being slowed down so that you can understand it.

When Nietzsche says that the prehistory of punishment is "present in all ages or may always reappear" (II.9), he is effectively stretching the deepest past he can talk about forward into the present. Things have always been this way. The man of *ressentiment* created the world you know, which makes him no devil figure any more but the father of civilization.

Nietzsche says no such overt thing about the man of *ressentiment*. The point is that his account of the past leads to this redescription. Nietzsche resists the thought that resentment could have fathered the only world he has to talk about. He wants to postulate a cheerful era before all the trouble started. But the story he would *rather* tell, a story of how things went wrong, calls for a powerful villain or at least a causal sequence that he cannot deliver. The single continuous history makes better sense: which is to say it does not disappoint the reader who wanted an explanation.

Without a villain, Essay II disappoints in another way. The regret for the species' fall into guiltiness has nothing to attach itself to. You were ready to kick with frustration. But now there is no cause for frustration and no one to kick, nothing went wrong because things were always just this way, what you see in front of you.

A possible resolution to Nietzsche's explanatory problems. It's always been known, though it is a recourse rarely chosen, that theodicy can take a shortcut through the problem of evil by denying that evil exists. God is then Cause of all. Genealogy likewise can avoid its explanatory thickets by abstaining from assertions about the time before the abrupt break in the past.

At least now and then the first two essays imply that view of history. There is no gap in the past, or else one that there is no discussing; therefore only the known world exists.

This recourse also resolves the epistemological question "How do you know there was a time of master morality or guilt-free punishment?" Nietzsche says nothing about the deep past from beyond the random break, therefore has no claims to defend. *Genealogy* does not posit a society that existed before guilt but inscribes the guilty bad conscience into its chronicle of even the most primitive community. Christianity never invented the moralized bad conscience. Nor was there ever a master morality.

This is the *monistic* reading. Everything manifests will to power. Every force and every action bespeaks positivity. The explanatory puzzles disappear—but where did that fury go that Nietzsche unleashes against the past? And how easily can Nietzsche himself accept the higher, more detached perspective from which every act bespeaks positive will to power?

Consider the ascetic priest; and consider Nietzsche's consideration of the ascetic priest. Of the three essays in *Genealogy*, III is easiest to read as a value-free accounting of the forms that the will can take. "Man would rather will *nothingness* than *not* will" Nietzsche screams at essay's end: It's all will (III.28). Essay III discloses that the priest does not turn life against itself (III.13) but rather does everything he can to enhance life.

In such passages Nietzsche manifestly wants to free himself from a lingering moralism of strength. Although he'd like there to have been a bad guy in history, and for that bad guy to have been the priest, he also knows that dualistic histories fail. (His preface reminded the reader of the traditional problem of evil: P.3.) So the putative bad guy turns out to have been everybody's father all along.

But even as he affirms the priest's fatherhood of all humanity, Nietzsche also calls him sterile and asexual. And no wonder: in such moments the thought that the priest had fathered him becomes an imminent danger. In such moments Nietzsche's philosophical predicament—to be caught between hopeless dualism and joyless monism—publicly sounds his private predicament. Nietzsche must exist and therefore must have been fathered; therefore must have been the priest's son. And yet it is unbearable to imagine the priest as his father.

Was there ever a master morality?   The worry about the slave revolt now also seems misplaced. A misplaced worry is still a worry about something, only not what it thinks. And what if the problem with Essay I should be not that it botches the explanation of the slave revolt's success but that it pretends to speak coherently of the revolt in the first place? Was there ever a master morality, or such a thing as a master?

Essay I could not recognize itself if it did not contain the claim that another morality once existed, before "morality" (the one that treats itself as the only possible morality) rose up and displaced it. And yet Nietzsche's explanations of the displacement keep finding master morality defeated before the battle.

The Crucifixion is bait for the Jews' masterful enemies only if they're already thinking like slaves. The lambs' absurd command to the bird of prey wound up being heard, as if there were some soul inside that bird as there had been in the lambs. Master morality could not have lost out if it did not contain some propensity for slave-thinking before it was ever "conquered."

Ackermann calls the masters "fully concrete Platonic ideals" (Ackermann 118), much what Porter (2000a) calls the Dionysus of *Birth*. Even without such extreme language you may wonder whether the masters ever existed.

Pericles.   Pericles uses *rhathymia*, "taking things lightly," to describe the Athenians' sense of their own warrior virtue (2.39.4). It's the right touch for a heedless master, says Nietzsche (I.11).

But is Pericles really so heedless? There is a jitteriness in his funeral speech, the jitters that come from pretending not to be jittery.

Pericles describes the Athenian penchant for debating every issue, "believing that actions [*ergois*] are not harmed by words [*logous*] but by our not being taught in words before coming to the time of action" (2.40.22). It is a claim you would expect from a master, if Nietzsche is not making this stuff up. The masters first stamped out the currency of moral language and made it say whatever they wanted to do with it. Why should words do them any harm?

But Pericles says that Athenians *differ* from other Greeks in their ability to dispute and still act effectively. Therefore other people risk paralysis if they talk things out. Debate does not have to support action. In those other cities with lesser citizens, the *logos* saps the strength of the *ergon*; on the threshold of a long war with Sparta the Athenians are starting to worry that it might hobble their own action.

Even if Athenians act boldly, in other words, they possess their boldness in spite of the Athenian culture of debate and not because of it.

Does the *logos* in Athens direct the *ergon*? That capacity for directing action shows what force the *logos* has assumed. Words have a life of their own now and it is not an attractive life; which is why it will not honor the fallen soldiers if words mark the occasion of their deaths.

The masters of Essay I had assumed not merely the perfect match between words and actions but also (as ground and guarantee for that match) the right deference on the part of their words. Their actions came first, the words at most showing where the actions had been. But Pericles among the masters of pre-Socratic Athens, at the height of the city's power, structures his greatest speech around an antithesis between word and action that pays reluctant tribute to the independent strength of words. The day of the masters' word making has already passed (still assuming for the sake of argument that it ever existed).

The incomprehensibility of master morality.   If Pericles's rhetoric and Aristotle's *Rhetoric* usher Nietzsche into a parlor of history from which the masters have already departed, those masters are Platonic ideals in a specific and demeaning sense: finding no such beings in the world, Nietzsche invents them.

Temporalization, *Genealogy* style, undermines any grounds Nietzsche might have for claiming that the masters existed. The chance, the break, the leap, and in fact it is a leap across a chasm—this gap that Nietzsche locates between master and slave moralities may shield him from demands for causal explanations. His forebears in genealogy "account for" past moral phenomena by overlooking the happenstance of history. They make the past comprehensible only by confusing it with the present; Nietzsche sees the radical disjunction between past and present and knows that no causal sequence will cover the gap.

But a break so complete and a past life for human beings so indescribable in present-day language makes it something like a miracle that Nietzsche could ever know about the masters.

Call this Nietzsche's premise: *If there were masters then no coherent account can be given of the time separating then from now.* It is unassailable, given how he has conceived the masters. And Nietzsche gladly draws the conclusion against petty historians' need for causality. But one man's modus ponens is another man's modus tollens and this premise cuts the other way too. If you must deliver a causal account of the past then there is no point in saying there were masters.

That broad doubt about what Nietzsche can know about the past takes particular form in readings of *Genealogy* I. It becomes the doubt that any "morality" like the one Nietzsche describes is worthy of the name. Thus Maudemarie Clark calls the masters' system of valuation a "proto-morality" at best. Slave morality "developed from something that existed prior to morality" (Clark 25). Nothing in the nobles' mode of valuing draws them to recognize moral qualities as such. "Calling commoners 'bad' is certainly making a value judgment about them, but it is not judging them to be 'morally bad' or 'immoral'" (24).

If Clark is right, then slave morality's arrival in the world does not have to entail talk of revolts or the devil figures who incited them or about revaluations and dice throws. Because Nietzsche is not really imagining master morality even though he thinks he is, slave morality has understood itself perfectly well. It is the only possible morality.

Now, Clark is probably *not* right. Her distinction between "bad" and "morally bad" denies morality to the masters only by equating moral judgments with the judgments that slave morality makes. For her, "bad" only means "immoral" when it implies something about blame: "the evil are blamed or thought deserving of punishment for being the kind of people they are, whereas the bad are not blamed for being bad" (25), she says—mistakenly. It may be a poor worker who blames his tools, but to say that is to grant that you *can* blame your tools. It's not the conceptually confused worker who blames. And if you can blame your blisters on a bad pair of shoes then the masters can blame their slaves, and when they do blame the slaves they are calling the slaves bad, morally bad.

If everything depends on whether one deserves punishment then again it is moral badness that master morality speaks of. The slave takes too long bringing dinner to the table and gets a smack and the master thinks that the slave deserves it.

"This isn't true blame or true punishment," an obvious defense on Clark's behalf. The blame a tool might get and the slap that a slave gets don't constitute morally charged expressions of value. So the noble still falls short of the moral domain.

But it begs the question to require so much from moral evaluation. Forcing blame and punishment to meet such specific conditions amounts to packing all of slave morality into the concepts of blame and punishment, and that neologism "proto-morality" (honorable mention for something that does not earn the title of morality) finally expresses only the thought that slave morality considers itself the only morality.

Master morality is not slave morality. Who thought it was?

And yet: even if Clark's argument against the idea of master morality does fail, and even if it fails because she is speaking from within slave morality, still the fact that she cannot force herself to call the masters' value system "morality" needs to be accounted for. Why *can't* she call it morality? Clark understands what morality is; her knowledge of Nietzsche is unimpeachable. What can the problem be?

Maybe that the masters' and slaves' perspectives lie so far apart that from within slave morality not only the battle between the two but even the morality of the masters' mores is doomed to remain invisible. If Clark's argument does not show that there never was a master morality, the diagnosis of her argument as internal to slave morality nevertheless suggests that even if master morality existed it cannot be known to have existed.

Nietzsche says he can see master morality as morality. No doubt he thinks he can. Does he see what he pictures himself seeing? He starts his history with master morality and moves to its vicious reflection—but then he flips back with fresh energy to speak of the masters again, having described slavish values so that he can say "The reverse is the case with the noble mode of valuation" (I.10), and again after another look at slave morality, that it's "the contrary of what the noble man does" (I.11). His portrayal of the masters gains so much concreteness from this contrast that one must wonder whether Nietzsche has simply decided to oppose morality any way he can to arrive at his own fantasy, the way he accuses metaphysics of inverting the visible world to produce "reality" or heaven. He inverts the morality he sees in front of him to create the reflection that *he* calls the original.

Etymology, corrected.   Nietzsche etymologizes like a cheerful pessimist who (to paraphrase the old definition of an optimist) runs through a barn of manure shouting, "There must have been a horse in here!" The evidence he finds only really proves that language is a blend. Whatever the word was in the beginning, it is now a jumble of first, second, third meanings, newly stretched metaphors of metaphors (what Aristotle said it was). The lost sense Nietzsche is seeking is one among the many senses of existing words.

Was the lost sense ever the only sense? Then the word would stand alongside its referent and etymology would stop moving within language when it reached the border between words and the things they name.

An illustrative joke.   It is told by philosophers: someone explaining how radio works. "To understand a radio you first have to understand telephones. A telephone is like a very long dachshund with its head in Paris and its tail in Berlin. Pull the tail in Berlin and the head in Paris barks.

"A radio is exactly the same thing but without the dog."

Compare Nietzsche's explanation of modern morality by means of master morality. The joke definition first posits an analogue to the telephone and then snatches the analogue away before it can do any explanatory work. The definition corrects itself into not saying anything. Essay I likewise offers to show the contours of slave morality by comparing that to master morality; then snatches master morality away in a final epanorthosis.

Temporalization, corrected.   The final disagreeable truth to emerge in *Genealogy* is that everything modern is a mixture.

If souls of today are marked by the ongoing battle between master and slave moralities then modern Europeans are mongrels; for master and slave morality

have been engaged in a fearful struggle on earth for thousands of years; . . . today there is perhaps no more decisive mark of a "*higher nature*" . . . than that of being divided in this sense. (I.16)

Without an original world populated only by masters, the mixture begins to look like the only world there has ever been.

Some of Nietzsche's readers take him this way. "Of course, there are *no* pure masters and slaves," inasmuch as "the races have been always mixed, and probably they *always were mixed*" (White 67). Or, more elusively: "Nietzsche's analysis does not preclude a multiplicity of degrees and intermediary stages, even mixed types" between master and slave (Haar 21).

It might disappoint the reader that Essay I delivers no unambiguous cases of masters. That disappointment is the reader's own problem if the master does not have to have existed. Physicists are not embarrassed that no actual gas exactly obeys the Ideal Gas Law. There are no ideal gases, that's all. Can't the myth of a confrontation between moralities play an elucidatory role even without describing a historical incident?

If the races were always mixed, Nietzsche's failure to produce a clear case of a master does not hurt his theory. As long as he can sketch two antagonistic evaluative modes he will have shown that "good" has no single meaning and also that it could mean more someday than it has so far.

Deciding that the types were always mixed benefits Nietzsche's history in other ways. The worry about how slave morality triumphed looks like wearisome i-dotting. If one pure type never yielded before another (and if no pure types existed, yielding becomes logically impossible), then no one needs to account for "evil."

But the aristocratic priest had appeared from the get-go as a mixed type and even the original mixed type. If everyone is mixed and always was, then he is no longer a devil conjured up to show how the world was lost. He made the only moral world there is to know—not master morality but also not just slave morality.

The mixed world now descends directly from its mixed father.

Is there a problem here? Mixed natures were supposed to be explained by the ancient war between two moralities and the priest was supposed to explain that war. Now, as an already-mixed figure, he explains everything you might have needed the war to account for. He explains the present jumble.

If Essay I tries to tell a different kind of story and falls into its disappointing narrative of lost innocence, that failure only betrays the desperation with which Nietzsche takes the father of the world as he knows it and tries to make that god-man a devil.

Genealogy I speaks the wish that the world had been otherwise in the form of the wish that the world's father is a false father.

Staten's moralizing Nietzsche.   Nietzsche would like the priest/god to be the source through which "evil" entered an innocent world. He keeps staging a Passion in which the Annas and Caiaphas of prehistory maneuver to destroy the old values. But if culture has always been a mixed bag of valuations, if all social existence is guilt-ridden—and remember the dramatic case ahead: if the earth is *the ascetic planet*—then that mixed figure of the priest is the father of all.

To the extent that breaks in history turn the times before them into fantasy, the truly disagreeable truth is that the one traditionally called "Father" is the only father that could have been. The mongrels of modern Europe descend from other mongrels. The romance of a better family collapses.

Staten's "psychodialectical" reading of *Genealogy* takes a different route from this chapter but discovers similar tensions, the book's "overall economy" of will to power sharing space with Nietzsche's advocacy for strength over weakness. Nietzsche recognizes all values and activities as operations of the will to power, and yet he moralizes in favor of those who make their power effective.

Staten tries to maintain equidistance from both voices. He gives the impression of writing out of a Nietzsche disappointment of his own, his being the letdown at finding the theorist of one power, identical everywhere, shifting gears to champion one of the two forms power can take. And try as he might he does regret the second voice, which he finds aberrant or repressed. To Staten, Nietzsche's sharp tongue subverts *Genealogy*. The will to power

> acts as a magnet for Nietzsche's most defensive or reactive impulses and brings out a partiality in his perspective . . .

language that already points to a problem, Staten's impartiality implying that partiality on Nietzsche's part betrays a failure of imagination. Nietzsche's partiality is

> fundamentally at odds with the "moraline-free" perspective to which he aspires . . .

contradicting Nietzsche's own methodology.

Though good and evil have now been crossed out, the essential charge of moraline has been in a sense transferred intact into the new categories of strength and weakness (Staten 21), which is to say that Nietzsche does not finish the task he set himself.

The failings that Staten detects in *Genealogy* come of Nietzsche's valuing master morality above slave morality. The real Nietzsche knows better. The considered Nietzsche takes the long view beyond strength and weakness, even if the irascible Nietzsche looks for weak villains.

On Staten's reading, whole sections of *Genealogy* are false to Nietzsche, the subtitle "A Polemic [Eine Streitschrift, quarrel-writing]" one more red herring, Nietzsche scurrilous in spite of himself. This quarrel writing is one thing and Nietzsche himself another matter.

If anything, Staten has things backward. To say this is to applaud his disentanglement of the two voices in *Genealogy*. But it is not the vitriolic Nietzsche who gets tamped down, instead it's the one who sees a single will to power at work everywhere. *Genealogy* tries as hard as it can to tell stories of loss and catastrophe—stories that evaluate and judge—and only delivers the loftier monistic assessment when those stories fail. Nietzsche comes to the economy of will to power after first doing all he can to find a slanderous devil in morality.

Why does he try so hard to fit history into the shape of a morality tale? What impulse does that satisfy that is frustrated by the monistic history of will to power in all things?

And look, not only Nietzsche is frustrated. The innocence and fall disappoint the reader intellectually, but that story lets you vent your anger on someone. Those Jews, the gods, the priests, they ruined it for everyone. What to do when there is no one to blame?

The ascetic priest.   *Genealogy* III raises much the same questions that the first two essays leave their readers with. In some ways it arrives at those questions more briskly. Nietzsche jumps right into his portrayal of the ascetic priest as a mixture, someone who

> must be sick himself, he must be profoundly related to the sick—how else would they understand each other?—but he must also be strong, master of himself even more than of others (III.15);

and this announcement of the priestly mongrelization that Essay I only implies sets the tone for the third essay's avoidance of fallen-innocence narratives.

Those narratives do turn up, there is still a drift toward stories of the fall. But the very fact that Wolfgang Müller-Lauter can point to a manifest contradiction—

> On the one hand, life *denies itself* in ascetic practice . . . [asceticism] employs force "to block up the wells of force." (11) . . . On the other hand the ascetic

ideal is an "artifice for the *preservation* of life." (13) . . . The ascetic simultaneously denies and affirms life (Müller-Lauter 44)—

this bubbling of the contradiction up to the essay's surface reveals Nietzsche's
effort not to tell a moralistic story.

At worst the ascetic priest is a physician who inadvertently makes his
patients worse. This description makes him one more adherent to the ascetic ideal, along with artists and philosophers, distinguished by what
sounds like incompetence: "when he . . . stills the pain of the wound he at
the same time infects the wound" (III.15). The ascetic priest administers
palliatives against the suffering rather than address its causes (III.17). He
inspires an outpouring of affect in the form of guilt (III.19), and in one way
that "orgy" has a salutary effect, for it reverses "the direction of *ressentiment*" (III.15); still "Who would want to maintain" that these moral pre-
scriptions for the followers "ever benefited any of them?" (III.21). Guilt explains suffering to the sufferer, but by explaining it as the sufferer's own
fault (III.15) it intensifies it, the relief as brief as when scratching a mos-
quito bite.

The ascetic priest brings harm to the species, but not diabolically. Essay III
does not begin in an innocent-animal past into which morality enters as a
corruption or even a sudden change.

For one thing, Nietzsche does not even try to make this essay a history. If
the artists are the innocents in their flighty uses of the ascetic ideal, they are
innocents of the present. The philosopher who makes the ascetic ideal a discipline also exists right now. Maybe something is about to happen (in the
next two hundred years, Nietzsche says), but Essay III barely acknowledges
anything to *have* happened.

The one exception belongs to an indeterminate past. The human species
is sick, Nietzsche says explaining the priest's appeal. How did the sickliness
begin?

[Man has] dared more, done more new things, braved more and challenged his
fate more than all the other animals put together: . . . he, still unvanquished
. . . whose own restless energies never leave him in peace . . . how should such
a courageous and richly endowed animal not also be the most imperiled, the
most chronically and profoundly sick of all sick animals? (III.13)

Why did the brave and strong animal become the quintessentially sick one?
Because he was so brave and restless, unvanquished—really because he was
healthy.

Is that like Zarathustra's *volte face* from moralism into immoralism—just because he'd been the one he is bound to be the other? Or should the reader only say that the human animal sickens for no reason at all? (See Staten 145.)

Now all through the third essay Nietzsche emphasizes something it is part of the essay's strategy for him to emphasize, that regret belongs to the ascetic way of life. "The ascetic treats life as a wrong road on which one must finally walk back to the point where it begins" (III.11), as a nostalgic genealogist of morals might also treat human history. Genealogy without regrets would have to have no villain.

The villain ruins things at a turn in history that might have turned the other way. So in Essay III the ascetic priest appears after the one most important historical fact, this "fact" of human sickness, in order that he not contribute any action to history that an onlooker might wish had gone the other way. An alternative history would only be more asceticism.

All right then, nothing happened that you could blame on the ascetic priest. There are only forms of the ascetic ideal, only sickness. As father-confessor to those already sick the ascetic priest is the only shepherd the human flock has ever had.

What clinches the emotional disappointment over this ascetic priest is that you cannot even hate him for his efforts. Nietzsche keeps turning his thoughts back to his doctrine of a unitary will to power.

> Every animal instinctively strives for an optimum of favorable conditions under which it can expend all its strength and achieve its maximal feeling of power. (III.7)

In keeping with this doctrine he repudiates the idea that asceticism dams up life. That phrase "life against life" describes an impossibility, he says now (III.13).

Too many readings play down III.13 even though it represents the book's decisive self-revision. See Alphonso Lingis, merely one example, who hews to language of external energy turned back on itself. "The rancorous life . . . begins in an inner dissociation of the will. . . . The active force of the will is retarded" (Lingis 52); but Nietzsche says that the ascetic priest does *not* take a healthy animal and pervert its movements, rather finds the sickened and worn-out old thing and gives it whatever movements it can stand to make. "The ascetic ideal springs from the protective instincts of a degenerating life" (III.13). Not only not evil, the ideal is not even negative. It is a positive force suitable to inspiring sick animals to stay alive.

If the soul does not turn against itself as it had seemed to, the power that the priest appeals to is indistinguishable from other power. You can't moralize about the priest now: you can't separate power into its active and reactive manifestations and deny the self-lacerating exercise of power just because it looks like inhibition. Power is power (power powers). The ascetic priest becomes "among the greatest conserving and yes-creating forces of life" (III.13), even if as the only caretaker that sick human beings know he can no longer serve as the object of Nietzsche's enmity.

"The No he says to life brings to light, as if by magic, an abundance of tender Yeses": but what's magical is the way the target of Nietzsche's hatred has slipped out of his hands.

The denial of a contradictory self.   Why should Nietzsche dig in his heels at III.13 and insist that a self can't be divided? And why does he make this point in academic-philosophical lingo? III.13 calls "life against life" a self-contradiction ("Selbstwiderspruch"), nonsense ("Unsinn"), merely "*apparent* [nur *scheinbar*]," the cover for something that hasn't been understood *in itself* ("*an sich*": this Kantian expression emphasized); "a mere word [ein bloßes Wort]" to be replaced now by a "formulation of the facts of the matter [Tatbestand]" (this "Tat" standing against the "Wort" as it had for Faust).

It is as if, when it comes time to stop moralizing and turn every act into a positive expression of life, Nietzsche reaches for traditional modes of resistance. But also as if his multiplicity of reasons for attacking "life against life" suggests some other motive that can't be spoken.

Nietzsche is taking back what he said about the bad conscience's being a war on instinct (II.16), representing ideals that are "hostile to life" (II.24). Essay II's entire analysis of guilty feeling as a will turned against itself depends on the possibility of what Nietzsche now calls a self-contradiction.

But the second essay's only hope for turning guilt into something better depends on the same possibility that Nietzsche now rules out. For Essay II, not simply heralding the future like so many of Nietzsche's writings, shows how to think about a real time ahead and move forward into it; and it uses the divided self to suggest how that forward movement might work.

Early in the essay Nietzsche says that nature breeds memory in the human animal so that promises will at last be possible. The autonomous man is the memorious man, whose memory has not the past for its ultimate object but the future. "Remember the future!" says the man who has earned the right to make a promise. Imagine this as Nietzsche's general plan for the time ahead, which becomes neither the automatically arriving utopia of modern progressives nor a mysterious afterlife accessible only to clairvoyants but the property of anyone who masters the real function of human capacities.

What about the bad conscience, also till now oriented toward the past? Near the end of Essay II Nietzsche suggests how it too might aim at the future. If you can take the guilt you feel about natural yearnings to power, aggression, and appetite, and you redirect that guilt to the inclinations that morality honors—if you can learn to feel guilty about every world-slandering aspiration you had identified with your better self—there might still be hope for you (II.24).

Feeling guilty about temptations to morality may lead to a better future even though guilt in its present form stays stuck in the past. Morality's ideals are false and therefore dispensable. Feeling guilty over natural desires is an endless task because it is unfinishable. Feeling guilty over externally imposed false ideals may finish them off.

The temple of the body.   Nietzsche knows that his hope for a more effective breed of guilt will strike his readers as destructive. Isn't it tantamount to tearing down everything holy?

But building a future will not look pretty. "If a temple is to be erected *a temple must be destroyed*" (II.24).

Given that the context of II.24 is the restructuring of bad conscience, it is not hard to take the temple that Nietzsche speaks of as an image of the human being—as in, "Destroy this temple and in three days I will raise it up. . . . But he was speaking of the temple of his body" (Jn. 2.19–21).

Jesus has just taken a whip to the money changers in the literal temple (2.13–17). A whip in the temple was nothing new when the place was full of sheep and oxen, but until now one had not been turned against the merchants. Same idea. If the metaphorical temple is the body then it needs clearing too, take a scourge if that's the only instrument you have and instead of whipping your pride and your aggression try driving out the metaphors of money-changing: "ought," "redeem," "duty."

Bad conscience as pregnancy.   The bad conscience is an illness as pregnancy is. This means that the bad conscience promises a future. It might also mean that what looks like a single misshapen person who can't walk straight actually comprises a pair of wills. Again guilt entails a self divided against its own will to life.

If pregnancy looks like illness because two lives are competing for control over a single organism, then separating the two lives will look and feel like a cure. So every pregnancy anticipates an expulsion of the dependent life; and

Nietzsche's proposal to aim guilty feelings back at unnatural ideals is a proposal for turning the unrelievable pressure of guilt into a fullness that can come to term.

The bad conscience as *pregnancy* is, in other words, the bad conscience as *human will turned against itself.* If you think "pregnancy" essentially means cultivation of some future being then that thought will lead you to the divided self, since Nietzsche's only plan for the future depends on seeing the self divided.

If what "pregnancy" more specifically has to mean to you is a discomfort owing to two beings' sharing a body, that cashes out into a divided-self picture of the bad conscience too.

Either way, when Nietzsche repudiates the thought of "life against life" and later half-apologizes for Essay II as "a piece of animal psychology" (III.20), he can no longer call the bad conscience a pregnancy. Guilt is no longer a new life growing inside another one, no longer the harbinger of something better for human beings.

Now suppose it were Nietzsche's *purpose* to suppress the figure of pregnancy. Then he has to move to the adjacent image of inner discord and quash that too.

Why should Nietzsche suppress his own former mentions of pregnancy? The important thing to note first is that he does. The ascetic priest preserves life (III.13), but preservation is not creation. The life that the ascetic priest preserves had already existed, and the obstacle it struggles against preceded him too. There is no concatenation of lives within the sinner but only a sickliness that does not resemble pregnancy. No wonder the ascetic priest's influence on philosophy amounts to "castrating" the intellect (III.12).

The sterile priest.   No longer demonized as a father of "evil," the ascetic priest finds himself no father at all. He provided "the repulsive and gloomy caterpillar form in which alone the philosopher could live and creep about" (III.10), something like a merging of the masculine caterpillar shape with the image of pregnancy. Then less than that:

> Nor does he breed and propagate his mode of valuation through heredity . . . a profound instinct rather forbids him to propagate. (III.11)

Nietzsche remarks on the priest's impossible yet regularly occurring birth. "It must indeed be in the *interest of life itself* that such a self-contradictory type [in another sense a mixed type] does not die out" (III.11)—that "must be" expressing surprise that the ascetic priest reproduces without participating in biological processes.

If anything the priest exists to deny biology. Nietzsche has cited Pope Innocent III torturing himself with those conditions of his own existence that he would rather forget, like "impure begetting, disgusting means of nutrition in his mother's womb" (II.7). Asceticism in its fullest form battles against the thought of pregnancy.

Read the ascetic priest's rebuke to his sheep.

> "I suffer: someone must be to blame for it"—thus thinks every sickly sheep. But his shepherd, the ascetic priest, tells him: "Quite so, my sheep! someone must be to blame for it: but you yourself are this someone . . . *you alone are to blame for yourself!*" (III.16)

His scolding parodies a talk about pregnancy. "Someone" got you pregnant? Come on, you were there. But it's a new kind of pregnancy: you are to blame for yourself because you made yourself. The ascetic priest has become a strange new father who represents the principle of self-birth, which is to say, *not really a father.*

Gospel genealogies.   Three gospels establish the Messianic status of Jesus with prefatory genealogies—or rather two do, while John replaces genealogy with a new story of parentage.

Matthew (1.1–16) and Luke (3.23–38) name the generations before Jesus in deference to the prophecy that the Messiah will come from the house of David (Isaiah 11.1, Jeremiah 23.5). Matthew starts with Abraham and passes through David to Jesus; Luke one-ups him, tracing the patrilineage in reverse through David and Abraham to "Seth [son] of Adam [son] of God" (3.38).

The Matthew and Luke genealogies are famously incompatible, giving different names for persons as recent as Joseph's father and running back through different sons of David. But those discrepancies make no theological trouble compared to the two lists' point of agreement, that both of them trace Jesus' lineage through Joseph's. For if Jesus' credentials rest on Joseph's patrimony, what makes him Messiah undermines his standing as son of God. Or else it gives him no more standing as God's descendant than everyone else has, if as in Luke's version Jesus only comes from God through "Adam of God."

The Messianic genealogies establish an unbroken series of births, every intermediary name supplied, only to arrive at a disruption of lineage between Joseph and Jesus of the sort that no traditional genealogy can bridge.

The Fourth Gospel opens with a different warrant for Jesus:

In the beginning was the word [*logos*], and the word was with [*pros*] God, and the word was God. The same [*houtos*] was in the beginning with God. (Jn. 1.1–2)

As the Evangelist who takes the greatest pains to declare Jesus' divinity (Thomas confesses at 20.28, "My Lord and my God"), John finds Joseph's place in the usual genealogy an occasion for mischief. Mention Joseph and a cynic might object as the Galileans do at 6.42: "Is this not Jesus, the son of Joseph, whose father and mother we know? So how can this same one [*houtos*] say, I came down from heaven?"

(It may again be for the purpose of avoiding mischief that the Letter to the Hebrews, having called "Christ . . . a high priest after the order of Melchisedec" at 5.6 and 5.10, later adds that Melchisedec was "without genealogy [*agenealogêtos*]": 7.3.)

Jesus says or implies that he is God's son at Jn. 1.18, 1.49, 2.16, 3.16–18, 5.17, 6.40, 6.69. The Fourth Gospel suggests even closer relations than sonship, as when John writes that "the word was with God." And Jesus says that the son does whatever the father does (5.19); his father "has sent me" (5.37); "as the living father has sent me, and I live by the father," he says (6.57). His words are not his own, for "my teaching is not mine, but his who sent me" (7.16; cf. 14.10–11, "I am in my father and my father is in me").

The trickiest element introduced by this new genealogy is that prefatory *logos* that Faust did not want to render "Wort." As the *logos* of God the son is practically indistinguishable from the father, or distinguishable only in principle. The *logos* in 1.1 may reflect a Hebrew tradition of separating God logically from His activities, by attributing the activities to God's word: see Ps. 33.6, "By the word of the Lord were the heavens made" (cf. Ps. 107.20). So you might call John's preface the translation of genealogy into the realm of *logos*—word, reason, speech, explanation—to account for the fatherhood by God that ordinary genealogies can't help leaving unexplained. The only genealogy you need is a genealogy of the *logos*, says John (and Nietzsche will look at the *logos* he's heard and try to carry out its genealogy).

The country parson.   Nietzsche smirks at Kant, who describes "the peculiar properties of the sense of touch with the naïveté of a country parson [landpfarrermäßiger Naivität]!" (III.6). Kant's aesthetic theories deny a place for desire, so he writes as if a theory of touch would not wander into country matters. He's being naïve about sexual contact, he doesn't know anything about it, as a country parson apparently also does not.

The parson returns later in Essay III looking just as feeble, and not only in his head.

> What would happen if . . . a real psychologist were to describe a real Luther, not with the moralistic simplicity of a country parson [nicht mehr mit der moralistischen Einfalt eines Landgeistlichen] . . . but, say . . . out of strength of soul? (III.19)

A Geistliche, a clergyman, is more or less a Pfarrer; a Landgeistliche like a Landpfarrer is one who serves in the countryside and speaks with moralistic simplicity. Nietzsche's slap at the man is bad enough on the face of it: the country parson doesn't have the strength of soul to write about the real Luther.

It gets worse. Earlier Nietzsche specified how someone *should* write about Luther, and the parson's inability to produce that type of writing suggests a more extreme insult. In III.2 Nietzsche says that during Wagner's happiest and bravest period, he had entertained the thought of writing an opera called "Luther's Wedding." Nietzsche wishes he had done it. A work like that—reproaching the ascetic ideal—would have showed what every good marriage does, that chastity and sensuality can go together (III.2).

But if no one has written such a thing about Luther yet, and if the lives of Luther thus far have had the smell of a country parsonage, then a country parson must be the type who cannot write about the sensuality in marriage. Like Kant he is naïve to the point of sexlessness.

The ascetic priest might be a mere type, as abstracted from daily experience as the slave of Essay I was. The country parson comes from right next door, if you want to put it that way: Nietzsche's father was one. A Christian clergyman and an asexual, the country parson makes a decent ascetic priest, which does not have to mean he chases down the sick and torments them but does mean he is no father.

No ordinary father.   It has become easy to find insults about women in Nietzsche's books and a commonplace to say he recoils from motherhood and birth. The truth is more specific. For if Nietzsche asks for ruminative readers it is also fair to call him a ruminative writer, which does not mean he knows everything he is saying—digestion is a paradigm of unconscious action (II.1)—but does mean that words look different each time he chews them over, and means regarding *Genealogy* that which essay an image appears in affects what that image is doing.

Consider the child in Essay II. To illustrate the irresponsibility of ancient punishment Nietzsche comments that it was imposed "as parents still punish their children, from anger at some harm or injury, vented on the one who caused it" (II.4). A child is a person who for no good reason can face its parent's flare of anger—probably the father's, as this aside fits his offense more than the stereotypical mother's.

Nietzsche also has a father in mind when he mentions "the notorious sacrifice of the first-born" to a tribe's ancestors (II.19), at least he does if he is thinking of the mythical versions of that sacrifice filtered down in the stories of Abraham, Agamemnon, and Jephthah. All three offer their children to gods. The first two keep what they are doing a secret from their wives; Jephthah's wife is not mentioned (Judges 11.30–40).

So there is real fatherhood in Essay II. The gods begin life as tribal ancestors who supernaturally sustain their children from beyond the grave; and then the one most powerful God that replaced them all, fathers (within Christianity) the first-born son he sacrifices to himself but also (within human history) fathers the crucial interpretation of indebtedness that turns bad conscience into the sense of guilt.

The other parents mentioned in Essay II are the warriors who founded the state (II.17). Nietzsche tries to exonerate them from blame for the bad conscience, but it "would not have developed *without them*, this ugly growth." The beasts of prey grind down their subjects with "that terrible artists' egoism that . . . knows itself justified to all eternity in its 'work,' like a mother in her child."

If Nietzsche's history of the bad conscience contains both villains and reminders of the potent father, it might count for something that *Essay III has neither*. The ascetic priest did not make humanity sick. The ascetic ideal represents not things gone wrong but things as they are and maybe always have been. As one more expression of the will to power no matter what anyone tries to make of it, the ascetic ideal shows that the history of humanity has been and must continue to be histories of the will to power; so there never was a villainy.

Meanwhile this unmoralistic nonhistory sweeps birth aside. The bad conscience is no longer a pregnancy (see earlier). The artist gets compared to a mother (as in II.17): the artist is only the womb out of which his work grows—or equivalently "sometimes the dung and manure" (III.4). Wagner couldn't be spared his psychological torments any more than a pregnant woman can "be spared the repellent and bizarre aspects of pregnancy—which . . . must be *forgotten* if one is to enjoy the child."

While not overlooking the aggression in "dung and manure," "repellent and bizarre," the reader should also notice Nietzsche's injunction to forget the pregnancy. In II.17 the artist's egoism knows *itself* to be justified in the work it makes: that mother artist is valorized, the one in III.4 best forgotten.

And where are Essay III's fathers? The philosopher refuses to become one: Nietzsche speaks of his maternal instinct (III.8). Philosophers would say what Buddha did at the sight of his new son, "a fetter has been forged for me" (III.7). Philosophers' apparent chastity masks their further agenda, because "this type of spirit clearly has its fruitfulness somewhere else than in children" (III.8).

Anyway philosophers pose as ascetic priests—like the spiritual sons of priests they imitate the priestly ethos—and the ascetic priest has forbidden himself to propagate. He too might ask himself, "Why should he desire progeny whose soul is the world?" (III.8), considering that the world has become "the distinctively *ascetic planet*" (III.11). The priest leaves new words behind. He performs his "name-changing and rebaptizing" not on real children but on his metaphorical children's acts (III.18). He gives these so-to-speak children not sin, as a devilish father might, but "sin," a new name for the bad feeling they are already living with (III.20). They adjust to their sickly lives by learning the priest's words for what they do—the new words take. So it is that the ascetic ideal "has inscribed [eingeschrieben] itself in a fearful and unforgettable way in the entire history of man" (III.21). Every page of the historical record you look at is covered with the priest's handwriting.

Nietzsche's lament that the ascetic ideal has thus far faced no competition (III.28) is therefore the lament that the priest has left the genealogist no words but ascetic ones, "slanderous" words in other words, no way to talk about the past and no past to talk about but the priest's.

What fatherhood is this? If there were even one father in sight or if there ever had been, then the one you originally took to be your father might be a stand-in and you'd have a true father somewhere else, maybe in the distant past. But if nothing has been ruined then there is no other father to hope for. You might as well accept that the words you are speaking come from the man that the world calls your father. You may deny your biological descent from him by refusing him the power to reproduce but now that denial sounds *desperate*, because it betrays the reaches you will go to trying to escape your patrimony; and also *pointless*, it's shutting the barn door after the horses are gone, you are a writer and the priest gave birth to every word you wrote and where it counts he is still your father.

Not speaking on your own behalf.   John says that Jesus says,

> I have not spoken for myself [*emautou*]; but the father who sent me gave me a commandment, what I should say and what I should speak . . . therefore whatever I speak, even as the father said to me, so do I speak. (Jn. 12.49–50)

This is one model for choosing the words you say, namely to choose the authorized ones. As a rule, "he whom God has sent speaks the words of God" (3.34).

The problem of "evil" reassures Nietzsche. A psychologist might say: "The problem of evil must be doing something for Nietzsche, when you consider the way he sniffs out every blunder and misfortune in history." True enough. However depressingly, the problem of "evil" reassures Nietzsche that he exists. Rethinking the Gospel of the Word, he looks for the primal literal words about morality that only he can speak.

I and the father. "I and the father are one" (Jn. 10.30); by comparison Nietzsche is one thing and his writings are another because his writings cannot help inheriting the moral vocabulary of the father's ascetic ideal.

Or rather more correctly speaking: he will speak the words of asceticism because those words are the only money in town even if you can't call this money "green" any more; but he so warmly wants to write better that he will mark the bills with inverted commas to mean something else by them. He is the quotation marks around the words he quotes. (See Derrida on Nietzsche's "epochal regime of quotation marks": Derrida 107.)

Nietzsche's effort not to speak the language he was handed down reflects in one way what Pierre Klossowski calls his "need to give birth to himself through himself" (Klossowski 188).

Nietzsche's need to have birthed himself is a response to a crisis. As long as some better model of a father exists he can dream of having been born to that father, lost, taken in by the uncomprehending false father, returning at last to the source. While the fantasy holds up, the false father is his slandering devil.

But the family romance retreats before the expanding economy of will to power. There is no room to speak of a false devil-father—until the only escape from his own genealogy that Nietzsche can muster is the denial that the step before him can reproduce. *What separates him from the possibility that the priest gave birth to him is the priest's asexuality.*

Nietzsche knows that the words for that denial have already been said before too. If his newness is a matter of virgin birth then it's already been talked about: even if Nietzsche has only himself to blame for himself his words are still not of his own making. If his words are those right there in front of him, then he will be something different from his words.

(Though it addresses a different text, one remarkable article about Nietzsche deserves a nod here. Richard Perkins, "An Innocent Little Story," reads a scrap from Nietzsche's notes of 1883, a Gospel parody that ascribes Jesus' theology to his fatherlessness. Perkins dexterously turns the allegory back to illuminate Nietzsche's fantasy of himself fatherless.)

Letter to Basel historian Jakob Burckhardt, maybe Nietzsche's last bit of writing. The letter alarmed Burckhardt. He showed it to Overbeck, who rushed to Turin.

> I have a writing business here . . . at root every name in history is I. . . . I have had Caiaphas put in chains; I too was crucified at great length last year. . . . You can make any use of this letter which does not make the people of Basel think less highly of me. (Middleton 347–348)

Mad it may be; also an allegory for writing, if you take "I have a writing business" as an instruction for reading what follows.

"*Every name in history is I.*" It's true that this letter proclaims Nietzsche to be identical with Carlo Alberto of Italy and Carlo Alberto's son Vittorio Emanuele II; with the French criminals Prado and Chambige (as well as with Prado's father); with a French diplomat and a papal state secretary—but this quip about "every name in history" that interrupts the string of identifications shows what point Nietzsche is pressing. It is a linguistic comment, a statement about words; people have always called themselves "I": "I" truly is everyone's name, for which other names are forced translations made to stroke effeminate ears.

When you boil people down to the words they use every name in history is I.

"*Caiaphas.*" If Nietzsche's business is a writing business, his books are his actions. "Caiaphas" represents the priest whose psychology *Genealogy* was the first to analyze. The book *Genealogy* ("I") put the priest "in chains," which is allegorically to say that it restrained the figure of the priest from working his effects on human history.

"*Crucified . . . last year.*" Nietzsche wrote to Burckhardt in 1889, which makes "last year" 1888, the year of *Ecce Homo*. *Ecce Homo* of course takes its title from the Gospel of John:

> Jesus came out wearing the crown of thorns and the purple garment. And he [Pilate] says to them, Behold the man [*Ecce homo*]. (Jn. 19.5)

And this book concludes (emphasis as always in the original) "Have I been understood?—*Dionysus versus the Crucified.*"

Has Nietzsche been understood?—he bears both these names: he bears them "at great length," over the course of a book. Last year he was (he called himself) "Crucified."

If Nietzsche is writing allegorically he is not really saying that he put Caiaphas in chains, he is saying that he wrote about priests in a way that constrains them; not really saying that he has been crucified, only that he has written about himself in terms drawn from the Crucifixion. Within the world of writing these putative ravings are as literally true as the linguistic observation that everyone's name is "I."

But the allegorical reading of Nietzsche's letter makes him sane only on the condition that Nietzsche collapse into his written version of himself. In *Ecce Homo* he distinguished himself from his writings; in this letter he dissolves the distinction.

From the man apart from his writings to the one as he has written himself is no small shift. (No little play on words either, even if you could call both of them "men of letters" in English.) What saved Nietzsche from identifying himself with Jesus was the difference he drew between himself and his writings. If he is his writings then he consists of words the priesthood has rebaptized and he really is the priest's son speaking as his father said.

The present reading resists Alexander Nehamas's claim that Nietzsche strives to "achieve the perfect unity and freedom that are primarily possessed by perfect literary characters" (Nehamas 1985, 195). That existence might suit literary characters, who have no identity separate from the words constituting them; Nietzsche's unity and freedom depend on his not having had words put into his mouth.

How will Burckhardt use this letter? If the letter makes people think less highly of the person who wrote it then its readers must be identifying the letter with the man; so Burckhardt must not use the letter in any way that permits that identification. But without equating the letter and the letter-writer, without reading "Nietzsche" back into the words he writes, a reader can't make sense of it. Either the letter allegorizes writing or it is lunacy. The people of Basel have to identify the letter with Nietzsche.

If Burckhardt may neither equate Nietzsche with his letter nor make the man's letter distinct from him, then he cannot make any use of the letter at all: the letter can't speak to anyone: it's not really a letter. Nietzsche ends in failure (he ends in Christianity) not because he is incomprehensible, he isn't that, but because his comprehensibility returns him to a family of language users whose founding father he told himself he had disowned.

∽

Some Remarks on the
Causal Sequence

Times. *Times change* is the message that *Genealogy* greets its reader with; it's there in the book's long-drawn-out ominous farewell, too.

"Times," plural: one unlike the other.

The religion that promised to make everything new was right about *that* (Rev. 21.5), even if the possibility of innovation means that values like altruism, feelings like guilt, and postulates of "the true world" are not what they seem to be—even if the fantasy of natural morals is unsustainable in a world of moral artifice.

Times change again in Nietzsche's philosophy. Now here is a really welcome novelty. New things are being said—*surprises*—and nothing will ever be the same again.

The disappointment in *Genealogy* emerges against this sense of newness, when unfinished genealogical business threatens the very idea of revolution in morality. For the core sense of "disappointment" in the Nietzsche disappointment comes down to *causal explanations called for but not heard from*; and extreme changes in history promise to make it impossible to explain those same changes.

"Extreme change" is vague, though. It forces the question: What *is* temporalization? Does it always imply breaks in past time? Do those gaps happen like the gaps in neo-Darwinian evolution, or does the unpredictability that Nietzsche speaks of exceed evolutionary surprises?

And given Nietzsche's overt and repeated contempt for "teleology," is it safe to say that the causation he attacks (in principle and in practice) is *final causation*?

172

Temporalization taken further. *Simple temporalization* means bringing references to time back into the study of what had been viewed *sub specie aeterni*. Time belongs in descriptions of formerly timeless things.

The eternal had once felt morally authoritative and magically efficacious. "Human nature" was a guide to which one could turn, also a force invariably returning to regulate behavior. But you will no longer find moral sentiments as gripping as you did, nor posits like human nature that shelter moral sentiments, once you see that such ideas have a past.

Simple temporalization might be *too* simple. Talk of eternal verities has been unfashionable for a long time. And the flat assertion that concepts and institutions change does not go far enough against habits of thinking eternally. Eternity is longsuffering and patient and knows how to reenter temporalized subjects, in teleological narratives that reconcile change over time with unchanging timeless essences. Change is progress toward the best and most real. Slave-owning societies were trying all along to turn into modern democracy, the right form of government.

Thus what is simply temporalized simply gets eternized again.

Against the gravitational pull of eternity Nietzsche therefore makes temporalization something more abrupt. Where time had flowed it now bursts. The gaps in history, chance happenings at crucial times, deny the possibility of a rationalizing explanation of the present. Then there can be no eternity.

What frustrates Nietzsche's readers is that these same gaps in history stand in the way of explanations of the past. Nietzsche's histories draw readers in with the promise of a new story of how the world came to be as it is. But when time's arrow begins to look as incapable of flight as Zeno's, it won't even deliver the thrill of thudding into its target.

After hectoring his readers to seek out contexts for the beliefs that philosophy had considered context-independent, Nietzsche turns around to declare the contexts inaccessible to inquiry.

Now, there are some interpreters who argue that the lacunae in Nietzsche's histories, far from forcing him to give up knowledge about the past, have been inserted expressly in order to deny such knowledge. The obstacle to knowledge is not a disappointment, it's the point. When James Porter writes that Nietzsche "has no single view of antiquity, and certainly no consistent view of it" (Porter 2000b, 225), he is not complaining. Nietzsche's "skeptical counterphilology" (17) examines a *constructed past*; his "self-disrupting frameworks" (166) demonstrate that all philology "mirrors . . . the philologist" (123).

Self-disrupting: don't suspect for a minute that Nietzsche is not doing this all himself.

Indeed the very idea of skips in history makes no sense. Nietzsche cannot be asserting that morality passed occultly from masters' hands to slaves', not when his counterphilology problematizes statements about the masters' existence. Drop the claim that there were masters and you have to drop any claim about masters and slaves.

Porter's merry skepticism has its appeals. Being a consistent view it is easier to defend than Nietzsche's back-and-forth between sometimes a knowable history, sometimes none. But Porter's position evades what it ought to confront, which is Nietzsche's problem of asserting a change to have occurred, that, if he is right, he is in no position to know about.

Don't just say that the deep past is perforce *under construction*. Nietzsche's main reason for saying that it is, is his belief that crises separate the past from the present. If you wave away that belief too you undo the constructedness of the past; you have a skepticism that eats its own mouth.

Blame Foucault? Foucault more than anyone else has brought readers to see Nietzsche's genealogies as epochal, "effective" (as he puts it) at subversive strikes against historical continuity.

For Foucault, the usual practice of history is constantly implicated in the assumptions that origins exist and need to be sought out. Genealogy, however, "disturbs what was previously considered immobile; it fragments what was thought unified" (Foucault 1984, 82). Interpreting "History" as an anticipation of *Genealogy*, Foucault finds Nietzsche both early and late sniping at coherent historical explanation. Monumental, antiquarian, and critical histories are really all manifestations of theoretical history. Only genealogy measures itself against its effects; only genealogy is really practice. (See Ansell Pearson 1991 on Foucault's politicization of Nietzsche: 268.)

By interpreting "History" as he does, Foucault can render questions of knowledge and method irrelevant to genealogy. Let theoretical history try to guess how the past's surprises could have happened so abruptly, or how anyone could claim to know about such singular events. Genealogy has fish to fry. "Effective history" takes whatever steps it must to undercut the justifications that history has thus far given to culture. Genealogy faces no truth tribunal.

Suppose you wonder how history ever turned into genealogy, given such differences in their aims. "How could history 'change roles on the same stage?'" is the way Foucault puts it; and he answers:

> Only by being seized, dominated, and turned against its birth . . . it is not the unavoidable conclusion of a long preparation, but a scene where forces are

risked in the chance of confrontations, where they emerge triumphant . (Foucault 1984, 93)

The genealogy of genealogy shows it to have come as a surprise as great as any pivotal event that genealogy finds in the past.

Foucault speaks of "gray, meticulous, and patiently documentary" genealogies (76). But when describing how history got subverted into genealogy he doesn't try to be meticulous, offers no documents (certainly not that "vast accumulation of source material" he promises: 76–77), pulls the story of genealogy's birth out of the blue. There went history on the road it had paved for itself and here came Nietzsche to knock it off course.

It is an old story, maybe the oldest in philosophy: universal error followed in a trice by the right approach. From Kant's Copernican revolution back to the impression that Anaxagoras gave of being the only sober man among drunks, the philosopher's legitimacy rests on his miraculous sunburst arrival in a world dark with idiocy. When Foucault's compulsion to radicalize the genealogical enterprise makes him set Nietzsche apart from all earlier histories and embattled against them with a preternatural strength, it feels like a domestication. (See Pizer on Foucault's appropriations of Nietzsche.)

A second problem with Foucault's reading is his allusive talk of chance. What does that mean exactly? What kinds of explanation is Nietzsche resisting, and how random a breed of chanciness does he have to assume for the purpose of resisting them? Is Nietzsche doing as little as denying a providential plan behind every bend and turn in history, or as much as denying the explicability of all events?

Analogy to Darwinism; limits to the analogy.   Darwinism speaks of the past too, and it too has had to account for gaps in its explanations. In *Genealogy* II.12 Nietzsche equates the biological and historical processes himself, with a sharp eye for how evolution works. (On Nietzsche's references to Darwin, see chapter 4.) The function of an organ "means nothing regarding its origin." Philosophers went astray believing "that to understand . . . the utility of a thing . . . was also to understand the reason why it originated — the eye being made for seeing, the hand being made for grasping" (II.12).

Stop daydreaming that hands were always here for handiwork and merely improved at their function. The hand was once a foot, before that maybe a fin, and that appendage did not become "the hand" by discovering its essence but at most by being available when a creature needed a hand.

True, a paw will grow into a hand faster than a nose can. To that extent you can reconstruct a rational story after the fact. But a nose will do when the creature weighs as much as an elephant and needs all its paws for standing. Aristotle thinks of the hand as a tool of tools, *organon organôn* (*De Anima* 432a2). Nietzsche can see the hand as a tool too, but he imagines nature picking up any instrument in a pinch, as workers do.

It is not surprising that a neo-Darwinian should recognize his own thought in *Genealogy* II.12 (thus Gould 2002, 1217). Modern Darwinism depicts evolution moving in fits and sudden stops. Evolutionary contingency begins in randomness (the randomness of mutations).

But then the analogy to cultural history fails. Astonishingly mutated living things are born in the usual way, namely in whatever way was usual to their parents' generation. Mutations amount to changes in DNA, but DNA remains the same and its changes follow regular patterns. *There can be a science of genetics and hypotheses about genetic mutation.* Nietzsche shows no sign of envisioning a comparable stable hypothesis about cultural change.

It is hard to imagine what kind of hypothesis would do. If you ask how the human animal originally got sick, or how it became philosophical, or where the inner life came from, analogies to evolution sound misplaced. Darwinian theory does very well at explaining why things might have happened that *did not have to*. That is the contingency in evolution. But when Nietzsche speaks of unexpected events he spends more time on developments that *never should have* happened. Parallels to the Fall and the problem of evil come to his readers' minds as they would not occur to someone contemplating a platypus.

The best theory of the unpredictable will not accommodate the impossible.

Mind you, if the chance that Nietzsche identified in historical junctures were the contingency that evolutionary theory speaks of, temporalization would still be remarkable. Decisive historical occurrences would still not be predictable on the basis of what preceded them. That much contingency brings all the power of full-bore temporalization and runs the same risk.

Temporalization derives all the power it needs from contingency because the unchartable birth of a moral sentiment bleaches the eternity out of it. If moral values were as contingent as horses they could not claim the allegiance that has been paid to them. As for the risk that Nietzsche runs when he temporalizes, which is the risk of making historical before and after so different that the before becomes a fantasy, that risk also follows from having historical events succeed each other with the spontaneity that characterizes evolution.

Thus the contingency present in evolution goes beyond the denial of teleology. References to Darwinism carry this discussion further than Foucault took it, because evolutionary spontaneity is more than the absence of a great plan.

The mutual causation of events. Nietzsche wants more than even the remarkable contingency known to evolution. He posits not only sudden changes but about-faces.

He invites disappointment in the first place by imagining transformations that no one should be able to account for; in the second place by suggesting explanations whose lavish inadequacy contributes to your sense that the events never happened. That is, the Nietzsche disappointment emerges not only out of the kinds of events Nietzsche describes but also to a great degree from the explanations he himself offers for those events.

(When substitute-explanations about birth are told to young children— the baby found under a cabbage—their implausibility encourages the suspicion: "My birth was not an event like other events. I was always here.")

Most peculiar to Nietzsche of all his twists on causal explanation is the mutual causation of events.

Given that Oedipus becomes more or less his own father it may be only natural (if it doesn't kink the word "natural" too much to say so) that Nietzsche's treatment of him in *Birth* 9 explains everything backward. But what does it mean that Socrates at the vortex of history both initiates Socratism and instantiates a Socratism that had been at work before him? Call Socrates another Oedipus, as Nietzsche does. Reflect on the coincidence that what sets his life in motion is an oracle that he tries to disprove but thereby proves true. Socrates and Oedipus are bound to exist despite all efforts including their own. And yet the existence of these men should not happen. (No contradiction there. Fate's big fingers poke in to reset machinery that would not crank out the right results otherwise.) Oedipus had to be present to usher himself into existence. Nietzsche's account of Socrates half presupposes the mighty force called Socratism and half explains it.

The reciprocal sequences in *Genealogy* likewise leave its reader that much more dubious about an already improbable event. You suspect that the slave revolt in morals could not succeed. Then Nietzsche tells you that the appearance of the soul makes that revolt possible, and also tells you that the slave revolt creates the soul.

In one place religion is a necessary condition for guilt. In other places Nietzsche uses preexisting guilt to account for religion. Were you wondering how the bad conscience could have struck this fundamentally healthy human type? Now that you have heard the explanation you will be sure it could not have happened.

The greatest improbabilities might be the ones that swirl around the execution of Jesus. In all three *Genealogy* essays, it is the Crucifixion that ful-
crums world history: the ruse by which slave morality triumphs (I.8), the
stroke of genius that brings guilt to a new crescendo (II.21), the beloved object of the ascetic ideal's self-abnegation (III.11). Each time the Crucifixion
explains everything, but also merely illustrates some other process that *was*
under way: in other words it is a cause but also an effect.

In Essay II Christianity had to be there, matured into a creative dogma, to
orchestrate this event that generated the fully moralized bad conscience. The
moralized bad conscience is the bad conscience that then goes looking for religion and makes a guilt-ridden Christianity possible, which in turn is able to
invent the Crucifixion.

In Essay I the Crucifixion enables slave morality to spread, but then it
only spreads into a world in which it has already triumphed.

Mutual causation as a rebuke to sequentiality. When *Beyond* 21
claims, "It is *we* alone who have devised cause, sequence," and so on, these
and other broad brushstrokes (see, e.g., *Gay Science* 127) can have the look
of self-defeating metaphysics. Why should it matter that "we alone" invented
the causal relation unless *some* causal relations matter, like the link between
the causality idea and its invention?

But Nietzsche does not leave his comments in that crude state. Along with
other products of human devising that he lists in *Beyond* 21, he cites not only
causation but also "sequence [das Nacheinander: the after-one-another]."
This word narrows down the problem with causal accounts, not only that they
link events but that they link them in a non-reciprocal order.

Gay Science 112 specifies that same "after-one-another" as the characteristic form that the lie of causality has taken. And at 374 Nietzsche remarks that
if some beings could experience time in reverse, or running alternately forwards
and backwards, their experience would entail "another concept of cause and
effect." Causal reasoning is inseparable from the sequential experience of time.

Sequence and efficient causation. The import of Nietzsche's attack on
sequentiality is that "chance" in his writings means a denial of efficient causation as well as of final causation.

Final causation, teleology, was one of Nietzsche's targets from the start.
Certainly if the important events in history happen by chance, there is no
sense in which history aimed for the present.

But if sequential thinking about cause and effect is itself part of the problem, more than teleology is at stake. Sequential thinking characterizes not

only narratives about the purpose of events but also the most mundane explanations in science.

Of Aristotle's four causes, only the "efficient" or moved cause has found a home in modern science. Aristotle defines it as "the immediate origin of a change or a state of rest: for example, the man who deliberated is a cause, and the father is the cause of the child" (*Physics* 194b30–32). In such relationships it is clear who is boss. The father makes the child and not the other way around; the man who deliberated made the philosophy. But that unidirectional movement from cause to effect, not just the movement toward a *telos*, is the subject of Nietzsche's attack.

For polemical purposes Nietzsche sometimes emphasizes the order in which things happen: thus it matters vitally that master morality comes first, before the parasitic morality that has to begin in a revolt. One morality has to be spontaneous and the other one reactive, and to demonstrate that they are Nietzsche orders the moralities in a sequence.

A contrary impulse informs *Genealogy's* second essay, which distinguishes the conscience from the bad conscience not by connecting them in a single story but rather by fitting them into two disconnected stories that may well unfold at the same time. The possibility of openly cruel punishment converts the human creature into a self-regulator; the impossibility of cruelty's expressions inverts the human into a self-flagellator. An ordered sequence that led from conscience to bad conscience would hide this difference between the two disciplinary forms.

Then too, if fatherhood exemplifies efficient causation, Nietzsche's doubleness of mind about that causation reflects his wishes both to malign the purpose (a purpose for which he must posit the father's existence) and to deny that the father was ever there. Causal order permits a story of fallen humanity in which the bad father plays Satan's role. The absence of causal order renders the father an unneeded hypothesis (see chapter 3).

The future sequence. In some passages Nietzsche disrupts historical continuity with a specific denial of teleology, or with an analogy to evolution that inserts unsuspected contingencies into narratives of the past. But his resistance to providing a causal back story can exceed either of those justifications. Explanations that make as much sense backward as forward suggest nothing less than an obsession with making past events inexplicable.

The past is not the only occasion for Nietzsche's obsessiveness. *Beyond* mainly assesses modern morality not against the backdrop of what morality has been but with reference to what it might become. The book rests its critique of the present on a projection from present into future, so that its reader will want to see if it maps the effects of the present any better than *Genealogy* mapped out the present's causes.

Then too, if *Beyond* falters in its causal reasoning, does it disappoint in the same way that the histories do? Why would Nietzsche display a new kind of resistance where the future is concerned, unless maybe the past and the future posed different threats to him?

Beyond Good and Evil: The Philosopher of the Future

"Our amazement and laughter would never end."   It suits a prophetic book, this promise of endless laughter. The sentence comes from the part of *Beyond* entitled "What is Religious"; so perhaps Nietzsche is imagining a new religion appropriate to the coming ages.

> Suppose we could contemplate the . . . comedy [Komödie] of European Chris-
> tianity with the mocking and aloof eyes of an Epicurean god, I think our
> amazement and laughter would never end: doesn't it seem that a single will
> dominated Europe for eighteen centuries—to turn man into a *sublime miscar-
> riage* [Mißgeburt]? (62)

He chooses the eyes of an Epicurean god because those gods maintain the greatest indifference to the world. Without being an Epicurean, Nietzsche shares the opinion that this would be the highest species of god, one who leaves the fate of humans in their own hands.

Comedy.   Nietzsche's god laughs at the sight of Christian history. But that comedy has not reached its conclusion yet. Comedy finishes with a wed-ding; the last line of the poem that concludes *Beyond* posits a finish up ahead: "The wedding is at hand of dark and light—"

So far the humor has taken a low road. Blame the species, so degraded that it's lost the power to bring forth a worthy birth: "Mißgeburt" means "miscarriage," as Kaufmann translates it, but also freak or abnormality. The breeding of the human has been so badly botched that only degenerate forms are possible.

Don't expect any help from Epicurean gods. The human being is both "*creature* [Geschöpf] and *creator* [Schöpfer]" (225), therefore to be blamed in both capacities, as misbegotten and as the misbegetter.

Nevertheless Nietzsche waits confidently for that future in which laughter never ends. He subtitles *Beyond* "Prelude [Vorspiel] to a Philosophy of the Future." This is no modern progressivist dreaming of more democracy ahead, easier travel and communication, longer life. *Surprises* are on the way.

Prophecy: laughter, evolution.   One surprise will be the punch line to a joke already heard but so far impossible to laugh at. Another will be the arrival of philosophers whose births even nature (in its present form) seems to be conspiring to prevent.

Nietzsche might appear at his most time-bound when he turns from ancient spectacles to look ahead. No need to find his interlocutor in Descartes, Saint John, or Plato: this is the nineteenth century, when everyone deals in futures.

Emerson for one imagines new days ahead, though his newness is not Nietzsche's.

[W]here Emerson speaks of *revolution*, Nietzsche speaks of *evolution*. . . . Nietzsche repeatedly asserts the exhaustion of the age and its culture, whereas Emerson as insistently calls for the discovery of America, whose culture has barely begun. (Cavell 2004, 213; emphases in original)

Nietzsche stands closer to evolutionists like Darwin or Bergson, who stake themselves to the future not with specific forecasts but rather in anticipation of the unforeseeable. The known world will produce the unknowable one. That is what "evolution" means. Emerson may wake up in a New World every morning; Old-World philosophers cannot think that the leap into tomorrow has already happened.

(In the twenty-first century the Disneyland outside Paris will emulate American Disney parks down to the untranslated place-names—"Fantasyland," "Frontierland"—and yet banish Tomorrowland, which in Europe becomes "Discoveryland": as if, for a European, it would be verbal impropriety to proclaim the present existence of a future place. Europe can only acknowledge an existent process of discovery.)

The Nietzsche disappointment regarding *Beyond* grows out of the ways that Nietzsche parts company with his contemporaries to become his own man. Bergson, for all his attunement to both comedy and futurity, never hears the laughter that the future will enjoy at the sight of the present. His evolution does not go far enough for Nietzsche. And Darwinian evolution does not go fast enough. Nietzsche sides with Lamarck because the vital impulse that drives non-Darwinian evolution promises a speedier transition to the new order.

What is that future, so far-off and yet so fast-approaching, that Nietzsche claims to hear? Given the pace and the range that Nietzsche envisions, it is not surprising that on his account evolution arrives somewhere indescribable. When things are really different they will sure be weird—but he rarely says *how* they will be different. Somehow today's floundering moral vocabulary makes a new kind of joke possible, and laughter to vanquish the old moral man. Somehow the exhausted species needs only a shake before new philosophical legions fall out of it telling those new jokes and laughing.

"Somehow"?

Nietzsche wants to tell, and he wants not to. He envisions himself snapping history in half over one knee, and if that's a clean break there can't be a present-day description of the future. And yet: if he is the one doing the breaking-in-half then he also stands in the future and ought to be able to recount what he sees there. He has one foot in the present while with the other he waves back at himself from up ahead (a feat even trickier to accomplish than it is to describe).

Nietzsche on the future.   Benjamin Bennett observes that Nietzsche's writings exhibit

> *free revolutionary thought*, thought that is revolutionary in its structure and problems, but despite its fondness for the metaphors of bridge and tightrope, is tied to no revolutionary project whatever. (Bennett 295; emphasis in original)

Georges Bataille said as much in 1945:

> What is odd in Nietzsche's doctrines is that they can not be followed. Ahead of you are unfocused, at times dazzling radiances. Though the way to them remains untraceable.
>
> Nietzsche the prophet of new paths? But *superman* and *eternal return* are empty as motives of excitement or action. (Bataille 87)

Bataille is not criticizing Nietzsche but spotting in his writings—in the pressure that Nietzsche puts on his own writing—something about prophecy, that it speaks of the future in a present-day language the future will brush aside.

What *can* you say about the future? The words that Nietzsche casts his message in have not yet come into their meanings. "Morality will perish," but since Nietzsche thinks his readers don't know what morality is, this is an as-yet-unreadable message.

Nietzsche will agree that he is making the gestures of pointing without identifying any objects he's pointing at. Call it the Heraclitus in him: given the flux of the world the ancient Heraclitean Cratylus gave up speech and only "moved his finger" (Aristotle, *Metaphysics* IV 1010a12), presumably to point.

Cratylus found fixed language inadequate to a contradictory world. Without affirming flux of such metaphysical proportions Nietzsche nevertheless foretells a world to come that will contradict the present world. How could he do *more* than point? As he says in *Ecce Homo*:

> Let us imagine an extreme case: that a book speaks of nothing but events that lie altogether beyond the possibility of any frequent or even rare experience— that it is the first language for a new series of experiences

(which means if not prediction then the advance taste of one).

> In that case, simply nothing will be heard, but there will be the acoustic illusion that where nothing is heard, nothing is there. (*Ecce Homo*, "Books" 1)

Nietzsche does not mean that specific words have disappeared from modern vocabularies—in that case he would just use the old words. Nor that the right words remain uncoined, because nothing prevents him from coining them. The same old words are at stake.

But then, what is Nietzsche doing with those same old words to create the illusion of silence? Is it his ability to create that illusion that produces the reaction many philosophers still have, "I don't know what he is but he's not a philosopher"?

Bergson on laughter.   One thing that can go unheard even when every word is audible is a joke. And the unheard joke is greeted with silence, which in turn implies that there must have been no joke (no one laughed).

Writing roughly when Nietzsche was writing *Beyond*, Henri Bergson acknowledges the threat that silence poses. "Laughter appears to stand in need of an echo" (Bergson 11).

Imagine a joke that no one laughs at for a hundred years, then becomes a knee-slapper. Would you say that it is a joke as soon as it's told, containing the jokiness today that tomorrow will recognize? People call art "ahead of its time." Can there be avant-garde humor? In that case laughter might crave an echo but does not logically demand the echo's existence.

But if laughter makes the joke, the joke of the future does not yet exist. If you say something now that no one else laughs at for a century, the future laughter will produce a joke where there had not been one. *This will have been a joke but so far is nothing.*

On the first interpretation the joke exists now ready to hear the echoing laughter even when the echo does not come. On the second interpretation the joke will only exist when the echo does bounce back. The wisecrack itself does not tell you which it is, a present being or the ground in which a future being grows.

Bergson can remind his readers of Nietzsche.   It was in the year of Nietzsche's death, 1900, that Bergson published *Laughter [Le Rire]*, but he had been thinking about the subject since a lecture he gave in 1884, "Le rire: de quoi rit-on? Pourquoi rit-on?" *Laughter* grew from that lecture enlarging its inquiry into what one laughs at and why (Sypher vii), even if the book still does not probe into who that "one" is who's laughing.

In 1886, meanwhile, Nietzsche published *Beyond*, which he had started writing the year before. Is it the two books' simultaneous gestation that brings them into occasional contact with each other? Because there are fleeting resemblances, like a potshot or two at the English. "English happiness—I mean . . . comfort and fashion"; Nietzsche leaves "comfort" and "fashion" untranslated from English (228). Bergson tweaking the same people writes that "to take some . . . low-class calling or disgraceful behavior, and describe them in terms of the utmost '*respectability*,' is generally comic." This euphemizing "is characteristically English," he says, so "the English word ['respectability'] is purposely employed" (Bergson 115; emphasis in original).

Maybe Bergson draws attention to the word he leaves in its original tongue because he is, more than Nietzsche, the type who explains every joke, preferably with a word like "purposely" that announces: I hereby make a joke. (Who would write a book called *Laughter* if *not* an explainer?)

There might be another echo when Bergson looks at a comic situation that "has fascinated the imagination of certain philosophers. To cover a good deal of ground only to come back unwittingly to the starting-point, is to make a great effort for a result that is nil" (Bergson 80). He is describing the elaborate journey that gives the impression of barreling straight ahead even as it spins in a circle, in other words the Eternal Return. Not describing it in the same spirit of course. Maybe Nietzsche can stare years into the future and find metaphysical comfort in time's revolutions; Bergson keeping himself rooted here and now finds the prospect funny.

But this is not about finding agreement between the two of them, or "influence." In Bergson's published oeuvre the name of Nietzsche appears twice, glancingly (Lawlor xi, and see 128n7): that is not the place to look for a connection. The relevant connection between *Laughter* and *Beyond* is that Bergson dedicates himself to telling how a joke works and Nietzsche dedicates himself to telling jokes, and *Bergson sounds as if he's describing the jokes that Nietzsche tells.*

At the same time there are aspects of the Nietzschean witticism that Bergson misses. He seems *to rule out the possibility of future laughter*, and the omission sets him decisively apart from Nietzsche, who cares less about being funny than about the circumstances under which he will have been funny.

Nietzsche's buffoonery is routinely acknowledged, less often examined. Nietzsche goes on and on about laughter; calls himself hilarious. Commentators at least acknowledge his intention.

Some do more, making room for horseplay in their interpretations. See Keith Ansell Pearson weaving references to Nietzsche-the-jokester into his story of Nietzsche's politics (Ansell Pearson 1994, 102, 144), or Laurence Lampert's commentary on *Beyond*, which calls it a comedy (Lampert 2001, 64, 263–264).

Lampert has an ear for Nietzsche's leaps into levity even when they fall flat, and he does not shirk the spadework. His article "Nietzsche's Best Jokes" catalogues the saws and sallies that Lampert finds in the Nietzsche corpus, including quite a few from *Beyond* (37, 78, 101, 104, 121, 157, 168, 172: Lampert 1999; cf. Lampert 2001, 138).

A lot of Lampert's examples fall *very* flat. You might not see them as even would-be funny. "Whoever despises himself still respects himself as one who despises" (*Beyond* 78)—true enough, but no joke. "The thought of suicide is a powerful comfort: it helps one through many a dreadful night" (*Beyond* 157): that one might be a *mot*, but between the *mot* and the jest there is a great *abîme*.

The fact is that Lampert is not after humor. He savors Nietzschean *joy*: "truth makes festive" (Lampert 1999, 75). It is comedy more than humor that he sniffs out in Nietzsche's writing; perhaps he contents himself with a *mot* because he finds comedy too important to waste itself in laugh-lines. The jokes he cites are "merely timely," Lampert says. "The true ground of comedy in Nietzsche . . . is the new understanding of the whole. The world viewed from the inside as will to power . . . is a world conducive to gaiety" (80).

When happiness becomes the honored guest in theories of comedy, funniness is sure to be sent around to the servants' entrance.

More ambitiously than the others, Kathleen Higgins writes a book about *Gay Science* whose title announces that it will pay persistent attention to Nietzsche's humor (Higgins 2000). As it happens, *Comic Relief* is a superb discussion of *Gay Science* but shies away from its humor. Higgins argues that *Gay Science*'s prelude parodies Goethe's "Joke, Trick, and Revenge" (21–31); she touches on such comic elements as the happy ending (94). She rarely points to a joking sentence or suggests that someone might be laughing.

An article of Higgins's comes much closer to an account of Nietzschean laughter when it makes the wisecracks a strategy for moving from the present into the future (Higgins 1994). Nietzsche recommends, says Higgins, that "we suddenly stand back from our previous experiences and distorting patterns and recognize their nonsense" (61). A good laugh makes that standing back possible, which is why Nietzsche considers laughter "the ultimate cathartic that can alleviate our overly poisoned systems" (61).

In connecting Nietzsche's jokes to the future of morality Higgins already supersedes a reading like Sander Gilman's, which restricts Nietzschean wit to the aim of "a recognition of the limitations of one's conceptualizing" (Gilman 1975, 60; see Higgins 2000, 71). Higgins does not keep Nietzsche attached to conceptual aims. His jokes are strategic. The right laughter will bring the future into existence if anything can.

But even if morality is nonsense, nonsense doesn't always get a laugh. Nor will laughter clean out a poisoned system simply because the system is poisoned: poison is even less funny than nonsense. Who is laughing, and why the laughter? Higgins needs to say.

Moreover, Higgins believes that laughter belongs in the present as its strategy for getting to the future, the way smallpox inoculations today promise a future without smallpox. But the future without smallpox will contain no inoculations. Is Nietzsche's laughter likewise supposed to repair the present and then disappear? Does the future laugh? On her account it would have no reason to: amazement and laughter would end.

The type of wisecrack in Beyond.   *Beyond* contains a type of wisecrack that is not an outright joke. It might be better to speak of *gags*, lines that an eccentric stand-up comic might deliver in some inconceivable future.

"One *has* to [*muβ*] repay good and ill—but why precisely to the person who has done us good or ill?" (159).

Notice the one-liner movement. In *Mr. Saturday Night* (Billy Crystal, 1992), the aging title character keeps describing that trajectory. "I led you one way and then I turned around and took you back the other way"—as you could say about a quip from Groucho Marx: "Outside of a dog, a book is a man's best friend. Inside of a dog it's too dark to read."

Nietzsche's epigram leads its reader into moral discourse. One *has* to repay good and evil: that sounds like boilerplate, no worse than what Polonius comes up with. Then the turnaround: "Why precisely to the person who has done us good or ill?"

The question runs the risk of sounding dim. What else would *having* to repay mean, if not that justice requires the reciprocation of benefits and injuries?

But "having to repay" could mean that when an animal receives any injury or benefit, it experiences a tension with the world that it needs to discharge. Call this biology. The gladdened animal responds to its contentment with a whoop; the one that just got a kick will want to bite. Repayment begins in the psychological reality of an animal's good or bad luck. Morality's relationship to that reality is the relationship of a skewed interpretation to a fact, for morality diverges from psychology with the proviso that the *right person* get repaid. You lost an eye? Then take one; no teeth; and make sure that the owner of the eye you take deserves the gouging.

To call morality a departure from psychology is to say that the moral "must" that seeks to control an act of lashing out is different from the psychological "must." *Beyond* 159 can lead you in one direction and then another because it has two meanings it plays off one another. The opening phrase can be read as containing either, so it might seem to introduce a platitude. That reassurance vanishes when the subsequent question "why precisely" reveals that Nietzsche has been using the psychological term.

Nietzsche's wisecracks-on-the-run can compress the same double movement into a phrase like "that tender composure which calls itself 'prayer'" (58). And this:

> We are—*accustomed to lying*. Or to put it more virtuously and hypocritically, in short, more pleasantly: one is much more of an artist than one knows. (192)

Here he threatens to make the oldest point in the philosophical book. Calling an artist a liar is Plato's line, and Plato wasn't joking. You lie a lot when you make art: dog bites man.

But "You are some artist, I have heard you lying" has the cadence of another demented one-liner. Nietzsche leads you one way with "lying" as if to shake his head over human mendacity. Then he cuts back the other way. No moralizing here! Lying slips between its grave moral significance and a neutral psychological meaning.

In another place the subversive effect befalls the word "miracle." How is it that criminals convert into saints? Nietzsche looks at the "saint" and the "bad man" and discovers that they share an uncanny strength of will (47). There is nothing supernatural about the conversion really, because really there's been no change.

"What?": Nietzsche's mock surprise. "The 'miracle' merely a mistake of interpretation?" (47). The divine perspective yields to one that sees only an error. The words that morality relies on appear with their nonmoral meanings tagging along like a Sancho who can't help undermining his master's pretensions.

And again: "A curiosity of my type," Nietzsche says, "remains after all the most agreeable of vices" (psychological assessment) "—sorry [turning the reader around], I meant to say [he meant no such thing but he might have, *given the plurality of available meanings*]: the love of truth has its reward in heaven and even on earth" (45).

Bergson's "the comic" describes Nietzsche. In the final letter to Burckhardt in which Nietzsche calls himself every name in the book, he takes God's name on too, and as God he finds plenty to laugh about. He says he's been telling people in the street, "son dio, ha fatto questa caricatura," I am God, I made this caricature (Middleton 348).

("Since I am condemned to entertain the next eternity with bad jokes," that letter already said, "I have a writing business here": Middleton 347.)

Bergson says that the caricaturist's art, "which has a touch of the diabolical, raises up the demon who had been overthrown by the angel" (Bergson 29). In that case Nietzsche's letter was right to claim credit for caricatures, even if you could not call his productions God's works. Instead the jokes in *Beyond* are little Black Masses conjuring up the psychological demons that angelic moralism had refused to recognize.

Beyond 45, for example, casts aside pieties about "love of truth" to reveal that agreeable vice, curiosity, that a demon had wakened in Eve before he was overthrown.

When Bergson speaks of "the angel," moralism is one of the things he has in mind too. Restrictive moralism is a type of the "rigidity . . . applied to the mobility of life" (39) that generates comedy.

And soon morality becomes Bergson's overt subject. "Any incident is comic that calls our attention to the physical in a person, when it is the moral side that is concerned" (50). Some of Nietzsche's lines call attention to the physical that way: "tender composure which calls itself 'prayer.'" What is physical is officially not there—morality has been setting the terms of every discussion—so that suddenly turning the spotlight on it produces a comic effect.

A corollary to the rule about physical and moral identifies an effect specific to language: "A comic effect is obtained whenever we pretend to take literally an expression which was used figuratively" (Bergson 106). Sometimes a witticism creates that effect by squeezing the literal and the figurative together so that you can't tell which one is meant: Groucho's "outside of a dog," Nietzsche's "one *has* to repay." The literal "has to" in Nietzsche is the psychological or literal truth of things, and the moral side, the "*muß*" understood as "ought to" or "should," is the figurative use of the word.

Taken together Bergson's generalizations home in on a fundamental comic ambiguity that contains both the moral and the physical, or the literal and the figurative. His rules practically generate those gags of *Beyond* that swing into moral language and back out (from "lying" to "artist"); or that begin in frankly naked literality ("curiosity . . . most agreeable of vices") only to slip on the coarse concealing burlap of pious metaphors ("lover of truth . . . reward in heaven").

Why should it be funny that the moral and the physical share a space? How is it that physical reality can show up in a moral description of things with the incongruity of an open fly on a fop?

Morality does not fit, that's the problem. Street wisdom advises caution (mixed with pity) around a man whose clothes are either much too loose on him or much too tight; but that is just what "modern man" looks like shoehorned into some of his moral imperatives and floundering loose in others.

The disproportionateness of morality might explain why Bergson can elide from the comic contrast between the physical and the moral to that between normalcy and deformity. A type of deformation—bad sizing of physical humanity—sometimes renders moral commands unnatural. When the virtue of thrift tightens itself beyond recognition it goes by the name of miserliness, which is when it belongs on the comic stage. On the occasions that moral rules do not fit human nature, they deform its actions comically.

Bergson trusts the social world to right itself. Moral errors will be small ones. He pictures a sane society that only has to fine-tune its moral sense. Holding basic principles fixed, the moral community can tell when a virtue has loosened into vice or tightened itself up into scruples. Laughter is the sound of having noticed the mismatch, as one laughs upon noticing physical flaws. And, as in the case of literal deformity, one laughs more easily at the mimicry of a moral failing than at actual appearances of it. "A deformity that may become comic is a deformity that a normally built person could success-fully imitate" (Bergson 26).

Nietzsche's language is more histrionic than Bergson's. "Whoever fights monsters [*Ungeheuern*] should see to it that in the process he does not be-come a monster" (146). But they both detect morality's potential for violat-ing the size and posture of a sound human nature; and they both have their eyes on the border between the group that's laughing and the excluded ob-jects of mockery, the monsters. Bergson, however, imagines a healthy society laughing at deviant members, while for Nietzsche it is the finest deviants and future deviations who laugh at a sickened society.

When Bergson first declares that "Laughter appears to stand in need of an echo" (Bergson 11), the thought is innocuous. It becomes a principle of ex-clusion when that echo turns out to be the laugh that a group shares as it mocks and humiliates whomever it has cast into outer solitariness.

It is not surprising that when Peter Kivy reviews theories of aggressive hu-mor he considers Bergson too complacent about the effects of public belit-tlement (Kivy 12). Bergson *trusts* the effects of laughter. "Laughter is, above all, a corrective," he assures his readers. "By laughter, society avenges itself for the liberties taken with it" (Bergson 176), and isn't such vengeance only fair? Bergson sees the mean teeth bared in the laughing mouth, but he closes his book with the placating thought that "nature has utilized evil with a view to good" (178), the good of improving society.

Bergsonian laughter aims at corrupted morals and corrects them. Sniping at morals gone astray, a society can keep itself flexible and sound. More or less whole and more or less healthy, the community laughs at its misfits.

When Higgins imagines a vomitive belly laugh sufficient to expel moralis-tic poisons and bring the body to a state you could call morality's future, she is just about summarizing Bergson's position. For Bergson and for the Nietzsche that her article describes, morality and nature reach crises of falseness to one another. Nature cuts a comical figure when it wears such an inapt morality: the asphyxiating crotch, the clown-floppy shoe. By mocking the incongruity, a so-ciety brings itself into a better condition, trading badly fitting morals for those that sit squarely, and don't get noticed (as if you weren't wearing anything).

But is this how Nietzsche pictures the origin and the proper functioning of laughter?

Nietzsche hears laughter from the outside, directed at the intact soci-ety. "The world now laughs [*Nun lacht die Welt*]," says the second-last line of the poem "From High Mountains" with which *Beyond Good and Evil* ends. Who is this world?

In *Beyond* laughter emanates from detached perspectives on European culture.

One example shows Nietzsche's distance from Bergson. "Why does one laugh at a Negro?" (Bergson 41). *One?*—he must mean not just *any* "one" but one who's standing on the inside. He says he learned the answer to his question "one day in the street," when an "ordinary cabby" tipped him off about the humor of African faces. Nothing runs through the middle of a civilization the way a street does, and no one belongs in the street like a cabby.

Then look at *Genealogy*'s list of the punishments known to antiquity. The delicate reader's stomach may turn. "Perhaps in those days," Nietzsche soothes,

> pain did not hurt as much as it does now; at least that is the conclusion a doctor may arrive at who has treated Negroes (taken as representatives of prehistoric man—) for severe internal inflammations that would drive even the best constituted European to distraction—in the case of Negroes they do *not* do so. (II.7)

Nietzsche separates Africans from civilization as much as Bergson does. But this time if anyone is laughing it won't be Nietzsche's fellow Europeans, distracted and doubled up with pain. The laughter over the Mediterranean comes from its southern shore, the few and misfit laughing at the normal multitude.

The laughter from *outside* is laughter from *above* because the highest perspective is merry. "Objections, digressions, gay mistrust, the delight in mockery are signs of health" (154). "We" in the detached position of an Epicurean god—a royal "we"—would have to laugh at the spectacle of modern Europe (62).

Gods are doubly elevated: they philosophize (295) and they laugh. Nietzsche proposes

> an order of rank among philosophers depending on the rank of their laughter. . . . And supposing that gods, too, philosophize . . . I should not doubt that they also know how to laugh the while in a superhuman [übermenschliche] and new way—and at the expense of all serious things. Gods enjoy mockery: it seems they cannot suppress laughter even during holy rites [heiligen Handlungen]. (294)

Holy rites.   These days, when "you no longer like to believe in God and gods" (295), holy rites take more corrupted forms than ever. They corrupt into jokes, for after all a joke is very much like a rite gone bad.

A joke has in common with a rite that both connect widely differing concepts. . . . The rite imposes order and harmony, while the joke disorganizes. . . . The message of a standard rite is that the ordained patterns of social life are inescapable. The message of a joke is that they are escapable . . . for a joke implies that anything is possible. (Douglas 369–370)

Seeing that rites now have no harmony to offer, Nietzsche can't suppress his own laughter at the sight of them.

Every philosophical system has been "the personal confession [Selbstbekenntnis] of its author" (6). Some confession, when it pretends to be nothing personal at all.

"The honeymoon [Honigmond] of German philosophy arrived" when Kant posited the existence of rational faculties (11); but what the honeymooners celebrated had never happened. "A time came when people scratched their heads. . . . One had been dreaming." Some wedding.

As befits Nietzsche's role in *Beyond* as forerunner and final prophet ("the last disciple and initiate of the god Dionysus": 295), the book's most frequently mentioned rite is baptism. It was John the Biblical Forerunner and last prophet who cried in the wilderness and is known as the Baptist. And in *Beyond* baptism first appears as a corrupted rite. Traditional philosophers fuss over "something that is finally baptized [getauft] solemnly [feierlich, ceremoniously] as 'the truth'" (2). Philosophers are called "wily spokesmen for their prejudices which they baptize [taufen] 'truths'" (5).

Elsewhere baptism serves a laudable goal: that is, Nietzsche wields the image diabolically. "[W]e gain the courage to rechristen [umzutaufen] our evil as what is best in us" (116). "Have not all gods so far been such devils who have become holy and been rebaptized [umgetaufte]?" (227). Like it or not you have taken the role of baptist on yourself and accomplished more with it than those spurious philosophers ever could.

If those mentions of baptism blaspheme its original intent, Nietzsche completely *inverts* the function of the sacrament when he appropriates it to anti-Christian ends. "A new species of philosophers is coming up: I venture to baptize [taufen] them with a name that is not free of danger":

these philosophers of the future may have a right . . . to be called *attempters*.

(The German is "Versucher," which as Kaufmann's footnote points out can also be translated "tempters" or "experimenters.")

This name itself is in the end a mere attempt

—a "Versuch," therefore also an experiment—

and, if you will, a temptation [Versuchung]. (42)

And this "baptism" of "philosophers" as "experimenters" turns up again later (210).
Calling the name "Versucher" itself an attempt and a temptation locates those philosophers in the future. It is a try because Nietzsche's naming serves as a first stab at capturing the essence of these still nonexistent types. There will be no really describing them until they're here. It is a temptation to the reader, being a seduction into future philosophizing.

And yet the philosophers do *not* belong only in the future. If the name that Nietzsche bequeaths is itself an attempt, then in bequeathing it Nietzsche too has done the work of attempting. *He has made himself an attempter by performing his baptism on the new attempters.*

"I christen thee" may as a rule be a performative utterance that makes itself true. Here, by enacting an experiment even as it calls someone else an experimenter, it makes a second performative true as well. "I christen thee" implies "I christen myself. By identifying tomorrow's attempter I become the attempter of today."

Sacramental comedy. It is telling that *Beyond's* sacramental imagery does not ridicule literal sacraments. Nietzsche has no time for petty anticlericalism that looks to jettison the supernatural touches in Christianity and keep its core morality. Instead of mocking Christian ceremonies, he mocks the ceremonies of thinking. The misfired baptism that leads to nothing but "truths"; confession that declares only metaphysical systems; a honeymoon to celebrate some consummation of philosophy that never happened: these doomed efforts at sanctifying philosophy only show how far from sanctification it has fallen.

So *Beyond* behaves not only comically but specifically like that Christian comedy, as old as *Commedia*, that carries the sacraments from their disabled or perverted forms forward to their reconstitution (Cunningham 1988, 1993, 1994). In this tradition the human world's disease is associated with malformations of the sacraments, its cure with the recuperation of the sacraments' true forms. And *Beyond* performs its own version of a recuperation on sacramental imagery.

The opening references to baptism, confession, and marriage put those rites in the hands of deluded truth-seekers, *Beyond's* clearest emblem of thinkers gone wrong. Nietzsche takes himself to be rehabilitating baptism when he performs it on his new philosophers. And the poem "From High Mountains" that closes *Beyond* builds to a finish that is both comedic and sacramental. "We celebrate . . . the feast of feasts," the closing stanza says. It is a feast that Zarathustra attended, "the guest of guests." (The complement to a guest is a *host*, and the feast that most distinctively has a Host is the Eucharist.) "The wedding is at hand of dark and light," good and evil to be joined together by the new philosopher where old philosophers had torn the two asunder.

In New Comedy the old man (senex) who blocked a wedding finds himself vanquished by the young bridegroom. Sacramental comedy depicts a senex who lurches toward his own destruction among perverted sacraments (Dracula, blood) until the New Adam supplants him. And the new philosopher of *Beyond*, once born, will defeat its philosophical senex with the help of this new baptism that makes him an attempter.

For of course Nietzsche doesn't hear gods laughing. The *high* laughter comes from *up ahead*. The world that laughs now is the world of future philosophers.

One day this will all be funny even if it isn't now; anyway it might be. Ideals of human kindness, democracy, it could all make good material. "Our" laughter will have a future (*Beyond* 223) if "we" do, if some group that Nietzsche can call "we" comes into existence by splitting moral discourse and recombining it for laughs and getting the joke.

Exceptional human beings.   Are Nietzsche's mentions of new philosophers concrete prophecies? But what Haar says about the Übermensch applies to all Nietzsche's expectations of future humans: "As the ultimate 'goal,' the Overman obviously cannot be identified with any type or level of humanity actually existing" (Haar 24). You might think you can pin Nietzsche down on *this* subject, given that the wrong type of human is present for all to see; but the right type, something "radically different" (Haar 24), will not let itself be specified by simple opposition to known humans. The new philosophers, being exceptions, will prove as hard to describe as the priests of *Genealogy* who break the rule of master morality and social superiority; so maybe it's only natural that in predicting their arrival the book enmeshes itself in questions of birth and origin as surely as "History" and *Birth* and *Genealogy* did.

Unlike those works, *Beyond* does not wonder how things went wrong. The puzzling origin is not that of degeneration or reactivity but something opposite. To speak with the angels (which in this context means speaking perversely), Nietzsche has to explain not the Fall but the Redemption.

Redemption is hard even for theologians, who can assume a dualism of supernatural forces that permits distinct origins for the way up and the way down. Nietzsche's task is to point to the possibility of *new forms of thinking about morality* with reference only to *the same forces that produced the present state of culture.*

Birth. *Beyond* opens with Nietzsche coming to interrogate the will to truth, or else (he concedes) coming to be interrogated by it (1), as if this final subversion of philosophy and resistance to European Christianity can equally be interpreted as the final outgrowth of Christianity and philosophy. So "Who of us is Oedipus here? Who the Sphinx?" The monster and the misbegotten are Nietzsche's reminders that abnormal births still happen in spite of their impossibility, and Europe's truth-fixation might give way to some barely predictable new tinkering with truth.

Oedipus represents an exceptional birth, but also one that almost didn't happen. Once Laius learned that his son would kill him he refused sexual relations with Jocasta, until according to one story she managed to seduce him. The baby son appeared and Laius ordered it exposed. If Nietzsche wants an Oedipus to come along he will have to wait for a birth that is *not only rare but also guarded against.*

Beyond 2 stays with the subject of monstrous births. Nietzsche mocks the metaphysician's question: "'How *could* anything originate out of its opposite? for example, truth out of error?'" or altruism from selfishness? Each origin is asked about by the old philosophers with the same gape, as if philosophy till now had begun in wonder at the arrival of some astonishing new baby. Knowledge and altruism must have come "'from the lap [Schoße, also womb] of being'" (2).

Nietzsche refuses to sympathize with the philosopher's bemusement. If altruism gives the appearance of having come out of selfishness, that's only because metaphysicians begin by sorting the two impulses into a false opposition. He won't have virgin births to puzzle over: it's all one generative force and one natural origin. And yet the end of *Beyond* 2 finds him waiting for

a new species [Gattung] of philosophers, such as have somehow [irgendwelchen] another and converse [umgekehrten: reversed, inverted] taste and propensity from those we have known so far.

"I see such new philosophers coming up," but he can only say that these turned-around philosophers will "somehow" stand apart from the old ones. The worry he ridiculed is worrying him too, how the favored objects appear among all these signs of disfavor—how something originates out of its opposite.

Nietzsche raises the question again when he daydreams of philosophical helpers who inquire into morality along with him. "But who would do me this service?" he asks and "who would have time to wait for such servants? They obviously grow so rarely"; these new philosophers that he sees coming up are "so improbable in any age" (45).

With the race debased the odds are against its producing better specimens. "The mediocre alone have a chance of continuing their type and propagating—they are . . . the only survivors" (262).

Darwinian evolution would predict further degeneration; but so would the Lamarckian heritability of acquired characteristics (see 264). Anyway Lamarck and Darwin agree *contra* Aristotle (see *Physics* 198b23–32) that new characteristics, however acquired, pass to the next generation. If the human species' new characteristics are as bad as Nietzsche says then so much the worse for the future.

Childbirth.   "Many generations must have labored to prepare the origin of the philosopher" (213). Nietzsche wants to talk about breeding. Still *Beyond* remains silent about the mechanics of procreation.

Consider the scandalizing sections 231–239. Nietzsche says he will talk "about men and women" (231); then he dissects the battles between the sexes barely acknowledging that the relationship between men and women has a biological outcome.

Feminists "threaten with medical [medizinischer] explicitness what woman *wants* from man" (232). "Holy Aristophanes!" Nietzsche interjects. (Feminists belong in the older comedy that did not end in a wedding.) As in *Birth's* snicker about the catharsis that might belong "among medical phenomena" (*Birth* 22), Nietzsche's "medical" here is a shy reference to orgasm. Still he makes no mention of pregnancy, let alone a medically explicit mention.

These passages speak as sarcastically as Nietzsche is able to (which is really saying something) about women's quest for emancipation (232, 237, 239) and yet with the exception of 232 they uphold women's maternal roles. Nietzsche fondly adduces Mme de Lambert's advice to her son (235), commends the strength exemplified by Napoleon's mother (239). *Beyond's* only derogatory word about childrearing appears in a different context, laying blame on father and mother alike (194).

You may want to smile knowingly at a man's dividing women into sexual partners and mothers and abusing them in one role while respecting them in another. (See Oliver for a reading of Nietzsche that begins with this distinction.) But whatever else it means to divide the gender this way, it also signals *Beyond*'s suppression of the biology of birth. Birth becomes something other than biological in, for instance, the sections that appropriate the language of pregnancy and parturition for intellectualist purposes. Nietzsche defines a genius as "one who either *begets* or *gives birth*, taking both terms in their most elevated [höchsten, highest] sense" (206)—those emphases are his, pointing with both hands at the biological language while he denies its lower biological sense.

"There are two types of genius: one which above all begets and wants to beget, and another which prefers being fertilized and giving birth" (248). But he doesn't mean it *that way*.

In such passages Nietzsche waits, fretting for a future being while denying any reproductive course to that being. "The degree and kind of a man's sexuality reach up into the ultimate pinnacle of his spirit" (75), but when Nietzsche keeps making birth a metaphor it can seem that a man's sexuality pulls itself up to the pinnacle of his spirit and stays there disdaining to come back down. If real procreation doesn't produce the new philosophers he's waiting for, where are they supposed to come from?

Disappointment in advance. The disappointment over Nietzsche's prophecies almost mirrors the one that strikes readers first primed by his histories to dig up the past and then denied a past to dig for.

In the historical works the point of temporalization had been that values arose when they didn't have to, and therefore lack the essences that philosophers look for. When Nietzsche's inquiries offer no causal mechanism for those values' arising they threaten to undo their own persuasive effect. It is almost as if Nietzsche first says that when you have seen enough history it loses its shape, then also says that history can't be seen.

The predictions in *Beyond* base themselves not on the cynicism of one who has seen too much but on the skepticism that results from knowing too little. Because thinkers *might* come to exist for whom religion carries no weight and for whom old philosophical problems dissolve away, what now feel like the boundaries of human thinking *might* turn out to be artificial fences, fences that shamble at a touch. A gulf like the one between the present and the Nietzschean past also lies ahead; a philosopher on its other side won't waste time on God and sin and the morally responsible free soul inside, so why should you?

But if Nietzsche offers no reason to believe that some such very different philosophers might arrive, the openness of his gestures toward the future suggests facile skepticism. "For all you know you might be wrong about everything."

Unphilosophical skepticism, for instance about nutritional fads, has the merit of generalizing from reversals that already happened. The Cartesian hypothesis that all experience might turn out to be a dream leaps beyond common sense, but it begins with the ordinary insight that some experiences have unexpectedly turned out to be dreams. If "I have dreamt" fails to justify "I might be dreaming" at least it makes the possibility something the skeptic can describe.

Nietzsche is promulgating a skeptical argument premised on the future existence of superior thinkers. So he likewise needs to make the case that they could come to be.

Birth in populations: rules and exceptions.   More than any proclamations about women do, *Beyond*'s references to patterns of birth in large populations come close to telling where the future's philosophers will come from. In those references Nietzsche at least talks about birth in a biologistic way. He is an evolutionist of the armchair variety but with instincts as scientific here as in *Genealogy* II.12; and he appeals to those instincts to show him a way to future humans.

For the most part patterns of birth invite a gloomy prediction. Peace and prosperity encourage mediocrity: "the opportunity and necessity for educating one's feelings to severity and hardness is lacking more and more" (201). The human animal develops best under harsh conditions. If "the plant 'man'" is to grow as tall and strong as possible, "the dangerousness of his situation must first grow to the point of enormity" (44), and that danger has disappeared.

Then too a regression to the mean helps the wrong type reproduce itself better than the right type does. "The accidental . . . manifests itself most horribly in its destructive effect on the higher man," so that "the higher the type of man that a man represents, the greater the improbability that he will turn out well" (62). The lower type faces no such challenges: "the herd instinct of obedience is inherited best" (199). And that would seem to be the end of things. Join the mediocritizing effect of comfort and peace with the stabler inheritance of common traits, and Nietzsche has every reason to lament the state of the species, no reason to hope for anything different.

That's what makes it noteworthy that he cites exceptions to his own rules of breeding; noteworthy in a way his readers will recognize. Describing religious asceticism, for instance, Nietzsche cautions against the assumption that univocal processes determine religion's effect:

The final doubt seems justified because among its most regular [regelmäßigsten] symptoms . . . we also find the most sudden [plötzlichste], most extravagant voluptuousness which then, just as suddenly, changes into a penitential spasm and denial of the world and will. (47)

If sudden exceptions turn up in religious worship, why not also exceptions to the rules that govern heredity?

Beyond sometimes suggests that exceptions come routinely. Take the commingling of races:

> In an age of disintegration that mixes races indiscriminately, human beings have in their bodies the heritage of multiple origins. . . . Such human beings of late cultures and refracted lights will on average [durchschnittlich] be weaker human beings.

But only "on average." For in this same section Nietzsche says that the bombardment by contradictory forces can also produce an occasional spectacular specimen:

> — then those magical, incomprehensible, and unfathomable ones arise, those enigmatic men predestined for victory and seduction. (200)

Magical strength and natural weakness "belong together and owe their origin to the same causes [den gleichen Ursachen]"—which makes the exception not a violation of the rule but somehow its equally true if unpredictable manifestation.

Hybrids and mongrels. Sometimes Nietzsche's talk of miscegenation and hybrids sounds literal: "the intermarriage [Blutvermischung, blood-mixing] of masters and slaves" (261). In other places he speaks figuratively. "The hybrid European"—"der europäische Mischmensch" Nietzsche says, the European mixed human—is one who can see a phenomenon in many ways (223). "The German soul is above all manifold, of diverse origins" (244; cf. 256). And

> we modern men are determined, thanks to the complicated mechanics of our "starry sky," by *different* moralities; our actions shine alternately in different colors, they are rarely univocal. (215)

In a passage like this one, Nietzsche is thinking of multiple cultural influences.

Whether the interbreeding happens among bodies or values, it makes for a population in which both higher and lower types flourish. Consider philosophical skepticism (208). Races and classes mix and make babies drawn to conflicting values, for whom "everything is unrest, disturbance, doubt, attempt." As a rule skepticism exacerbates the weakness of the average person. But a strong skepticism in the same culture, energized by "the unconquerably strong and tough virility of the great German philologists and critical historians," can turn the groundlessness of modern values into an occasion for new discoveries (209).

The interbreeding by itself does not *produce* both extremes of character but only *permits* the full expression of both. Weak and strong natures come along for their own reasons. The blending that is modernity shapes the forms they take.

Even when *Beyond* tries to suggest that hybridization as such *produces* both types of human, it reverts to finding the blended state a contributing factor rather than a cause. In his most explicit treatment of Europe's evolving hopes, Nietzsche describes the continent's democratization as the end-product of a mixing that washed away ethnic differences. The "*evolving European*" is a more adaptive type than ever, mostly for the worse; still:

> The very same [Dieselben] new conditions that will on the average [im Durchschnitt] lead to the leveling and mediocritization of man . . . are likely in the highest degree to give birth to exceptional human beings [Ausnahme-Menschen] of the most dangerous and attractive quality.

A few sentences later he writes that

> while the democratization of Europe leads to a type that is prepared for *slavery* in the subtlest sense, in single, exceptional cases [im Einzel- und Ausnahmefall] the *strong* human being will have to turn out stronger and richer than perhaps ever before—

(the strong possessing their strength in advance of the democratization that makes them "turn out" even stronger: they are single and exceptional cases and both adjectives deny that any rule governs their appearance)

> thanks to the absence of prejudice from his training, thanks to the tremendous [ungeheuren: also monstrous] manifoldness [Vielfältigkeit] of practice, art, and mask. (242)

Manifoldness, tolerance, freedom from ingrained values, all stimulate the exceptional case.

Like Plato in *Republic* 8 (557c–d) and Pericles in his funeral speech (Thucydides II.37), Nietzsche equates democratic culture with the proliferation of values and behaviors. Like Plato he considers that mixture degenerate; but even if his Europe is short on the heroes that Pericles found around every Athenian corner, still like Pericles Nietzsche sees the blend of democracy hastening the growth of any heroes that do appear.

If the varied origins of modernity make its extreme expressions possible, one has some reason to hope that special philosophers will come along. But again: Where will they come *from?* Nietzsche's argument needs another step that tells how the exceptional beings originate in the first place.

Darwin on mixed populations. Darwin too finds in mongrelization a return to the norm. He speaks of "the effects of intercrossing in eliminating variation of all kinds" (IV.3.iv). Sexual reproduction undoes the effects of variation.

Even a monstrosity, which Darwin defines as "some considerable deviation of structure" (II.1.i), will not last long. The monstrosity's preservation in nature "would be a rare event . . . if at first preserved, it would generally be lost by subsequent intercrossing with ordinary individuals" (IV.3.ii).

Exceptions to homogeneity. One passage in *Beyond* suggests a mechanism that would produce future philosophers:

> A *species* comes to be, a type becomes fixed and strong, through the long fight with essentially constant *unfavorable* conditions. Conversely, we know from the experience of breeders that species accorded superabundant nourishment and quite generally extra protection and care soon tend most strongly toward variations of the type and become rich in marvels and monstrosities [Monstrositäten] . . .

So when a culture finds itself suddenly liberated from hardship,

> variation, whether as deviation (to something higher, subtler, rarer) or as degeneration and monstrosity, suddenly appears on the scene in the greatest abundance and magnificence. (262)

Surprisingly, the same ease of life that had made human beings flabby (201) now also brings fancier experiments in living, and possibly the excellent types who take advantage of modern hybridization to achieve something unusual with themselves. Comfort breeds laziness and cowardice but also their opposites.

Darwin on variation.   Darwin introduces the "struggle for existence" as "the doctrine of Malthus applied . . . to the whole animal and vegetable kingdoms" (III.3.i). Scarcity is the motor of evolution. And yet scarcity is not what makes variations arise among organisms. Unless useful variations come into existence in a species, "natural selection can do nothing" (IV.1.iv). Natural selection makes efficient use of the variations that do arise but operates independently of whatever process creates them (IV.1.ii).

Darwin remains agnostic about where variations do come from (V.1.i) but has observed some patterns. Domestic plants and animals vary more than their cousins in the wild: they "often have a somewhat monstrous character" (I.3.i). This greater variability "may be partly connected with excess of food" (I.1.i).

Generalizing as Nietzsche does from the experience of breeders, Darwin finds that in nature "it is the most flourishing, or, as they may be called, the dominant species . . . which oftenest produce well-marked varieties" (II.4.ii), or as he also puts it "the greatest number of varieties" (II.7.ii). The security and plenty of domesticated life, and comparable well-being in the wild, incite a living thing to improvise with its young.

Nietzsche and Darwin.   Such parallels in their thinking make Nietzsche's swipes at Darwin puzzling. Surely he should find "struggle" and "the fittest" more congenial than the appeals to God that are latent in pre-Darwinian evolutionism. Darwin points out, for example, that according to Lamarck, species improve themselves so inerrantly that nothing remains at the bottom of life's ladder. Lamarck must therefore posit new single-celled creatures constantly coming into existence via spontaneous generation (Historical Sketch ii). Why should Nietzsche take that side of the debate as energetically as *Beyond*'s Lamarckian comments seem to show him doing (213, 264)?

Nor is it only in retrospect that Darwin and Nietzsche look compatible. Darwin's Russian critics, to pick one group, objected to his vision of a natural world roiling with aggression, countering it (mid-1880s) with a "theory of mutual aid" that Nietzsche would have sneered at. In 1896 the Russian morphologist A. F. Brandt even called the struggle for existence "the philosophical system of Friedrich Nietzsche" (Todes 544). Did everyone see the resemblance except Nietzsche?

On one interpretation Nietzsche opposed Darwin because he did not *read* Darwin, knew only secondhand teleologizing synopses (Cox 224; Ansell Pearson 1997, 86–87). Christoph Cox speaks of "Darwin spin doctors" (Cox 225n25). But that claim hardly goes without saying, and some readers press the contrary—Dirk Robert Johnson for one, arguing that Nietzsche did not misunderstand Darwin (Johnson 63); Alfred Kelly who says that Darwin's German popularizers "usually did a fairly accurate job" (Kelly 8).

Those who think Nietzsche was ignorant of Darwin also have to account for his accurate descriptions of him.

Beyond mentions Darwin twice. Nietzsche calls him an "anti-teleologist" (14), a thing Nietzsche likes to call himself. Why would he say that if he identified Darwin with Darwin's teleologically minded expositors?

Also in *Beyond* 14, Nietzsche connects Darwin's name with ways of thinking he considers degraded. Like positivists and other modern free thinkers, Darwinians limit their descriptions of the world to what their senses tell them, admitting only "the 'smallest possible force'" into their theories.

Later Nietzsche makes Darwin a typical Englishman rather than a positivist, but it comes to the same thing. Darwin has the "narrowness, aridity, . . . industrious diligence" (253) that one needs for reaching the discoveries that Darwin reached—pinched little discoveries, in other words, that rarely dare to venture beyond observation.

So *Beyond* portrays Darwin as opposed to teleology and to most other grand speculations. That is not a complete account of natural selection but it's not uninformed either. The question of Nietzsche's antipathy is not trivial.

Richard Schacht sees the Darwinism of cautious methodology as a foil to Nietzsche's will to power. Adaptation to the environment means the simplification of organisms (*Will* 685); will to power calls for them to outgrow their environments in the direction of greater complexity (Schacht 1983, 245; see also *Will* 647, 681). And whatever will to power is, presumably it exceeds that smallest possible force that Darwinians permit in their theories.

If Darwin *qua* antiteleologist and Englishman belongs among the workhorses of thought who lack both nerve and imagination, his theory must specifically fail in rejecting anything that looks like the theoretical posit of the future's nervy and imaginative philosophers (22, 211; also 44).

But why should will to power matter so decisively to Nietzsche's assessment of evolutionary theories?

Darwin against Lamarck. When Nietzsche rejects the Darwinian inclination toward a smallest possible force, he returns to the nub of Darwin's disagreement with evolutionists before him.

Origin rejects Lamarck for holding to faith in inevitable progress. Less respectfully it dismisses the anonymous *Vestiges of Creation* for basing evolution on supernatural "impulses" (Historical Sketch ii, xi). Darwin's theory distinguishes itself in its own eyes as the one that calls for no inner forces and no drive toward development.

The heritability of acquired characteristics plays a part in the change from Lamarckian to Darwinian theory but an indirect part. Historians routinely point out that Lamarck considered the acquisition of new traits a minor part of his theory, and that Darwin never denied the possibility of that mechanism. Darwin names "the use and disuse of parts" as one factor governing variation (V.2.i, XV.xiv). Evolution has been "aided in an important manner by the inherited effects of the use and disuse of parts" (XV.xxxvii). The giraffe stretches up for leaves and bequeaths a longer neck to its children; the mole burrows and in time it has blind descendants.

It is important to tread carefully here, where there is less agreement than meets the eye. *Darwin refers frequently to both use and disuse but rarely gives giraffe examples.* He cites case after case of degeneration: blind cave animals, the withered unavailing wings on flightless birds. At times accordingly he speaks of this source of variation with only the word "disuse" (XV.xxxvi).

One acrobatic sentence even begins with the question of how "to judge of the effects of long-continued use or disuse" and concludes observing that "many animals possess structures which can be best explained by the effects of disuse" (V.2.i), "use" having dropped away before the sentence could finish.

Disuse by itself is not much. It might account for vestigial organs; it will never explain how eyes or long necks formed. Really it handles only the evolution that everyone's always acknowledged: even ancient theories had species' degrading into lesser versions of themselves (Plato, *Timaeus* 91d–92c).

Why should Darwin avoid the effects of *use* but not disuse? There is a sense of effort in the acquisition of traits, as there is a feeling of laziness about needless organs' shriveling to appendices. To picture the elephant's snubber-nosed ancestor reaching down for water till its trunk stretched out is to posit a "trying" among organisms that fits well with the inner force that pre-Darwinians spoke of and not at all with natural selection.

The appeal to an organism's effort in turn implies a prediction that Darwin could not even pretend to countenance: that *significant changes can come in a single generation.*

Certainly the anonymous author of *Vestiges of Creation* (its tenth edition appeared in 1853) linked evolutionary impulses to species' *rapid* development. And Darwin believes rapid development to be a central claim for the theories he rejects. *Vestiges*' author "apparently believes," he writes, "that organisation progresses by sudden leaps" (Historical Sketch xi). The pre-Darwinians conclude that something besides adaptation has to have driven species onward if their toes very quickly fused into hooves.

Darwin grants a crucial premise: *natural selection makes for much slower evolution* (XI.1.iv). Creeping change *is* the change he's talking about. Natural selection, denied the intervention of inner forces, "acts slowly by accumulating slight, successive, favourable variations," which means "it can produce no great or sudden modifications" (XV.xxii).

Origin's penultimate paragraph takes enough of "a prophetic glance into futurity . . . to foretell that it will be the common and widely spread species . . . which will ultimately prevail"—again, because evolution makes no sudden moves; minor genera don't leapfrog ahead of the dominant species. "We may feel certain" on the same grounds

> that the ordinary succession by generation has never once been broken, and that no cataclysm has desolated the whole world. Hence

(Darwin taking the next claim to follow: the future will resemble the past)

> we may look with some confidence to a secure future of great length . . . all corporeal and mental endowments will tend to progress towards perfection. (XV.iv)

All endowments progressing toward perfection; a secure long future as everyone's wish and every animal's birthright; no break between generations—there couldn't be a less Nietzschean view than evolution by incremental steps.

Nietzsche on the evolutionary leap.   Darwin cares enough about the appearance of leaps in evolution's history to devote an industrious chapter to "the imperfection of the geological record" (X). One way or another that chapter has to explain away the fossil record's jumpy story as a misleading representation of the incremental process. For otherwise evolution does proceed quickly, one big step after another, and natural selection yields to talk of impulses and guided evolution and an organism that takes charge of its own progress.

Suppose that what stuck in Nietzsche's craw was not the organism's undignified subordination to its environment but the snail's pace of natural selection. "Who would have time to wait for such servants" as the new philosophers? Nietzsche asked (45), and got no satisfaction from Darwin.

Just as Thales took the deep past of myth and made it follow the same natural principles as the present, Darwin looks with confidence to a long future that leads out from the present in an unbroken string of generations.

Isn't that better than nothing, to foresee the human species' steady progress toward new philosophers? But a long way short of their sudden arrival. So when Ansell Pearson says that Nietzsche's anti-Darwinianism serves the cultivation of "higher types" (Ansell Pearson 1997, 100–101), he could take the point further. Higher types are wanted *right now*.

Will to power might propel an individual straight into its remarkable future state, not only for its descendants' sake but even for its own. The philosopher for example can give birth to the philosopher of the future.

Philosophy of the future.   The syntactical ambiguity works in German as in English: "philosopher of the future" can mean a thinker of today who sees the times ahead but also a thinker who will have come to be tomorrow.

As a book *Beyond* enacts that ambiguity. It alternates between standing in the present looking ahead to a future philosophy to be practiced by some new breed of men, and practicing that philosophy itself, in other words standing with one foot in the future. Nietzsche wants human evolution to go further than Bergson could envision but faster than Darwin would allow. And wanting such a great change but also wanting it now leaves him in a bind.

Beyond will have been a joke on morality when the future finally laughs; other times you think it's a joke already that lies in wait for echoing laughter.

Nietzsche could not write a not-yet-existent philosophy. It couldn't be future philosophy if someone today were capable of producing it. Indeed, given the revaluation of values that Nietzsche predicts, an entirely future philosophy could not even be intelligible in the present. An account of that philosophy would sound as if Nietzsche weren't saying anything at all.

At the same time it would not do for *Beyond* to call for future philosophy and never exemplify it. Describing a way of philosophizing entirely from the outside amounts to trafficking in empty possibility.

But if *Beyond* partly moves down into the promised land that it sees from its own mountaintops then Nietzsche is a self-fulfilling prophet. He calls for new philosophers already being one himself.

To paraphrase the abusive old joke about Brazil: Nietzsche is a philosopher of the future and always will be.

New philosophizing.   To the extent that *Beyond* does occupy philosophy's future and enact a new philosophical practice, it accomplishes that by refracting a fixed concept into a multiplicity. Philosophy thus far has relied on refutation and counterproof to bring error to an end. What *Beyond* calls "the prejudices of philosophers" instead collapse under the weight of complexities that simplistic philosophical concepts had suppressed.

It makes sense to call such fragmentation the work that Nietzsche thinks future philosophers will occupy themselves with.

In *Genealogy* the new method appears, e.g., when Nietzsche teases apart the meanings of the ascetic ideal. *Beyond*, treating a looser category it calls "religion," similarly details the many forms that "the passion for God" can take (50). Nietzsche scorns any analysis of religious feeling that would discover that feeling's origin in a single impulse. He lists the very different purposes to which the varieties of people put their religious beliefs (61–62).

When *Beyond* addresses the problem of free will, Nietzsche jigsaws the apparent contradiction between free and unfree wills into a wider range of phenomena. The act called willing "seems to me to be above all something complicated," he says, "something that is a unit [Einheit] only as a word—and it is precisely in this one word that the philosophical prejudice lurks" (19). *Beyond* as a new philosophy *shows the one word to be many things already.*

If new philosophers are distinguished by their freedom from prejudice (242), they will escape this prejudice too. They will not let the word "will" lull them into simplifying the will. Rather than rest when they see that word and generalize about its meaning they are the types who will get to work, playing the word's many referents off against each other. The thing "will" names is after all something "manifold [vielfach]." The new philosophers will notice that "in all willing there is a plurality [Mehrheit] of sensations" (19): one willed act by one person emerges not from a unified soul but out of an inner community.

Nietzsche has already described the "new psychologist" as one who finds plural communities in the soul (12). Simple talk of souls like talk of wills stands in need of "new versions and refinements" in the direction of greater complexity: "'soul as subjective multiplicity,' 'soul as social structure of the drives and affects'" for instance (12).

"The way is open" Nietzsche says, meaning that the way has been prepared. Having no time to wait for new philosophers he begins their work himself.

"Our laughter may yet have a future." The new philosopher's way of playing with old concepts might be what will give the future its ease of mind. For when *Beyond* imagines the weightiest words of the present striking future ears, the words have lost their gravity; they will fall lightly against those ears.

> Perhaps the day will come when the most solemn concepts which have caused the most fights and suffering, the concepts "God" and "sin," will seem no more important to us than a child's toy and a child's pain seem to an old man. (57)

For a version of "us [uns]" in that unspecified future these ritually invoked concepts will continue to exist but without their ceremoniousness. ("Feier-lichsten Begriffe" are the most *solemn* concepts but also the most *ceremonial*.) If the people of the present day are children squabbling about toys they over-value, future humans will likely get a laugh out of those same toys.

Nietzsche hears a pre-echo (if that's a word) of the same future laughter in his era's historical spirit. Today's hybrid European compulsively tries on moralities from different historical periods. This compulsion is a symptom of despair, but one day it might yield the fun of donning and doffing moralities at will. In that case the study of history could be

> where we shall still discover the realm of our *invention*, that realm in which we, too, can still be original, say, as parodists [Parodisten] of world history and God's buffoons [Hanswürste]—perhaps, even if nothing today has any future, our *laughter* may yet have a future. (223)

People put morality on but they don't know how to make it a put-on. The inhabitants of the right future will laugh at the civilization (today's) whose morality will have gone from being the only morality possible to being one among many.

First-person pronouns imply their antecedents' existence. So this "we" ex-ist already, even given that "we" will only laugh in the future.

What are the new philosophers like?   Hard to say: "it cannot be taught," Nietzsche says, "one must 'know' it, from experience" (213), even if the problem with the existing world is that it lacks experience of philoso-phers.

In such passages Nietzsche postpones the new philosopher's arrival to a later time; he speaks of the philosopher's "readiness for great responsibilities . . . the pleasure and exercise of the great justice, the art of command, the width of the will"—inspiring words, but really just the promise of a description.

Real philosophers

> *are commanders and legislators*: they say, "*thus* it *shall* be!" . . . With a creative hand they reach for the future. (211)

This doubly removes philosophers from the present: not only not yet exist-ing, they define themselves in terms of their own future. Nietzsche pins his hopes for the future on figures he then calls "forerunners [Vorausgesandten] . . . men of the future [Menschen der Zukunft]" (203), their hopes pinned still further ahead.

(He is also talking about himself. If what characterizes the new philosophers is an orientation toward the future, then by looking forward to these beings Nietzsche guarantees that they will carry on at least one activity he's doing now.)

The philosopher will have to wear other hats too, playing the "critic and skeptic and dogmatist and historian and . . . and . . . and almost everything" (211). Thus the philosopher can "pass through the whole range of human values and value feelings and . . . be *able* to see with many different eyes and consciences" (211). Trying out one perspective after another shows the philosopher what function each morality plays in a life. Pagan virtues look like splendid vices to a Christian, Christian hostility looks shifty to a Roman provincial governor, and so on.

It now appears that being an attempter or tempter must include the work of trying out perspectives. What is "still necessary" is to start with the experience of many perspectives and then "conceptualize and arrange a vast realm of subtle feelings of value and differences of value" (186). Not for nothing will future philosophers call the soul a community. Their own souls will have to contain a whole society of voices and let each one have its say. Not for nothing will a philosopher ("if today there could be philosophers")

> be compelled to find the greatness [die Größe] of man, the concept of "greatness," precisely in his range [Umfänglichkeit] and multiplicity [Vielfältigkeit], in his wholeness in manifoldness [Ganzheit im Vielen]. (212)

You may translate "die Größe" plainly as "largeness": the new philosopher will find those human types who are large enough to contain multitudes.

Devils. "My name is legion, for we are many," the man with the unclean spirit introduces himself (Mk. 5.9). Anyone baptized an experimenter would have to be many too.

Canonical baptism exorcises devils. It assumes a real opposition between good and evil and seeks to drive the evil out of a soul and leave a better, simpler person. Nietzschean baptism casts demons into the soul; good and evil live together; no wonder it makes philosophers tempters.

Nietzsche's philosopher has to possess what *Nietzsche's Perspectivism* calls a "bundle" self (Hales and Welshon 157–182), "a loosely organized confederation of functional states and dispositions" (159). Being many people, as Nietzsche is, makes for the *willingness* to speak with many voices and also the *ability* to do so. When he describes his method of perspective, engaging any number of points of view on a single "fact," he is not advocating some sympathetic or objectivist "getting outside of oneself," he is digging deeper into him*selves* to find all the perspectives he represents.

Variations in language. *The etiology of the multiple meanings that a joke calls for parallels the etiology of human characterological variation.*

Under harsh conditions—those under which a species tends toward uniformity—a language tends toward maximal intelligibility. "The greater the danger is, the greater is the need to reach agreement about what needs to be done" (268). Everyone says the same words and means the same things by them.

When people vary in character and strength their vocabulary varies too. When meanings proliferate most people will mean less by what they say. Words mean too many different things to different people.

But some of the additional meanings that attach themselves to words will be the psychological senses of moral terms. Now and then in the indulgent present "miracle" openly means miscalculation; such second meanings turn up in Nietzsche's witticisms jumbled among morality's officially sanctioned words.

The second meanings provide the punch line for a joke that the future will laugh at. And now the lucky appearance of a moral prankster has a purpose it could not have had in the hard old days. The prankster looks for odd double meanings and cracks wise about them. All the words are the same as in everyday conversation: this is why some readers will not laugh and others will swear that nothing was said.

What's new is that new philosophers are calling a thing by all the names it bears. Their gags will be the first sign that they have ungagged themselves.

The illusion of a joke's silence. The illusion begins when the audience cannot hear the joke's play on words. When a joke brings the moral close to the literal, the two make a risible odd couple only on condition that morality has begun to appear unnatural. Morality's vocabulary first has to sound like figurative language, and that is not normal; words like "honest" and "virtuous" do not ordinarily give the impression of being figures of speech.

What would it take to find honesty and the other virtues funny? You would need a perspective from which morality at large appears wanting and false. Maybe only far-future humans can take that perspective and maybe they are the only ones laughing, because only they can take today's solemn moral concepts as lightly as children's toys.

Where Bergson thinks that a joke's second meaning is easy to identify, Nietzsche suspects that the moral meaning has overridden all others for so long that the alternatives have vanished from sight. The solemnity of moral concepts consists in their seeming literal. People think "sin" is a word for something. The predominance of *unconditional morality*, in which one code among many represents itself as the only morality possible, has ensured that the misfit between morality and nature cannot be seen from within a common language.

You can only spot a double meaning when neither meaning feels like the only one possible. As long as the moral words for things are fixed and seem obvious, the joker who plays the moral meaning of a phenomenon off against its non-moral meanings will appear to be saying nothing.

Abusio. The practice of substituting or juxtaposing words with great impropriety.

Abusio is not always called a figure of speech. What distinguishes it from literal language, that it takes words away from their proper uses, is what by virtue of its excessiveness makes it *not* a trope.

"Supposing truth is a woman" from *Beyond*'s preface; "immodest fat errors" (229); "the slowly revolving swamp of sounds" (246).

The purpose is as much to end communication as to communicate freshly. So Bataille makes Nietzsche a new John the Baptist preparing for the disappearance of the *logos*. He

> knew he was a voice crying out in the wilderness. To be done with obligation and *good*, to expose the lying emptiness of morality, he destroyed the effective value of language. (Bataille xxi)

We, you, and they the free spirits. In the course of a single section *Beyond* can refer to free spirits in the first, second, and third person. Nietzsche says that "they [sie] will not be merely free spirits" (44). He turns to face his audience: "And perhaps *you* [ihr] have something of this, you that are coming [ihr Kommenden]? you *new* philosophers?" (44).

Nietzsche says "we" too, "that is the type of man we are [sind wir], we free spirits!" More elusively he speaks of the we "who are their heralds and precursors [Vorläufer, forerunners], we [wir] free spirits" (44), as if free spirits were a kind of human only foreseeable by their own kind.

Nietzsche as the philosopher of the future. Procreation and nourishment are the same problem (36). That explains all actions: for whether an act is "self-directed" or "other-directed" it flows from the will to power. But it also implies that Nietzsche's task of sustaining himself is indistinguishable from that of making a future philosopher.

For Nietzsche to count as an original philosopher, there must be more coming after him and existing because of him. At the same time Nietzsche feels the pressure to count himself among future thinkers, because philosophical thinking can't be described except by the philosophical thinker. If it is future thinking at stake the thinker must come from the future too.

The opposed imperatives threaten any coherent sense of time. And in the final autumn of his sane life Nietzsche kept promising a fissure between present and future. To Paul Deussen he wrote in September 1888 of his "task, which, *when it is understood*, will split humanity in two halves" (Middleton 311); to Franz Overbeck a month later, "I am shooting the history of mankind into two halves" (Middleton 315).

Later still, December 7, Nietzsche to August Strindberg: "I am strong enough to break the history of mankind in two" (Middleton 330).

But to break anything in two you have to grab both sides.

And again: aside from how to describe what these new philosophers will be thinking there is the problem of saying where they come from. You can't count on men and women to propagate properly. Large mixed populations in times of peace and ease will produce their occasional exceptions, but not in any way that a rule can explain. So *Nietzsche cannot guarantee the new philosophers' arrival unless by force of will he becomes one himself.*

In a way nothing will happen. "I do not wish in the least that anything should become different than it is" (*Ecce Homo*, "Clever" 9). If what inhibits the free spirit is civilization's relentless herding and penning—community, communion, communication—then the counterforce of idiosyncrasy does not dream up coherent new worlds but wakes up to the incoherencies in the same old one.

Imagine that the future's communiqué to the present inhered in the miscommunication born of present multiplications of meaning. Then exploiting the abuses of meaning that those multiplications make possible might produce the strange sound of nothing's being said but might also be the voice of the future speaking.

A joker in motley. Presenting himself as leading man in the comedy of the future (*Ecce Homo*), Nietzsche swears off any desire to invent moral systems. "I do not want to be a holy man, sooner even a buffoon [Hanswurst].—Perhaps I am a buffoon" ("Destiny" 1). He combines inclinations in himself, as a joker would have to:

> ... my life is simply wonderful [wundervoll]. For the task of a *revaluation of all values* more capacities may have been needed than have ever dwelt together in a single individual—

(which makes it a wonder that he ever came into existence)

> above all, even contrary capacities. . . . An order of rank among these capacities . . . ; to mix nothing, to "reconcile" nothing; a tremendous variety

—the German says "ungeheure Vielheit": an "Ungeheuer" is a monster, literally this is a monstrous muchness—

> that is nevertheless the opposite of chaos—this was . . . the long, secret work and artistry of my instinct . . .

And Nietzsche's instinct for shaping his instinct proved to be a canny one:

> I never even suspected what was growing in me—and one day all my capacities, suddenly ripe, *leaped forth* in their ultimate perfection. ("Clever" 9)

Kaufmann's note underscores the obvious reference: Athena's birth out of her father's head. Zeus had foreseen that Metis (her name means "cunning") would bear the son that overthrew him. He tricked Metis into taking the form of a fly, and swallowed her. Metis gave birth to Athena who matured inside Zeus's skull until she leapt forth fully grown: another rare birth resisted by the father.

Nietzsche did not even have to swallow an outside source of cunning. The mix of war and wisdom is his own, not his daughter's. He swallowed his own self back to give birth to his own self who leaped forth out of his own head.

Morality dies laughing.   Is that too strong a way to put it? Then say you will know morality has died when jokes about moral evaluation become possible.

The jokes will not be about moral *evaluations*, plural, as one might smile at this or that belief. The atheist chuckles patronizing the believer's idea of a duty (imagine considering *foods* to be "wrong"!), but *that* laugh does not extend to moral evaluation as such. The coming laughter does.

As for *morality's death*, this phrase too juxtaposes words with impropriety and might be misunderstood.

Because "morality" has come to mean an unconditional demand—a demand pressing back against the force of human nature—its death means not the disappearance of all rules, more like the disappearance of the illusion that some superhuman reality stands behind those rules.

Analogously, Hume's attack on causality did not aim at outlawing *laws of nature*. Hume wanted to end the illusion of a mystic force that reached out from the cause to compel the effect.

"Death" is therefore a misnomer for morality's future. "The death of pointillism" means that after some date one could no longer (authentically, automatically) paint as a pointillist. The movement lived and then died. When *phrenology* was finished, though, there was nothing left to any life it had ever known. It is not that one can't learn phrenology after some date; rather, after that date one sees that there never had been phrenology. *"Death" means there had never been a birth.*

When a philosopher like Wittgenstein or Nietzsche inspires movements to root out philosophy, its end too is pictured as retroactively effective. Philosophy is dreaming of itself alive: when it wakes up it'll have been dead.

What passes out of human existence with "the death of morality" is the possibility that moral principles can be imagined as holding universally. The dream of morality will end.

And when a dream is harsh escaping it is a delight. The thought that you used moral terminology to classify psychological events will be as funny as the idea of diagnosing personality disorders with gropes of the skull. Error is amusing. One smiles. But looking back to a time when moral classifications felt like duty will bring the much giddier laughter that comes with liberation. Imagine if the phrenologists had also been the cops.

Dionysus. In *Beyond* even Dionysus becomes "that great ambiguous one": "Zweideutige" Nietzsche calls him, "possessed of two meanings" (295). No wonder he's also the "tempter god [Versucher-Gott] to whom I once offered . . . my first born [meine Erstlinge]" (295).

Nietzsche has learned a lot about "the philosophy of this god" and not secondhand either but "from mouth to mouth [von Mund zu Mund] . . . and I suppose I might begin at long last to offer you, my friends, a few tastes of this philosophy?" (295). Fertilized with his mouth against the god's, Nietzsche takes the place of sibling-spouse to Dionysus that Apollo had held in *Birth*: he's the prophet now giving birth out of his own mouth.

How one becomes what one is. Under conditions of proliferating varieties the new philosophers are not one more wild type but themselves the multiplication of varieties. Being already a whole community of souls and multiply named they can call a thing by all the names it bears. They will have the last laugh on morality; they will convict morality out of their own mouths.

But if that's what a new philosopher is then to see one as possible is already to live among and recognize those variations the recognition of which makes you the new philosopher. You have to be one of them to have reason to hope for their arrival; and Nietzsche wants to be able to hope for himself.

"Alas, what are you after all, my written and painted thoughts!" Nietzsche asks on the eve of the wedding (296). He has delivered his children "and some of you are ready, I fear, to become truths," which would make him the old man falling back into the corrupted old baptism. Nietzsche has given birth to something in his book but it wasn't a new philosopher.

As he could not bear to have been borne by his father or really by anyone but himself, so too he cannot tolerate the thought of a son unless secretly that son is Nietzsche.

Conclusion:
To Finish with Nietzsche

"All this trouble and care that you are taking on my account." Nietzsche's readers' disappointment leads pretty quickly to other kinds of reflections about his books. From the disappointing experience of reading him one moves to questions about how in general one *ought* to read him; then to questions about what reading is.

The inquiry can take a biographical route. When one misstep keeps tripping an author up it is natural to ask why he should keep being clumsy in this way. The first query

—Why does Nietzsche start these stories that he doesn't finish?

focuses into

—Why does this person who can write two hundred extraordinary pages then botch the most ordinary relationship that holds between two things (cause and effect)?

And the reader who asks *that* might want to psychologize an answer, in the interests of making some sense of Nietzsche that he had not made of himself.

"All this trouble and care that you are taking on my account" says Nietzsche in a thank-you note to Overbeck. If he'd lived he might have replied with the same words to his reader's psychological answers: trouble and care to square Nietzsche's account with his reader and present his writings as a coherent whole. After all it does take an investment of trouble to explain why Nietzsche writes as he does; Nietzsche might thank you for the trouble.

(Or the reader might only dream of being thanked. The interpretive fantasy often conjures up gratitude from writer to reader.)

A reader's disappointment might lead *away* from the author's person. If Nietzsche is inconsistent in his search for a lost moral innocence, does something about *him* have to be the cause of that inconsistency? Maybe every project so ambitious and amoral is doomed to fall apart. Then a different question comes up:

—Given that these books are incomplete as they stand, what do I do with them next?

The reader's obligation might be that of the philosopher who tries to answer the discipline's dangling leftover questions. Maybe you will try to be a more careful historian than Nietzsche and fill in the causal answers that he's merely sketched.

The enterprise that carries Nietzsche's books further than they take themselves is an enterprise that requires getting free of Nietzsche—not necessarily rejecting him, but learning to back away and breathe in his presence. You can get free of Nietzsche and go on agreeing with something he said, but you will not agree solely for the reason that he said it.

A final question finds its voice:

—How can I ever be done with Nietzsche?

and that question bespeaks both the effort to carry on with his philosophical enterprise and the constant temptation back to his person.

"Everything has arrived safely."   A letter that speaks for Nietzsche's sense of his own predicament as a writer should be worth a look from any reader wondering what to do next with Nietzsche. (A letter is technically a publication; sent out to be read.) "Why I haven't written," as he sometimes says; that I ought to write; that I have a writing business here: these are all reports from the front that come in Nietzsche's correspondence.

Even consider the note that speaks of "this trouble and care." He dashed it off in late March 1885, no more than a thank-you (Middleton 239). "Everything has arrived safely." Nietzsche needed certain supplies in Nice and Overbeck arranged to have them shipped.

For a minor correspondence, the Overbeck letter manages to land on a lot of Nietzsche's worries. His sister back from Paraguay. Will she keep her distance? No publisher yet for the last part of *Thus Spoke Zarathustra*—.

And one thing about this note, it keeps turning around not quite contradictorily but in a way that undermines what it just said. Nietzsche emphasizes his indebtedness to Overbeck "for all this trouble and care that you are taking on my account," then remarks that his eyes are worse, "Schiessen's medicines have not helped"—he seems to mean medicine in the package that Overbeck sent, the stuff had no effect. Thanks so much and thanks for nothing; you worked on my account but the accounts are clear.

Something similar happens with the news about *Zarathustra*. No publisher yet for the last part but Nietzsche shrugs. "*I* am satisfied with it, and even enjoy it as a new stroke of fortune." The book is not yet becoming the gift he had planned to bequeath to the world but it certainly is the gift he received.

"Stroke of fortune" will continue to be Nietzsche's line about *Zarathustra*. Years later writing *Ecce Homo* he will still be enchanted by the inspired state he had been in when the book spontaneously came to him (*Ecce Homo, Zarathustra* 3). He did not go looking for *Zarathustra* and still he found it—apparently the way an animal finds itself with child, for he gestated *Zarathustra* in an eighteen-month pregnancy, as elephants do with their young (*Ecce Homo, Zarathustra* 1).

The spontaneity is so perfect as to leave Nietzsche without a benefactor he has to thank. He wrote *Zarathustra* in wretched health, living in a noisy damp room.

> In spite of this and almost in order to prove my proposition that everything decisive comes into being "in spite of" [trotzdem], it was that winter and under these unfavorable circumstances that my *Zarathustra* came into being. (*Ecce Homo, Zarathustra* 1)

If "in spite of" means the opposite of "because of," Nietzsche's "proposition" asserts that important things happen without cause, even elephantine pregnancies. Nietzsche did not labor to deserve *Zarathustra*. The book may have been given to him but there was no giver and no one he owes. If he is the mother there's no father.

Nietzsche's luck brought him not only the ideas in *Zarathustra* but even the words he said them in. In the inspired state,

> one no longer has any notion of what is an image or a metaphor [was Bild, was Gleichnis ist]: everything offers itself as the nearest, most obvious, simplest

expression. It actually seems . . . as if the things themselves [die Dinge selber] approached and offered themselves as metaphors. (*Ecce Homo*, *Zarathustra* 3)

All coming unbidden, even the language to write in.

And now he will give the book away to humanity, though this time around the donor's identity will be clear to everyone. Except that—getting back to the letter to Overbeck now—he hasn't found a publisher who'll *take* the last part. Ah well, that is to be expected.

> If a man draws up the sum of a deep and hidden life, as I have been doing, then the result is meant for the eyes and consciences of only the most select people. Enough, *all in good time*. My desire for pupils and heirs makes me impatient now and then, and it has even, it seems, made me commit during recent years follies that were mortally dangerous. . .

The treasure trove is too big to parcel out like pennies to an urchin. Nietzsche has drawn up a stupendous sum: this is a matter of inheritance, testaments, what passes along after one's own death ("all in good time"). It is a legacy; he will have heirs.

The letter's next paragraph shifts into a chummy tone to undermine the maudlin self-regard of that talk about heirs and mortal danger.

> I have been reading, as relaxation, St. Augustine's *Confessions*, much regretting that you were not with me. . . . How I laughed! . . . What psychological falsity! (for example, when he talks about the death of his best friend, with whom he shared a *single soul*, he "resolved to go on living, so that in this way his friend would not wholly die." Such things are revoltingly dishonest). Philosophical value zero! (Middleton 239–240; emphasis in original)

Despite the joking, it is in this paragraph that Nietzsche gives away his most tenacious anxieties about writing philosophy. It is a chatty passage but it worries the question of what kinds of books there are, what their merits consist in, and which kind of book Nietzsche wants to write.

After all he wants to differentiate *Zarathustra* from the *Confessions*: to ward off the possibility that *he* wrote anything of philosophical value zero.

But what really makes the paragraph stand out is its nervous alternation between invoking intimacy and belittling it. Nietzsche says he's been regretting that Overbeck was not with him—for what purpose? Don't worry, it's nothing personal. Only so they could laugh at Augustine together. And what is the joke that Overbeck would have enjoyed? Look, here is one example: the idea that Augustine and his friend shared a "single soul."

Why does Nietzsche underline those words "single soul"? The phrase is not funny. The emphasis makes him seem to be pointing the sentiment out to his own close friend in the moment of disavowing it.

And again, what is so funny about sharing a soul with a friend who's died? Apparently Nietzsche is amused by the dishonesty of claiming to feel that one has absorbed the loved one. Does the lie reside in Augustine's proposal that one stays alive for altruistic reasons? Is the real joke that no one would stay alive altruistically? But Nietzsche is defending himself against more than cheap altruism. He is taking back the intimate image he had just put forward, of himself reading Augustine with the sense of his own friend Overbeck in his own soul. He seems to want to laugh away the idea (the idea that this could be *his* wish) of one soul's absorption into another.

The defensiveness in the paragraph about Augustine, the way it recoils from the idea of souls merging, contrasts touchingly with the paragraph before. "My desire for pupils and heirs makes me impatient." An heir will be someone who owes him, to such a degree that Nietzsche would resolve to go on living—with reassurances to himself: "all in good time"—for the heir's sake.

That side of Nietzsche's authorial anxiety will resurface in *Ecce Homo*. Who will receive the gift he's given? When *Ecce Homo* contemplates *Zarathustra*, the book is again a stroke of luck, as in the Overbeck letter, and again the reason that Nietzsche will have heirs. *Zarathustra* is the greatest present that anyone has ever given humanity (*Ecce Homo*, preface 4). The species is in Nietzsche's debt, as a people are to their ancestor.

Nietzsche even tries to bootstrap *Zarathustra* into the position of an ancestral book. "This work stands altogether apart"; "none of this has ever been dreamed of" (*Ecce Homo*, *Zarathustra* 6). It is the first of its breed and cause of all subsequent examples.

"Nothing like this has ever been written, felt, or *suffered*: thus suffers a god, a Dionysus" (*Ecce Homo*, *Zarathustra* 8)—therefore an ancestor. *Genealogy* II.19 taught that the gods in general are projections of ancestors; Dionysus in particular plays the father to all humanity in stories of the suffering Zagreus, whose torn body provides the raw material from which humans are made. Everyone is *that* god's heir and everyone ought to be his pupil.

Zarathustra is ancestral in a more direct way. "There is no wisdom, no investigation of the soul, no art of speech before Zarathustra" (*Ecce Homo*, *Zarathustra* 6), but above all no art of speech. The sentences that follow mention the "unheard-of things [unerhörten Dingen]" in *Zarathustra*, its "epigrams [Sentenz]" and its eloquence. Nietzsche concludes:

> The most powerful capacity for metaphors [Gleichnis] that has existed so far is poor and mere child's play compared with this return of language to the nature of imagery [diese Rückkehr der Sprache zur Natur der Bildlichkeit].

What makes Zarathustra's voice so much better than every other—even why you would call it a new voice—is that it's *the oldest voice of all*. Its originality makes it both new and old, as an evolutionary throwback is both the fresh appearance of its phenotypes and a reach back into antiquity.

There has never been an art of speaking before Zarathustra because he lets language return to its first nature. That first nature is a condition of pure imagery that Nietzsche has already pictured as natural things' procession up to the human speaker (3), the way the animals walked up to Adam to receive their names (Genesis 2:19).

Nietzsche's words for his relationship to his reader. The reader who agrees to meet Nietzsche on his own terms is bound to feel overwhelmed. The terms are demanding and they favor Nietzsche. If *Zarathustra* has returned to the first emergence of language, for instance, then Nietzsche's readers learn everything they know from reading him, including the language it takes to read him. To read Nietzsche is to become his pupil.

One becomes Nietzsche's heir, too. "The greatest gift" has been passed along, and *Ecce Homo* is the invoice leaving no doubt about who the debtor is and who intends to collect.

Ancestors and creditors both enjoy the right to eat their inferiors. So when Nietzsche imagines his readers as his heirs and debtors it is with the thought of consuming them. Even when he offers to redeem his reader from all debts, he has absorption in mind. It is a governing fantasy in Nietzsche's writing and a governing fantasy he has *about* his writing: he can speak for everyone. His reader is inside him as if swallowed whole: as if by a snake.

The fantasy of containing the reader moreover is the fantasy of being a cause. The cause contains the effect—or rather, what contains the effect must be its cause.

Here you have the Nietzsche reader's predicament, as invented by Nietzsche himself, but also frequently accepted and lived by his readers. The readers might be "the most select people" but that compliment still reminds you that they are being selected by someone else. The writer makes the reader. Authorial priority is causal priority.

Debt.   If Nietzsche posits debt as one form of the relation between his readers and him, they in turn are very often eager to accept his terms. But being cast in the debtor's role by Nietzsche is rough treatment, for he understands debt as a debased condition.

Genealogy II tells a morbid history of debt according to which all original power is vested in the creditor. Punishment begins with the creditor, for one thing. Insofar as primal punishment leads to the appearance of the promise-keeping animal, the creditor precedes all promises and every other component of morality. The debtor in this relation is a sorry creature.

The point has been misunderstood, mainly because Nietzsche has some respect for the debtor who pays up. The "sovereign individual," he is "autonomous and supramoral," has the right to make a promise (II.2). In Essay II's most hairy-chested passage, Nietzsche says the promise keeper "is bound to reserve a kick for the feeble wind-bags who promise without the right to do so."

The congratulatory language has encouraged readers to equate the sovereign individual of II.2 with Nietzsche's own ideal and hope for the future, so that Christa Davis Acampora rightly complains about the near-unanimity of this mistaken reading (Acampora 2004). The sovereign individual has been assimilated to a Kantian or existentialist hero ("make up your own morality and stick to it"). But Nietzsche values something that is incommensurable with the promise-keeping individual he calls "calculable [berechenbar]" (II.2). Granted you can reckon with a man like this—you can count on him—but as Lawrence Hatab says, Nietzsche "displaces" the moral ideal that the promise-keeping animal represents (Hatab 37). This is not what he would call either the happy future of humanity or its glorious past.

The fluctuant human type that Nietzsche *does* honor is quite different (Acampora 2004), someone like the wild beast of prey of II.17 who exceeds legalistic grasp and *will not be known.* And judging by the frolic that warrior makes of swooping down on innocents and mocking the very idea of a contract, he would make a bad credit risk. He is not a debtor, but if he were to become one he would be the great promise breaker instead of an industrious trusty.

The promise-keeping sovereign individual is at most the finest type of that low breed the debtor and can boast of only debtors' virtues, which are complaisant vices.

The indignity of the indebted state might be most perfectly represented in the debtor's vulnerability to "the most dreadful sacrifices . . . (sacrifices of the first-born among them), the most repulsive mutilations (castration, for example)" (*Genealogy* II.3). Those abuses amount to power over the debtor's bloodline; they are more appropriately the work of an ancestor. When *Genealogy* II speaks of such horrors again (II.19), it is to observe that tribes perform the sacrifice of the first-born to their ancestors, who demand the offering as acknowledgment that the people could not have existed without the ancestors' bequest. Thus *the ancestor is a creditor*, the perfect creditor as a matter of fact, considering that the ancestral debt is so great and no propitiation ever repays it.

"The civil-law relationship between the debtor and his creditor . . . has been interpreted" says Nietzsche in the same section "into the relationship between the present generation and its ancestors" (II.19). But if the ancestor becomes a type of creditor, it is equally true that *the creditor becomes a type of ancestor*. The creditor gets such delight from cutting off the debtor's bloodline because it is what a father would do.

The father remains the only possible ancestor when he prevents his son from becoming an ancestor in turn. In the ancestral case the logic of power is exact: this is why castration and child sacrifice are emblems of ancestral power. The creditor who can cut off the bloodline is therefore the creditor who functions as an ancestor. And what an ancestor! He can take your reproductive organs, take your wife, and then fundamentally *take credit* for everything you are.

The creditor contains the debtor, as cause also contains effect.

Genealogy II sometimes inclines toward a literal picture of the debtor's containment in the creditor. Many of the old German punishments butcher the body, such as

> breaking on the wheel . . . piercing with stakes, tearing apart . . . boiling of the criminal in oil or wine . . . flaying alive . . . cutting flesh from the chest, and also the practice of smearing the wrongdoer with honey and leaving him in the blazing sun for the flies. (*Genealogy* II.3)

The primitive creditor had a free hand with the debtor's body, could "for example, cut from it as much as seemed commensurate with the size of the debt" (II.5).

For a plebeian creditor the enjoyment can appear "as a most delicious morsel, indeed as a foretaste of higher rank" (II.5). And between Nietzsche's talk of tastes and morsels and culinary particulars about honey and wine and boiling and carving, it sounds very much as though the creditor eats the debtor, as mythical forebears eat their children.

The preface to *Genealogy* almost entertains the reverse possibility for the relationship between reader and writer, namely the possibility that the *reader* becomes the devourer; then Nietzsche dismisses the thought. P.8 closes with contempt for modern readers:

> one thing is necessary above all if one is to practice reading as an *art* . . . something that has been unlearned most thoroughly nowadays—and therefore it will be some time before my writings are "readable"—something for which one has almost to be a cow and in any case *not* a "modern man": *rumination.*

You have to be able to eat what you read. Modern readers do not eat—which is to say that the ruminative reader who devours the author is an *ancient* man, i.e., an ancestor.

The father eats the child and the creditor eats the debtor. The cause, which in a way contained the effect, could reach out to take it back in again. The only question is who will be in debt to whom: who eats and who is eaten? Any chance the reader might have teeth (be an ancestor)? No, such animals have not been spotted in these parts for centuries.

Genealogy P.8 delivers one of the Nietzschean criticisms that his readers should take with a grain of salt. He is only pretending to complain about readers who no longer know how to eat. Often enough he relishes the thought of his incomprehensibility. "Every profound thinker is more afraid of being understood than of being misunderstood" (*Beyond* 290). *Ecce Homo* denies any ambivalence: "*non legor, non legar*" (*Ecce Homo*, "Books" 1), I am not read and I will not be read (I refuse to be read, Nietzsche is saying).

Genealogy P.8 too hardly wrings its hands wondering how to help readers understand. On the contrary Nietzsche sets the bar higher. To comprehend *Zarathustra* you have to have been profoundly wounded and profoundly delighted by every word in it. To read *Genealogy* you have to read everything else Nietzsche wrote. No one will really be able to read this book.

No father will come back to eat Nietzsche. Nietzsche remains the only ancestor and his indebted readers of inadequate digestion will remain his children.

Nietzsche's person.   Nietzsche has an effect on the reader, or would like to, related to something he says about his own personality, namely that he contains other people. He is Wagner and Schopenhauer and his own dead father. He's the king and also the king's dead father.

Ecce Homo tries to retain some separateness for Nietzsche but words fail him. "I am such and such a person . . . do not mistake me for someone else" (*Ecce Homo*, Preface 1). But those words "I am such and such a person" sound more as if they proclaim his *identity* with everyone else: "ich bin der und der,"

I am he and he. I am this one, I'm the other one too. (Rimbaud with comparable syntax "Je est un autre" meant to assimilate himself to others, not set himself apart.)

Nietzsche does not write ventriloquously, and readers do not mistake his writing for someone else's or watch him disappear into personae. Rather than the simulation of other vocal modulations, what attests to Nietzsche's plurality is that unmodulated animation that makes his writing so recognizable. That way Nietzsche has of writing like a man never completely in control of himself could mean that he is more people than he can manage, as if the real Nietzsche added up to a crowd at a demonstration in which one person after another grabs the megaphone and talks fast and loud not knowing when it will be the next guy's turn.

The wonder is not that Nietzsche does so many voices but that he should be able to say everything with the one voice he has. His readers hear their own fears and lusts suddenly shout out at them. If he had his way he'd bring the reader into the same crowd. He knows you, he contains you.

Not being a god.   In his most messianic moments and trying to be better than a creditor (namely someone who expunges debt, namely a redeemer), Nietzsche in the person of Zarathustra gives voice to the same fantasy.

At first Zarathustra sounds like any other modern atheist when he denounces God as a "conjecture" (*Zarathustra* II "Upon the Blessed Isles"). The world has to make sense to a human being, he says. Human desires should be reflected in it.

Then the antitheism enters new territory. "You could not have been born either into the incomprehensible or into the irrational," Zarathustra tells his audience, and "what could one create if gods existed?" Now the divine is not just an affront to human knowledge but also a limit to what humans can create. This attack goes beyond positivistic arguments inasmuch as the creating that Zarathustra envisions is practically an assimilation of persons. First of all, the creation at stake is a reproductive enterprise of astonishing ambition.

> Could you *create* [schaffen] a god? . . . But you could well create the overman. Perhaps not you yourselves, my brothers [meine Brüder]. But into fathers [Vätern] and forefathers [Vorfahren, forerunners] of the overman you could recreate yourselves.

Then Zarathustra takes another leap. One becomes the child one bears. "To be the child who is newly born, the creator [Schaffende] must also want to be the mother who gives birth [Gebärerin] and the pangs of the birth-giver [Schmerz der Gebärerin]." Reproduction looks like an activity in which the maker and the made run together. If creation means reproduction in this sense then it is a merging or identification.

No wonder Zarathustra speaks of having passed through "a hundred souls." As a creator he is repeatedly making versions of himself. If A causes B then A becomes B—in which case, however, one might say that A causes A.

On this reading, Zarathustra's question about what a man could create if gods existed means that God also stands opposed to the power to merge with what one produces. *God sets a limit on identification.* If there are things that one cannot become, then there are things (they are the same things) that one cannot create.

It is as such a limit on identification that Zarathustra famously denies himself the conjecture of God. "If there were gods, how could I endure not to be a god? *Hence* there are no gods." That argument sounds as if it's giving voice to Zarathustra's envy of possible gods: he could not stand possessing merely human powers when someone else had more. But Zarathustra has not been enumerating the joys or powers of godhood. He has been calling God the Being that humans can't create, the incomprehensible and irrational and the Being essentially distinct from the human. That's not enough to inspire envy, and envy is not the point. Zarathustra is saying that if gods existed there would be something he could not be. Gods do not have to be happy or powerful for that argument to work. Their separateness already torments Nietzsche. How could I endure there to be *someone* I am not? If God existed there would be a figure Nietzsche could neither take in nor bring forth in childbirth.

Redemption.   If assimilation is a name for Zarathustra's fantasy-action as an ancestor, it also describes the redemption he offers.

Zarathustra (*Zarathustra* II, "On Redemption") sees the humanity of the present as specimens in need of being redeemed. "Redemption [Erlösung]" means the end of indebtedness here as it also did for Christians, but in very different form. The Gospels' lame and sick and blind sufferers end up walking and healing and seeing. Zarathustra refuses to treat the cripples who gather around him. There are much more disadvantaged humans to worry about. *These* beggars are short an eye or a leg; but

> there are human beings who lack everything, except one thing of which they have too much—human beings who are nothing but a big eye or a big mouth or a big belly or anything at all that is big. Inverse cripples I call them,

because there is only one thing they can do, whether it's eyeball other people or mouth off or belly up to the bar. "I walk among men as among the fragments of limbs of men."

The future will see these footloose parts reassembled into a complete body.

> I walk among men as among the fragments of the future. . . . And this is all my creating and striving, that I create and carry together into One what is fragment and riddle and dreadful accident;

as if the brokenness of the human will end when Zarathustra fits every part together into One big body.

And now something perplexing happens. Right after developing his metaphor of body parts Zarathustra changes the subject, suddenly equating this reconstructive redemption with an act of will: "to recreate all 'it was' into a thus I willed it." The psychological act of declaring "I willed it" is the same act as the assemblage of loose parts.

This odd equation of the two redemptions implies that one who does *not* say "I willed it" is an inverse cripple. Obsession with the past is a way of existing only incompletely. "All 'it was' is a fragment," Zarathustra says, "until the creative will says to it, 'But thus I willed it.'" *The positive spiritual act of willing to bring the past into line with present wishes is an act of gathering fragments together.*

The converse also holds. Gathering today's part-humans together only requires acknowledging them as one's own wish and desire. The fragment becomes part of a new One when there is One who calls it his own or identifies it with himself. Think of that ear-man as your own ear, and you will have given him the purpose he lacked.

Zarathustra will (will *will* to) become everyone else. He will declare himself to be and to have been everyone. No wonder he could not bear the thought of a God beyond his assimilative reach. He will redeem the ear-man by making the man Zarathustra's ear, and he'll make the big belly-man his own big belly, and in general he will discharge the indebtedness of these broken human beings by consuming them as a creditor has the right to.

"All this trouble and care that you are taking on my account" the redeemed will want to say. Everything will have arrived safely in the future when everyone arrives at Zarathustra and enters him.

Personal effects.   What do Nietzsche's readers do with *him*, then? To idolize Nietzsche is of course to elevate him to the highest causal status. The god contains the human and creates every human, the god is everyone's ancestor and teacher: the god is every kind of cause that Nietzsche wants to be, including the *causa sui*.

Although there is something acquiescent about making Nietzsche the first cause of all your thoughts, this surrender to his causal arrangement is still unstable. For the two responses to disappointment can come into conflict with each other, namely the response that homes in on the figure of the author and the other response that works free of that figure to pursue the questions that the author raises.

What happens when Nietzschean modes of argument come into conflict with Nietzschean doctrines? What if he falters in executing his own theories? How does the loyal reader *stay* loyal? For like other philosophers Nietzsche gives his readers a combination of doctrine and argumentative method. (Hume has his ever-ready complaint about the emperor's new clothes; Aristotle collects wise and popular opinions; Nietzsche thought-experiments with eras precisely opposite to the present.) Therefore, one question about Nietzsche is the question that a reader could come to about other philosophers: "How do I take this and go on with it?"

Does continuing with what a philosopher wrote mainly consist in holding to the doctrines that these methods first led to, or in carrying on with the methods even when it means overturning the doctrines? Going on with a philosophy can set up a battle between that philosophy's potential and what the philosopher actually said. When do new applications of Kantian epistemology start looking like rejections of Kant? There is no one answer. You can't always tell when the road you're on is the road to Damascus. A disciple can turn into a heretic overnight; heresies become new denominations and even new religions.

When the philosophical project is going well, interpretive worries are marginal. But when the philosophy (as wielded by the philosopher) does not succeed, personal issues come to the fore.

What Nietzsche's readers expect is a kind of explanation for morality and psychology that no one ever gave before.

In the philosophical tradition as Nietzsche interprets it, not only low and dishonorable origins threaten beliefs but most talk of origins in general. He looks for what is bound to feel repellent and unclean to philosophy, which is why he portrays himself as a snake, no doubt the kind that peddles knowledge of good and evil (*Gay Science* 8). Nietzsche describes the snake as an animal that eats earth and he gladly takes that description on himself, because he wants the dirt on human morals and the taste of the dirt that moral values grew up in. He is looking for the birth of ideals where philosophers deny that any histories of birth need recounting.

"History" does not mean optimistic Whiggishness, nor any just-so science stories like the sociobiological account of altruism that makes it out to be adaptive. When *he* asks why the world is as it is, the answer is: for no good reason. Temporalization might reveal dirty little secrets but it does not have to. Any news about the past will do as long as the past event connects accidentally to its moral effect. (Michael Levin's questions and conversation very much clarified these paragraphs.)

Nietzsche's followers are the readers who have been gripped by the power—even when it is only a promised power, power so far existing potentially—of new ways to explain morality, science, and the rest, to explain them away if possible. Having been gripped by that power his readers also face the occupational hazard of attachment to his person. Even discussions of the gaps or the impossibilities in his philosophy keep the attention on him, his self, his hidden life.

One asks: "Does *Genealogy* aim for a disengaged account of morality but then take sides against the ascetic ideal? Isn't that a contradiction?" Then interpretive machinery starts running, maybe to drill into Nietzsche's posthumous notes for a word that resolves the contradiction; or to weld together an explanation of the reasons Nietzsche has for saying every bit of what he says, including what might seem to be a failing or an oversight.

Nietzsche's very recent biographer Rüdiger Safranski acknowledges this drift of attention to Nietzsche's life and especially the last kind of attention, the Nietzsche-has-this-all-planned-out faith. Safranski takes his biography's epigraph from a letter Nietzsche wrote to Carl Fuchs (July 29, 1888):

> It is absolutely unnecessary, and not even *desirable*, for you to argue in my favor; on the contrary, a dose of curiosity, as if you were looking at an alien plant with ironic distance, would strike me as an incomparably more *intelligent* attitude toward me. (Safranski, emphases in original; see p. 298)

Opening with the credo of ironic distance the biographer pledges himself to remain a philosopher.

But if you lay claim to ironic distance on Nietzsche, can you also justify the pose with an appeal to Nietzsche's instructions? "Ironic distance" becomes the approved reading of Nietzsche by virtue of this word from the man himself. But desiring Nietzsche's approval for the method undoes the ironic distance; preserves only unintentional irony.

Where does this appeal come from, back to Nietzsche's own far-seeing mind? Why the quest to check back and square a reading with Nietzsche? Is this the debt that Nietzsche's readers think they owe him?

In another case, Daniel W. Conway argues that Nietzsche never got the heroic readers he wanted, only scholars and disciples. "He envisioned," as Conway puts it, "a vanguard of warrior-genealogists," but as it happened "his actual readers are nook-dwelling creatures of *ressentiment*" (Conway 37–38). This is why he's read so charitably. Heroic readers would have cast the old man aside; the nook-dwellers, god love them, preserve his memory. He does not lose control.

But wait, because it turns out that manly conqueror readers are serving Nietzsche too.

> Nietzsche may very well have known that he would quail before the transfigurative task he set for himself and that he must enlist others who would inflict on him the violence that he would, in the end, spare himself. (Conway 41)

Suppose a tough reader did come along who was careless of Nietzsche's feelings and intentions. That is all right too: Nietzsche may very well have known that. He had it all planned out.

To finish with Nietzsche.   A liberating work of philosophy would be one you could turn away from when it had served its purpose. And Safranski's most concrete recommendation about reading Nietzsche tries to point the way to such liberation:

> Nietzsche was *well aware* of why he did not present [his logic] in a pure and simple form, but instead . . . dropped hints and clues. . . . He *organized* his gardens of theory in such a way that anyone on the lookout for their central arguments would . . . fall flat on his face. Nietzsche hid out in his labyrinth, *hoping* to be discovered by means of long, winding paths. And why should we not lose our way on the search for him? Perhaps it would even be the best thing that could happen to us. . . . Hence he *arranged* his books in such a way that the *ideal outcome* of a reader's search for ideas would culminate in an encounter with the reader's own ideas. Discovering Nietzsche in the process was almost beside the point; the crucial question is whether one has discovered thinking per se. (Safranski 234; all emphases added)

Maybe readers *should* lose their way looking for Nietzsche. Maybe they will only find themselves thinking. And yet in spite of himself Safranski defers to Nietzsche's wishes even in his fantasy of getting free. Nietzsche was well aware, he planned the whole reading process, readers' final face-to-face with themselves is Nietzsche's ideal outcome.

232   Conclusion

The impetus toward psychoanalytic reading.   David Allison's preface to *The New Nietzsche* opens with an exhalation of relief at the end of psychological treatments of Nietzsche (Allison 1977, ix).

Thirty years after the appearance of *The New Nietzsche*, it is hard to name another collection that has done as much for Nietzsche studies. And maybe the respect the book has earned contributes to one's suspicions about psychoanalytic reading: if Freud's Nietzsche must be blotted out so that all these other Nietzsches can become visible, that is worth the price.

The persistent appeal of psychoanalysis to readers might be its effectiveness against those figures who have produced disproportionate effects, or figures to whom one is excessively attached. Doesn't psychoanalysis take a man like Nietzsche down a few pegs? And that diminishment of an author might feel as close as you could want to liberation from the author. But then too, if psychoanalytic interpretation means the examination of a work's author, it would seem to guarantee more time and energy focused on the author than ever before. This might be a rebellion, but rebellion is still a long way from liberation.

Plato, psychoanalytic reading, and the figure of the author.   Plato's dialogues contain the first clear attempt at a psychological reading of literature. They are also the first place to see the shortcomings of that attempt.

What especially makes Plato a cautionary example is that modern psychoanalysis has tended to stumble, in its efforts to speak of literature, in many of the same ways that Plato stumbles.

Republic Book 10 anticipates the psychoanalytic interpretation of literature first of all by bringing a psychological theory to bear on tragic drama. Book 4 worked out a division of the soul into rational and irrational parts; earlier, Books 2–3 condemned mimetic poetry and its effects on a community's citizens. Book 10 combines the two concerns, positing that a psychological theory should have something to say about the complex psychological phenomenon of poetry.

So far so good. Wouldn't it be worse for the psychology if it could *not* explain anything about literary writing?

It might be that Plato lacks the tools for the job. In deep ways his psychological categories have been called inadequate to capturing the elusive effects of literary mimesis (Nehamas 1982; Nussbaum 1986). But long before exploring those depths you can see an immediate failure of Platonic interpretation that again anticipates modern psychoanalysis. For besides the question of whether Plato is entitled to apply his psychological theory to the literature he wants to censor, there is the blunter question of *whether he applies the theory in the right place.*

Grant that mimesis is pathological (399e, 595b, 608a). Does the sickness inherent in a tragedy consist in the *audience's* entrancement, in the tragic *character's* psychological imbalance, or in some already existing neurosis of the *author's*? Whose soul is sick?

In some passages *Republic* 10 diagnoses the audience (605b–c, 606a–c), in others the poet (603a–b); the characters in a work are also cited as the loci of psychological disorder (605c). (See Pappas 1999.)

The issue is not whether Plato's diagnoses are individually plausible but why he makes so many of them. He applies his psychology to poetry as if nothing in the theory dictated where to apply it—applies the theory *unmethodically*, in other words.

Here is a second foreshadowing of psychoanalytic interpretation, and it is not just a version of the loose-gun accusation that anything goes and everything symbolizes every other thing. Rather *the simultaneous presence of conflicting applications of the psychological theory* foreshadows the history of psychoanalytic interpretations. For in the course of the history of psychoanalysis too, some readings of literary or artistic works treat the author as analysand (pathographic readings), others the work, still others the audience at large.

Besides the move to interpret literary works with a psychological theory and the methodological anarchy of those interpretations, there is a third anticipation of psychoanalysis having to do with pleasure—the interpreter's pleasure, and the respect that the interpretation pays to pleasure. As long as the interpreter plays the part of an analyst, psychoanalytic readings are apt to repeat a Platonic orientation toward poetry.

In the *Republic,* Socrates admits to his long-standing love for Homer (595b–c), but he says that a philosopher has to fight such feelings. He advises suppressing one's love of poetry as one resists falling in love with the wrong person (607e). The psychologist who would understand the psychology of poetry must remain uncorrupted by its delights.

Freudian analysts meanwhile steel themselves against reciprocating transference-love. Therefore the interpreter who wants to wear the analyst's cap when talking about art and literature will have to renounce the love normally experienced by an audience member.

This time it is a lay accusation that hits home hardest. Psychoanalytic interpretations *ruin the pleasure of art and literature*, people widely say, even if they don't know about countertransference. If the accusation is untheoretical it is not crude or false, and not to be despised by psychoanalysis. Freud's own "Autobiographical Study" takes the trouble to deny that analyzing a work of art spoils the enjoyment of it (Freud 1935). Today an analyst who writes about film can still gripe about those theorists who "view pleasure at the movies as a seduction away from clarity" (Greenberg 1993, 14).

True or false, the accusation of anhedonia is neither a marginal complaint nor disconnected from the problem of the analyst's place in art's audience. What is so annoying about affected disaffection? Is it only the distasteful sight of a puritan's refusal to have a good time? Or the professional pose of scientific rigor when psychoanalysis has no right to that pose? Or does the pretense of standing above love and pleasure betoken something deeper?

There is a further problem with the tradition of psychoanalytic readings. Stanley Cavell pinpoints it when he writes that

> psychoanalytic interpretations of the arts in American culture have, until quite recently, on the whole been content to permit the texts under analysis not to challenge the concepts of analysis being applied to them, and this seemed to me to do injustice both to psychoanalysis and to literature. (Cavell 1996, 91)

Too many interpretations have assumed the right to do all the heavy lifting. Put the screws to the book until it says what you want it to—as if only the interpreter, never the book or movie, knew anything about human souls. The habit of refusing to enjoy the book has appeared together with the habit of refusing to believe that the book has anything to teach; which makes sense. The willingness to be pleased takes some deference, maybe not always the same deference found in the willingness to be taught, but some acknowledgment that the art knows something.

In *Republic* 10 the one who refuses to love Homer, Socrates, is the same person who will not admit that Homer might have something to teach him (599b–600e).

For any tradition of psychologically informed reading the stance of superiority also promises that the interpreters *will not examine themselves.* Their responses and their irrationality are not at stake. No wonder they examine the author, the work, the character, even every other audience member—no wonder at the accompanying wildness of application. These interpreters will focus on anyone's soul but their own.

Plato's Ion: the problem of the author. Like other short Platonic dialogues—*Charmides, Lysis*—the *Ion* presents a scene of instruction that also looks like a scene of therapy. (When Plato's *Sophist* describes Socratic cross-examination it therefore calls that process "the greatest *katharsis*": 230c.) Ion, a rhapsode who recites Homer professionally, is attached to Homer above all other poets, and Socrates begins with probing questions to show that the attachment is irrational.

Look at *how* Ion loves Homer. He can quote every Homeric line on a subject—vigorously: the verses thrill him—while the sound of any other poet talking about the same subject puts him to sleep (532c). Homer speaks of military strategy and medical technique, cooking, all the most familiar acts of life, but not the way anyone else does. The subject may be cookery; the object of Ion's affection is always Homer.

Socrates responds with what will one day be called wild analysis. He jumps in and tells Ion how irrational he's being and makes the man defensive. You possess no skill or knowledge, Ion (532c). Some divine power is moving you (533d), as it moves poets and revelers who like you are quite deranged (534a–b; 535d).

Socrates calls Ion's madness "divine" in case the compliment helps, but only as sugar frosting on the bitter truth that Ion's love of Homer makes no sense (Pappas 1989a). Ion resists, denying that he's crazy (536d), so Socrates has to take a longer path to demonstrate that Ion lacks rational knowledge. Think, he says: Homer's no doctor, no fisherman, he's taught Ion nothing and Ion is ignorant (537a–540e). Ask any middling charioteer about race-winning strategies; who'd ask a poet?

Wouldn't Ion rather give up his claims to knowledge now and accept the crown of divine possession (542a)? In the end he admits that does sound better.

The Socratic questioning forces Ion to cede ground to reality. Still the therapy fails: Ion loves Homer as blindly in the end as he did when they started talking. Like an infantry movement that keeps the invading fleet from docking but cannot sink it, Socratic cross-examination protects itself against the person of the author but has no purchase against the reader's already existing attachment.

What is Socrates missing? A sign comes in the dialogue's concluding and oddest exchange, in which Ion and Socrates (both of them unyielding) debate whether the reading of Homer makes someone a good general (540d–542a). It is not hard to see why Ion believes it does. A general has to size people up and motivate them, and Homer fills his poems with tips about the things people say and the words they listen to. Thanks to Homer, the rhapsode knows what a man or woman would say, a master or slave, and so on (540b), and so does the general.

Socrates does not see the worth of Homer's observations. Presumably this is because they remain isolated points. Homer has an eye for human idiosyncrasy, and idiosyncrasy is what Socrates refused to respect in Ion's nontransferable affection for Homer. What Ion feels for Homer looks like madness to Socrates because he begins by finding any attention to one individual over another inexplicable. But *this neutrality anesthetizes Socrates against recognizing Homer's savvy.* If there is nothing special about the idiosyncratic other, there must be nothing in Homer's value to the generals who have to lead large groups of idiosyncratic others.

Despite the way Plato has organized the *Ion*, it does not show that because Homer is ignorant Ion must be crazy to love him. Instead it is because Socrates first sees Ion's love as madness that he can then declare Homer to be ignorant. Socrates dismisses the understanding of human beings that remains at the level of their particularity; so he can easily deny that Homer understands anything.

Socrates has won, in the sense that if you numb your tongue to the taste of sweetness you will win every debate against pastry lovers. There is no *reason* to eat an éclair. Hitler breakfasted on éclairs and other ultrasweets and then planned German troop movements, and see what happened to him. The pastry chef might be a species of nutritionist, but a very poor and even deranged species. (You can say "divinely possessed" if that sounds nicer.) Every human who can't taste sweetness will find the argument decisive, and the argument won't be worth a nickel. The person who can taste sugar will keep liking cookies whatever the argument says, as surely as the reader in thrall to an author can admit to every ignorance that Socrates brings to light without feeling any bit less attached.

Therapy in reverse. Cavell charges the psychoanalytic pose of interpretive superiority with betraying the spirit in which, for instance, Freud spoke of being anticipated by creative writers (Cavell 1996, 91). In saying such a thing he is identifying the Socratism of the psychoanalyst.

If you pretend to be a book's analyst, or you make the book a symptom so you can pretend to be its author's analyst, you are denying the possibility that the author or the book might teach you, let alone the possibility that it might treat you. Acting the analyst presupposes an asymmetry. One analyst can psychoanalyze another but the two of them do not simultaneously analyze each other.

When Cavell proposes reversing the analytic model—the book in the analyst's place, reader on the couch—the act of reading is to give up its pretensions to superiority. As Timothy Gould writes in his book on Cavell, the reversal "converts the philosopher from the position of *reading* the prior text into the position of one who is . . . *being read* by the prior text" (Gould 1998, 148; emphases in original).

Cavell sees something fundamental about reading and healing. Surely one sign of a book's effectiveness is its ability to inspire talk from its readers; and

the talk that usually comes does not sound like the cryptic interrogative fragments of psychoanalysts in legend and stereotype, but very much like the
analysand's long-delayed and finally unstoppable outflow. The challenge is to
find the best words to describe the reader's vulnerability, or the best analogy.

In clinical language: it is the analysand, the one experiencing transference, to whom interpretations and the cost of getting them wrong will matter most. Why not see a book's reader, or the spectator sitting in the audience
of a play, as working out an interpretation in ways that a psychoanalytic patient does, and from comparable motives? Perhaps you come to a book in
search of a new pleasure reminiscent of old ones. This is transference. You are
projecting. And in a turn like the analyst's recalcitrant quiet, the narrative
refuses to say what it's supposed to, the book will not lend a hand to make
the interpretation of it true. By blocking the interpretation it trips up the
transference. It does not let the transference continue to be what it had
thought it was. So you begin to see which elements of this new love were fantasies. Your interpretation falters but you see it as fantasy, and in place of the
knowing first excitement there is room for a more innocent self-examination
(Pappas 1989b).

Gould draws attention to the "silence and stillness" with which Cavell
pictures the text performing such a therapy (Gould 1998, 38–39). The occasions of silence and stillness draw the reader out. Words come where no
words had seemed possible.

It is interesting that Gould himself, who plaits together the elements of
Cavell's comments on reading with kindred passages in Emerson, should
mark one connection he will *not* pursue:

> we are unlikely to share Emerson's concern with the texts of scripture. Nor are
> we as likely as Emerson to mount an argument for the tropological nature of
> the sacraments and of the Eucharist in particular. (Gould 1998, 199)

And what is interesting about this one point of differentiation is that Gould
is presenting a model for reading according to which the text imposes a *pressure to confess*. That is: he is speaking sacramentally of reading.

Does too much attachment to the author Nietzsche persist?   Letting
the book be therapeutic provides answers to some of the complaints about
psychoanalytic interpretation.

Take the objection that psychoanalytic readings are no fun, that having
been born of deliberate unpleaseability they issue in unpleasure. Absence of
pleasure really has been the interpreter's tool, and like any heavy tool it has

left its mark on everything made with it. But the reader being analyzed is free to love the book, idolize it, identify with it, do a dozen irrational things.

The analytic fantasies "I will not be gratified" and "I'm the one in charge" both lose their chance to express themselves when the reader gives up on being the analyst.

There might be new problems in place of the old ones. If the authorial person had served as a constraint on interpretation, this reversal might be promising free associations, self-obsessed rambles. (The contributors to William Irwin's anthology *The Death and Resurrection of the Author?* take on this abstract question from all sides.) Readers will do openly and without shame what they usually deny that they're doing, which is talk about themselves. Can an interpretation collapse into narcissism and still claim to interpret?

Second: If this is interpretation, why should anybody care?—as callous types say after hearing the breakthrough moments of your therapy. Maybe someone who had the same analyst would care (or loved the same book), but only in order to compare solipsistic notes. "Is that your autobiography? Nice. Here is mine." If that is how people speak when they have been liberated, one may forgive the impious wish that they return to servitude.

There is a third reason for resisting the proposal of the therapeutic book, and it goes beyond any worry about undisciplined readers. The author's authority continues to loom. What often accompanies a therapized broadcast of the self is a valorization of the therapeutic author who made it possible. You talk about yourself while deferring to the book that got you talking. "See how Nietzsche dragged this out of me."

The author knows where you will go when you put the book down and run. Nietzsche is waiting at the end of the road for you to arrive at his deepest thoughts. "Causal lapses? You should ask what the lapses mean. He wants you to think outside the causal paradigm."

And what happens when the urge to analyze the author is too strong? It is a live problem for Nietzsche's audience. A reader might want to reverse the interpretive approach in all good faith but not be able to overlook certain observations about the author. Do you just fight the urge?

The challenge will be to accommodate two impulses that strike the reader of an author like Nietzsche: *to recognize his pathologies of thought* not letting pity or misplaced piety stay your hand, but also *to give up the pose of superiority* and disaffection: to hear the other's confession and yet to let it induce your own.

And if the other does not seem to be confessing? That might be an even better opportunity. If you have to bring out a confession that was not already there, maybe the act of articulating it will create the words for stating your own confession. And the distance between the other's silence and the confession you find in it might build a pressure in you too, to say something.

Lacan on being analyzed.   An early essay by Lacan meditates on the problem of psychoanalytic interpretation as such. The manifest subject of this essay ("Aggressivity in Psychoanalysis") is the beleaguered state of modern analysis, not any specific puzzles about how to apply the doctrine but the ground-floor question of whether it is legitimate to speak of subjective states. Psychoanalysis has come under attack for its subjective vocabulary, positing inner lives everywhere when scientific psychology rejects them.

Looking for an ally, Lacan seizes on Augustine. "Because he lived at a similar time," says Lacan, "without having to suffer from a behaviorist resistance in the sense that we ourselves do, St. Augustine foreshadowed psychoanalysis." Augustine was free to interpret, as in the scene that Lacan calls an

> exemplary image: "I have seen with my own eyes and known very well an infant in the grip of jealousy: he could not speak, and already he observed his foster-brother [at the mother's breast], pale and with an envenomed stare."
> (Lacan 20)

Augustine attributed an affective or subjective condition to someone incapable of describing that condition. So too should all psychoanalysis.

Augustine's psychoanalyzing consists in what Augustine himself would call a confessional reading. He identifies the baby's sin in order to discover his own, "the sin of my infancy" being the first stage covered by his confessions.

But the confessional function of Augustine's interpretation deepens Lacan's use of this predecessor. What Lacan identifies as pure primeval psychoanalysis already belongs to a process of self-discovery.

Being read does not always call for a reversal. The attractive implications of the passivated state that Cavell proposes might be available even to the interpreter who's playing the analyst. If Augustine licenses modern analysis, he also leaves it the directive to practice analysis as a means to self-analysis.

Augustine's confession.   Lacan's appeal to Augustine falls short of being serious, but it is not just a joke. Augustine would understand why Lacan quotes from his observation of the infant, what the observation has to do with mirrors, and why there should be so much at stake in ascribing a hidden motive to someone. He is certainly an analyst in those respects, as well as in one more crucial way: Augustine sees his confessional practice as a precondition for thinking.

In the first place Augustine understands that despite the parade of information in a confession, its purpose is not to inform. Because God already knows him, a confession to God does not consist in reporting news (X.ii, XI.i). Because human readers do not even know themselves they run the risk of finding out facts about Augustine only to remain unknown to themselves. And if they read a confession wanting to learn about Augustine it will not have served its purpose. The role of confession is quite distinct from its communicative effect.

Successful confession requires both good confessional writing and good confessional reading. Bad writing encourages bad reading, both of which draw readers away from themselves, and confession is a way in which readers come to themselves. Good writing (Scripture; Augustine's confessions) will not always save the reading. What has been written well can be read badly. But the good reading of good writing takes someone else's confession and makes it the occasion for one's own. Good reading creates the pressure to confess.

Bad writing and reading are deplorable because they estrange the soul from itself. When learning Latin Augustine had to read about the peregrinations of Aeneas, "forgetting my own." He wept for Dido "while I tolerated with dry eyes the death of my own miserable self" (I.xiii). In the grip of bad reading, Augustine did not even notice how peculiar the emotions of theatergoers are, when people sit and savor the sympathy they're feeling for characters in a play (II.1).

Doesn't the audience's sympathy exonerate theater? After all these spectators are weeping for someone outside themselves. No, there is no "someone outside." Indeed going to a play must be the nadir of reading, given that its "persons" do not even exist and yet the audience stares at them. Theatrical attendance is a looking for the sake of looking (given that there's nothing to see). From Augustine's point of view it is cupidity, the morally and pragmatically empty distraction of the self away from itself. Surely this sympathy for fictional characters is not getting the audience up on its feet and rushing to help those characters. So what kind of sympathy is it? A *feeling*?

Later in life Augustine is still perplexed by voyeurism. Why are his own readers eager "to hear from me what I am when they do not hear from you what they are?" he asks God (X.iii)—which shows that not only decadent pagan verse can be badly read but even the best-intentioned Christian apologetics. Try to point bad readers the way to their own salvation and for all you know they might stand there gawking at your index finger.

Augustine himself used to be a bad reader. Before becoming a Christian he went to hear Ambrose's famous rhetoric with the plan of ignoring *what* Ambrose said and only learning "how he spoke," how this one orator formed his sentences and not the doctrine the sentences transmitted. The main difference between good and bad reading is therefore that good reading imparts a pressure to confess. Good reading turns into self-examination. Augustine could not separate the matter of Ambrose's speeches from their art, and like it or not he began absorbing Christian doctrine (V.xiv).

Good reading, confessional reading, figures in Augustine's account of his decisive conversion. The story begins when he hears Ponticianus telling about his own life. The confessional gesture works on a prepared reader by inspiring a companion confession. Ponticianus speaks:

> but you, Lord, while he was speaking, took me from behind my own back where I had put myself so as not to attend to myself . . . and you set me facing myself and I saw how foul I was. (VIII.vii)

Because the story has stopped being about Ponticianus it can work on Augustine. Augustine's confessional method turns the act of looking at someone else into self-observation.

(Writing the *Confessions*, Augustine accordingly feels the liberty to move fluidly between other subjectivities and his own. In that passage in which Lacan scents depth psychology, Augustine divulges that he must have sinned before he could move or articulate his foul desires. The proof of his guilt? "I have witnessed even a baby being envious"—the speechless child's tense white color, its bitter look at the foster brother: I.vii. *The baby is envious, so I confess that I must have been envious too.*)

After Ponticianus finishes telling his tale, Augustine goes to sit in a garden. The story has shaken him. He overhears the voice of a child chanting "Take up and read [*tolle et lege*]" (VIII.xii). He opens Romans at random and interprets the closing sentences of chapter 13 as a message sent specially to him. Chance or the hand of God brings Augustine to words that he can read rightly.

Even before his conversion, Augustine has begun working toward a good reading of books. He found Christian doctrines in Platonic works "although it was said in other words and in many ways" (VII.ix). He doesn't regret subverting the Platonists' intentions to make them quasi-Christians. Rather than leave the Platonists in their otherness he takes them up and reads them as Christian allegorists, speaking to his concerns.

Does the willful translation of pagan philosophy into Christian language sound far removed from the peaceable listening that is more often associated with receiving confession? Augustine takes himself to be supplying the vocabulary that Platonists would use if they could. This way of directing a confession—probing for the sins one has grown too numb to mention; naming the spiritual excrescences that had appeared in consciousness unremarked-on—is if anything more characteristic of sacramental confessional practice.

Reading Genesis after he has entered Christianity, Augustine explicitly defends a method of reading like the one that confirmed his own conversion. It doesn't hurt anyone when people draw different interpretations from a book, as long as the interpretations are all truths (XII.xviii). Indeed there is no profit in fixing an author's meaning when any truth that can be taken from a book is worth finding in it. "As we do not battle over the light of the Lord God, why battle over the thoughts of our neighbor?" (XII.xxv). The most inspired authors are not the ones who fix their intentions but those whose words regardless of intention are open to being interpreted into indefinitely many good doctrines (XII.xxvi).

If, despite its surface form (the form of a secret being released), confession works best when it becomes more about the reader than the writer, then looking for a confession in Nietzsche does not have to conflict with the enterprise that Safranski imagines, of bringing yourself into his books to finish them. They will be indistinguishable projects. A good confessional reading will start out being about Nietzsche but wind up about his readers too.

You may call this being read as you read, or you may call it reading yourself in a reading of the other.

The pressure to confess.   Augustine's own example shows that the pressure to confess does not have to work hydraulically, as if one were bursting to release secret information.

In his terms: a sin may reside hidden in a soul and yet not as a secret yearning to be told, not as a stress or strain. It never occurred to the wordless boy that he should somehow let out his jealousy. He is not keeping the envy sealed up—he *can't* report it, any more than he could report a pain in his foot.

The pressure to confess can derive not only from the weight of guilt but also from the arrival of words for what had been crimes untold. Once given a name, the sin will have been there: that is what its silent present existence actually amounts to.

The confessional reader begins by finding the confession in the writing, not always an easy task. Nietzsche might confess despite himself. Or he might think he is confessing to one thing and give something else away. But the reader finds a confession. And in the process of eliciting this confession, the reader feels a new pressure to confess. Maybe you now sense the discrepancy between what the text is saying and what it cannot say; maybe this discrepancy as a model of self-blindness writ large helps you see the same difference in yourself. So now you can articulate what your own confession might look like.

Confession is a communion. The confessional reading is not a technique for battling Nietzsche's incorporation of his reader. If anything it embraces the incorporation. The reader rushes to be absorbed; for the possibility of confessional reading implies that there is no conflict between letting Nietzsche speak and speaking for yourself.

"Do you intend to speak for me?" the confessor says. "Very well then, speak," but watch out what becomes of your words.

The envious baby in *Confessions* is pretty voracious himself. He would like to be devouring that breast, for one thing; for that matter, if he were to swallow down his rival and sit in that little guy's place, he would be returned to the happiness that he's been shut out of. As his confessor Augustine can be seen as yielding to the boy's will to consume. The boy has been putting his own desires first, so Augustine puts them first. He speaks the desires. He is jealous. I am jealous. He (Augustine) makes himself (Augustine) a mouthpiece. "I will speak whatever words you give me, and where you lack the words I will lend them to you to give me." It is not Augustine's fault if "'I am jealous'" sounds so much like "I am jealous."

Nietzsche is even more of a jealous god than the boy with the envenomed stare. He claims ownership over every idea his words express and also over the words. These are his own metaphors, culled just now from nature's herd. A confessional reading ought to make sure that Nietzsche's words are not masticated by the reader in the course of being reported. The jealous fantasy is fulfilled—and also betrayed, because someone else now speaks your secret of individuality. He calls himself the great philosopher, so you as his confessor spokesman say "I am the great philosopher."

This chapter so far. This chapter has come a long way already, on what feels like a mountain path—not (as Nietzsche might have it) because the chapter is moving high above settled opinion, merely in the sense that mountain paths twist every which way to fit the terrain, and this discussion likewise has bent and detoured accommodating the trickiest of Nietzsche-terrains, the region of *conclusions.*

In all the traveling, what happened to the Nietzsche disappointment?

This chapter started with the loose impossible question of what to do with these enticing books that finally let you down. It looked into Nietzsche's letter to Overbeck, a letter that crawls with disappointment, to see what *he* thinks disappointed readers do.

First of all he seems to think that one denies disappointment, though how the denial happens is of some interest.

It is hard to find a better word than "disappointment" for Nietzsche's feeling about his books being neglected, or his sympathizing friend's distance from him; and yet the note does not confess to its disappointment. Nietzsche partly shouts the feeling down with his partisan scorekeeping: Nietzsche *something, anything*; Augustine *zero*. Mainly he drowns his disappointment in a fantasy of absorption. Nietzsche might take Overbeck's soul into his own. Nietzsche's selected readers might inherit his books, which makes him both ancestor and creditor—and in his book the creditor and ancestor both consume their dependents.

The one-sidedness of Nietzsche's fantasy promises a tough contest for his reader. He's not the easiest guy in the world to read, this aggressive way he sets the terms. Eat or be eaten; you owe me big time. Does the reader have to fight back and conquer Nietzsche in order not to owe him?

Readers do know how to get the upper hand, if it comes to that. Pointing out a writer's self-sabotaging tendencies is a maneuver of remarkable power. And yet diagnosing Nietzsche does not feel like enough. All it can bring is victory, and the disappointed reader doesn't want just to *win* (even if like the *Symposium*'s lucky lovers Nietzsche readers find it hard to say what they *do* want). Nietzsche got you asking for the causes and effects of morality as you never had before: it's hardly satisfying to respond to his disappointing non-answers with dismissal, refutation, or some other sneaky agonistic overthrow.

Nietzsche himself does not only read agonistically. The Overbeck letter conjures up an image of him on solitary evenings, Augustine's *Confessions* on his lap. It is true that as he reads Nietzsche fights back against Augustine's demands on him: Augustine insists on reciprocating confessions, and Nietzsche refuses to confess to anything—which might tell you why he does not confess to disappointment. But he is also watching his thoughts wander to his absent friend. Though Overbeck is far away, reading Augustine spirits him back into Nietzsche's heart. Augustine speaks of sharing a soul with his friend and Nietzsche admits that he wishes his own friend were there.

If reading can set off sympathetic sentiments in Nietzsche along with his aggressive ones, why can't it do the same for Nietzsche's reader? In search of some way of reading that will allow that kind of sympathy, this chapter's excursus into Platonic reading seeks an alternative to models of interpretive victory.

Plato established the legacy of the combative reading, and although psychoanalysis refrains from expelling the poets as he did, it preserves more of his antagonism toward literature than it acknowledges. Take Plato's ambition to assume poetry's cultural place (pseudo-Longinus, *On the Sublime* XIII.4). People will read philosophical dialogues instead of tragedies; but when Freud speaks of having been preceded by literary authors he is voicing a very similar ambition, what you once found in novels you will see spelled out much better in books by psychoanalysts.

Then too the Socratic refusal to become attached to literary authors finds a parallel in the analyst-interpreter's anhedonia. Given the antipathy behind Socrates' refusal, it rests on psychoanalytic readers to show that their own detachment does not grow out of defensive hostility as well.

Fortunately, Plato is not the only early psychoanalyst: the discussion of how to read psychoanalytically not only preceded psychoanalytic writing by 1,500 years but was a much wider-open conversation than moderns might think. For Augustine's confessional reading points a way out of the Platonic constraints.

It is true that Augustine sounds as hostile toward poetry as Plato. Why did I care what happened to Dido?—there's the Platonic contempt and also the familiar Platonic reason for the contempt, that poetry stirs up the emotions. Against Plato, however, Augustine diagnoses corrupt reading as essentially not the *excess* of emotion but its *lack*. In the most important sense bad readers are numb: curious to read someone else's newsy memoir, racing their pulses along with Aeneas's adventures, but blind to the sin and suffering inside themselves.

Good confessional reading as Augustine describes it attends to the other's confession as a means to finding words for one's own. That might be the reading a book calls for when it seems to force its readers to speak of the soul and its disorders, and yet they lack the nerve, or feel they lack the right, to diagnose the book from a superior perspective.

And now as if rounding the last hillside bluff that had blocked the hiker's view of home, the trail of this chapter's thought turns back toward the Nietzsche disappointment. That undirected nothing of a question about books that let you down has gradually become the challenge to pick up the letdown by both ends, as it were, Nietzsche the authorial letdown and you the letdown reader both fessing up.

What follows in the spirit of that challenge is an attempt at hearing the confession of disappointment.

The promise of a confession. Nietzsche's revelations about the past promise to undermine the present by showing what dubious bloodlines have led to it. The blundering past will be shown up as a patrimony that the present wants to reject.

Nietzsche's prophecies promise to belittle the present in another way, by imagining splendors ahead compared to which nothing has happened yet.

But to reveal the bathos of the past Nietzsche has to link that past to the present. To reveal the pathos with which the future will regard the present, he has to link this present to a glorious future. And he breaks his promises in both directions. Sometimes wrapping himself modestly in a critique of causality, often enough nakedly without it, he omits the crucial steps of his narrative.

Nietzsche cannot abandon his prophetic and historical accounts. History is his antidote to the eternity that philosophers take refuge in. His principal strategy is to take a phenomenon that philosophers assumed to be eternal and redescribe it as historical. Because the historical must have started somewhere his redescription invites the reader to listen and hear an origin.

But then Nietzsche denies that origins can be known. The possibility of the origin disappears soon after its necessity was conjured up.

What would a professional interrogator do with a narrative, touted as overdue, that faded away unfinished? Or that sounded like a straight story until you got wise to the contradictions in it? Or started out with confident steps before stumbling into silence with the equivalent of hands thrown up and "I can go no further"?

Whether interrogators belong to the police or the priesthood, they watch for failures like those in a story. Gaps and inconsistencies; tokens of incompleteness (enthymeme, aposiopesis, epanorthosis); the hysteron-proteron that U-turns a narrative; the rhetoric of intimacy—"you've guessed what happens next"—that prepares to sell you something unbelievable pretending it's as natural as dirt. One snag in the story and the questioners know they can press for a confession. "You owe us more."

Nietzsche's confession: philosophical debt. Settling up calls for some dickering between the writer intent on overwhelming his reader and the reader who is holding out.

The bargaining begins when the reader looks for a confession in Nietzsche's books but realizes that Nietzsche will never offer one of his own free will. It is debts that you confess, and from Nietzsche's point of view he has nothing to declare. The *reader* occupies the debtor's place.

Indeed the force with which Nietzsche refuses to confess is the force with which he tries to establish his reader's indebtedness to him. He will not accept the role of debtor. Indebtedness makes one known, better-known the better a debtor one is—the finest debtors are *calculable*. And when Nietzsche speaks of being unknown to himself (*Genealogy* P.1) and incomprehensible to others (P.8) he is saying that the "deep and hidden life" that underwrites his books will remain deep-hidden. The reader does not have *his* number.

But that is not the whole story of *Genealogy* II.2, regarding which Acampora and Hatab say that the sovereign individual is not Nietzsche's ideal; that his praise for the man who keeps his promises should not misguide his readers.

Hatab and Acampora are right; and yet the language does misguide readers. Is it just that people read carelessly? But Nietzsche's emphasis on the great leap forward into personal sovereignty, his damp eyes when contemplating this proud new animal, at the very least encourage the "careless" reading. Why does Nietzsche make it sound so unequivocally good to deliver on promises that you can close your eyes and hear Kant talking? It's as if something were *tempting* him to praise the economy of debt and obligation.

It might be that unlike the fantasy of the incomprehensible warrior, the language of debt and good debtors will bring readers' minds back to what they owe Nietzsche. He has single-handedly footed the bill for modernity's education about itself. Speaking of debt and obligation now will redound to his benefit. Not only is he no debtor, Nietzsche is your grand creditor and hence your ancestor and hence your cause or your ground of being.

By hailing the conscientious debtor as he does, Nietzsche also calms the jittery reader. "It won't be so bad, being indebted to me. Look at these fine debtors."

(In one respect Conway is right. Nietzsche's panic does make him call forth heirs inconsistently. Only it is more accurate to describe the process as follows. Nietzsche would have liked to be the incalculable warrior who blows through civilization destroying everything familiar and inspiring future warriors to go forth and do likewise. But he wonders if the next generation would recognize what he was doing. So he falls back on morality, he binds his readers to him by reminding them of the favors he's done them.)

Where is the great gift? (The strategy of reading Nietzsche as a Nietzschean debtor comes from Damien DuPont 2002.) Nietzsche *promises* a lot of gifts, no question. *Genealogy* alone is full of those promises, whether Nietzsche says he has a book about art on the way or he is setting a date for the end of morality. But if the reader has to be upright and agree that a gift incurs an obligation, Nietzsche has to admit that his presents never arrived. Morality has not ended; his books have not cracked history in half.

Broken promises aren't the end of the world, though. When the gift turns out to have been only the promise of a gift, disappointment marks the debtor's transformation into a creditor. Where one fantasy ends a new one might begin.

"A creditor? What did you ever do for Nietzsche that he should owe you?"

—I believed that he would explain the present age: its morality, religion, politics, art. I thought that more was coming.

"Are you sure it isn't?"

—His histories fail and so do his prophecies. This book has done its best to demonstrate the failures. And when Nietzsche fails to deliver on his promise then all the joy that the promise had brought is lost and he looks like a debtor.

Genealogy observes that the creditor's "enjoyment will be the greater the lower the creditor stands in the social order" (II.5). Likewise when the debt is intellectual: the creditor-reader is all the more pleased at exacting punishment from Nietzsche when standing below him on the rank of philosophers.

The honest reader ought to admit to the potential for delight that is contained in the model of debt and repayment, if only Nietzsche can be maneuvered into the position of a debtor. Once Nietzsche disappoints me, he owes me. As his creditor, I become the one to complete his explanation of the present. His philosophy is here with me, everything has arrived safely. All this trouble and care you are taking "on my [Nietzsche's] account" has brought the philosophy into the present—"his" philosophy if you still want to call it that, but I am the philosopher. Disappointment is not such a bad thing: see what Nietzsche says in *Will* 16. If we are "disappointed," it is at least not regarding life.

Nietzsche's confession: philosophical vanity.   A second confessional moment is occasioned by one memorable line from *Beyond*. "Vanity is an atavism [Eitelkeit is ein Atavismus]" (261).

An atavism is a genetic inheritance that gives the appearance of coming not from one's parents but from one of their ancestors. An atavism revives congenital traits without any evident means of transmission, as if your parents did not exist.

Beyond 261 as a whole is about the slavishness of vanity. A true noble will never understand the depth of a vain person's interest in what other people respect; certainly the noble won't understand the vain habit of honoring oneself only to the degree licensed by other people's opinions. And so 261 builds to its closing pronouncement that vanity is an atavism.

But what is remarkable about that concluding line is that Nietzsche's discussion does not need the point about throwbacks. He wants to analyze vanity in terms of debasement. Does he also need to insist that debasement has disappeared? Quite the contrary: if vanity belongs among slaves and slave values, then burying it in the past will lead to contradiction.

The preceding section introduced Nietzsche's distinction between master and slave moralities, and it is as clear there as it will be in *Genealogy* that master morality is the older form, what he calls "this first type of morality" (260). As Nietzsche will spell out in *Genealogy*'s first essay, slavish thinking ("the second type": 260) arrives later, opposes the already present masterful form of valuation, then lingers down to the present day.

But in 261 Nietzsche is speaking as if explaining the otherwise baffling appearance of vanity among today's people. He speaks as if the more improved human beings of the present needed to have vanity explained to them; as if everyone today were too noble to experience it firsthand. Causally speaking the claim cannot work. To understand vanity one needs to situate it among slaves. But then the steady disappearance of vanity would have to imply a steady improvement of the modern human being, along lines that the master-and-slave story would seem to rule out.

That is: Nietzsche says two things about vanity in 261, that it is incomprehensible to a noble mind, really more suited to the slave's mentality; and that it harks back to an earlier time. The first claim rings true. But it is the more implausible assertion that Nietzsche makes more noise about. He wants with all his might for this section to be about the throwback, whatever its natural subject matter might seem to be.

Why the unexpected and unwarranted language of atavism? Why this psychological pressure on that point?

Suppose you read "Vanity is an atavism" as if it called for a confession in the same way that Nietzsche's causal lapses generally do. The words of that confession would have to include "vanity" and "atavism." The confession might say that undue concern over one's own person is a matter of leapfrogging genetic inheritance. Nietzsche might be saying: my undue self-regard consists in the idea that my parents are not responsible for my being.

To use the words he does say, maybe to decode his confession: Atavism is my vanity.

Is Nietzsche a philosopher?   Sebastian Hausmann wrote of having met a solitary walker in Sils-Maria in 1883. The stranger mumbled his name, something like "Nietzsche."

> "Are you perhaps a relative of the famous philosopher Nietzsche?" He looked at me sharply for a moment then answered: "No, I'm not related to him." . . . After

a few paces the man suddenly stopped and turned toward me with a good-humored, gentle smile: "Let us not play hide-and-seek. You were quite right to think of the philosopher Nietzsche at sight of me. I am really not related to your Nietzsche, for I am the man himself, whom you chose to call a famous philosopher." When I stopped, full of surprise, and greeted him with clearly visible reverence, I had very much the feeling that this involuntary praise from so insignificant a young man touched him, let us say, not unpleasantly. From which I concluded that even great minds are not completely free of the general ingredient of human vanity. (Gilman 1987, 134)

Nietzsche's vanity is tied up with being a philosopher. (This is not to mention how tickled he is to deny that he is related to himself—almost as if because he is beyond human relations, like an atavism.) Hausmann's reverence delights his vanity; and it doesn't even require praise or a word like "famous," most philosophers will testify to the awkwardness of those moments in which they tell a stranger their profession. It is awkward because it touches them, not unpleasantly, to be seen as philosophers. Within their discipline, at least, "philosopher" is a term of praise.

According to one way that philosophy conceives itself there is no cause for embarrassment. The philosopher is no one special because philosophy is a pursuit available to all. On the other conception philosophy is a storehouse of strange ideas, things that you would never have thought of yourself, and the philosopher is a singular creature.

The first kind of philosophy has no history, does not happen in history. It is always possible and can always arise again. The second kind is nothing but its history, or cannot live without its history. And somehow both visions of philosophy are plausible. Philosophy seems to be always available, and yet—to a greater degree than any other discipline—it has a tiny number of heroes who define its nature and possibilities.

Maybe Plato wants to keep both visions open when he writes the line in the *Theaetetus* that is rendered, "Philosophy begins in wonder." For what he actually does in that passage is describe the philosophical passion of wonderment and then say, literally, "no other beginning [*archê*] of philosophy but this" (155d), which is incomprehensible in English without a copula. Which copula do you add, then? Do you say that to wonder *is* the *archê* of philosophy or do you say that it *was* the *archê*, that philosophy *begins* with wonder or *began* there?

Is the inauguration of philosophy a historical event or a metaphysical possibility always ready to be repeated?

If the *archê* in philosophy can come to everyone naturally, then why was there a specific and now celebrated event when it first happened (Thales for instance: *Metaphysics* 983b20)? Shouldn't the first philosophizing have the standing of the first handshake, a curiosity it is nice to find out about but irrelevant to the present-day phenomenon?

Conversely, the more it matters that philosophy began on some ancient occasion, the less it counts that every human being now contains the potential to embark upon philosophy. The original first philosophy creates an indebtedness not discharged by subsequent practices of philosophy but increased with every subsequent practice.

Philosophy dedicates itself to both self-conceptions. But if philosophy lives this kind of contradiction, then the vanity of considering oneself a philosopher looks like the vanity of being an atavism. For a philosopher becomes someone who exists now, carrying on with the thinking that is everyone's birthright, and also someone who had been there in the first place. A throwback is a return to a pre-existing possibility—which is to say that being a philosopher means being yet another one; it is to say that being a philosopher comes to being philosophy personified.

But then too, if philosophy essentially has a history, if philosophy began on a specific occasion, then the pleasure of being an atavism is the pleasure of leaping back to the moment of philosophy's founding. It is the pleasure of having been *the* philosopher.

For the philosopher who reads Nietzsche.   Nietzsche's atavistic fantasy hits close to home. That's how it is with confessional readings. (Augustine did not just see the young boy's envy, he saw his own envy written all over the boy's face.)

For the philosopher who reads Nietzsche, his fantasy of having founded a bloodline and then returning as its ever-present possibility expresses *an incompatible pair of guilty wishes* that the reading philosopher had been having.

Nietzsche is the philosophical forebear in the sense that Thales is every philosopher's ancestor, or in the sense that philosophy has been promissory notes to Plato. But then his vaunted causal explanations fail, and their failure is his personal failure.

Nietzsche is no one special, in the way that no philosopher is anyone special. But then causal lacunae are not crises. If Nietzsche's versions of history and prophecy run into trouble, someone else's will plug the gaps. Where Nietzsche left philosophical debts unpaid, some other philosopher—you or I—might have better luck.

That is the happy thought whose unhappy twin is saying, "Those histories and prophecies fail because they have to, nothing peculiar to Nietzsche, morality cannot be spoken of this way." This gloomy thought sees the failure of Nietzsche's theories not as an invitation to further philosophizing but as a slammed door in every philosopher's face. Nietzsche's failure as a philosopher is philosophy's failure.

For the philosopher who reads Nietzsche is no one special as much as Nietzsche is (and yet that philosopher dreams, as much as Nietzsche does, of having invented philosophy). You read Nietzsche valorizing his person's uniqueness and also taking up his claims and theories as communicable: you digest them: as if you did no more than overhear the words (like Augustine chancing on the sight of the furious jealous baby) and now you think "What shall I do with these ideas?": *take them and run*—and it appeals to your vanity to appeal to his because you reading Nietzsche are a philosopher too, disappointed in philosophy but always hopeful.

Bibliography

Acampora, Christa Davis. 2004. On sovereignty and overhumanity: Why it matters how we read Nietzsche's *Genealogy* II:2. *International Studies in Philosophy* 36 (Fall).

Acampora, Christa Davis, and Ralph Acampora, eds. 2004. *A Nietzschean bestiary: Becoming animal beyond docile and brutal.* Lanham, Md.: Rowman & Littlefield.

Ackermann, Robert John. 1990. *Nietzsche: A frenzied look.* Amherst: University of Massachusetts Press.

Allison, David, ed. 1977. *The new Nietzsche.* Cambridge, Mass.: MIT Press.

———. 1990. A diet of worms: Aposiopetic rhetoric in *Beyond good and evil. Nietzsche-Studien* 19: 43–58.

———. 1994. "Have I been understood?" In *Nietzsche, genealogy, morality: Essays on Nietzsche's "On the genealogy of morals,"* edited by Richard Schacht. Berkeley: University of California Press.

———. 2001. *Reading the new Nietzsche.* Lanham, Md.: Rowman & Littlefield.

Ansell Pearson, Keith. 1991. The significance of Michel Foucault's reading of Nietzsche: Power, the subject, and political theory. *Nietzsche-Studien* 20: 267–283.

———. 1994. *An introduction to Nietzsche as political thinker: The perfect nihilist.* Cambridge: Cambridge University Press.

———. 1997. *Viroid life: Perspectives on Nietzsche and the transhuman condition.* New York: Routledge.

Aschheim, Steven E. 1988. After the death of God: Varieties of Nietzschean religion. *Nietzsche-Studien* 17: 218–249.

Aulén, Gustaf. 1969. *Christus Victor: An historical study of the three main types of the idea of atonement.* Translated by A. G. Hebert. New York: Macmillan.

Bailey, Tom. 2002. Review of Simon May, *Nietzsche's ethics and his war on "morality." New Nietzsche Studies* 5: 161–163.

Barnes, Jonathan. 1986. Nietzsche and Diogenes Laertius. *Nietzsche-Studien* 15: 16–40.

Barrack, Charles M. 1974. Nietzsche's Dionysus and Apollo: Gods in transition. *Nietzsche-Studien* 3: 115–129.

Bataille, Georges. 1992. *On Nietzsche*. Translated by Bruce Boone. St. Paul, Minn.: Paragon House.

Behler, Ernst. 1996. Nietzsche in the twentieth century. In *The Cambridge companion to Nietzsche*, edited by Bernd Magnus and Kathleen M. Higgins. Cambridge: Cambridge University Press.

Bennet, Benjamin. 1994. Bridge: Against nothing. In *Nietzsche and the feminine*, edited by Peter J. Burgard. Charlottesville: University Press of Virginia.

Bergmann, Frithjoff. 1994. Nietzsche and analytic ethics. In *Nietzsche, genealogy, morality: Essays on Nietzsche's "On the genealogy of morals,"* edited by Richard Schacht. Berkeley: University of California Press.

Bergson, Henri. 1999. *Laughter: An essay on the meaning of the comic*. Translated by Cloudeseley Brereton and Fred Rothwell. Los Angeles: Green Integer (reprint).

Berkowitz, Peter. 1995. *Nietzsche: The ethics of an immoralist*. Cambridge, Mass.: Harvard University Press.

Bishop, Paul, ed. 2004. *Nietzsche and antiquity: His reaction and response to the classical tradition*. Rochester, N.Y.: Camden House.

Blondel, Eric. 1977. Nietzsche: Life as metaphor. Translated by Mairi Macrae. In *The new Nietzsche*, edited by David Allison. Cambridge, Mass.: MIT Press.

———. 1994. The question of genealogy. Translated by David Blacker and Annie Pritchard. In *Nietzsche, genealogy, morality: Essays on Nietzsche's "On the genealogy of morals,"* edited by Richard Schacht. Berkeley: University of California Press.

Bloom, Allan, translator, notes. 1968. *The Republic of Plato*. New York: Basic Books.

Booth, David. 1992. Nietzsche's legacy in theology's agendas. *Nietzsche-Studien* 21: 290–307.

Branham, R. Bracht. 1996. Defacing the currency: Diogenes' rhetoric and the *invention* of Cynicism. In *The Cynics: The Cynic movement in antiquity and its legacy*, edited by R. Bracht Branham and Marie-Odile Goulet-Cazé. Berkeley: University of California Press.

———. 2004. Nietzsche's Cynicism: Uppercase or lowercase? In *Nietzsche and antiquity: His reaction and response to the classical tradition*, edited by Paul Bishop. Rochester, N.Y.: Camden House.

Branham, R. Bracht, and Marie-Odile Goulet-Cazé, eds. 1996. *The Cynics: The Cynic movement in antiquity and its legacy*. Berkeley: University of California Press.

Brunius-Nilsson, Elisabeth. 1955. *DAIMONIE: An Inquiry into a mode of apostrophe in old Greek literature*. Dissertation, University of Uppsala.

Burgard, Peter J., ed. 1994. *Nietzsche and the feminine*. Charlottesville: University Press of Virginia.

Burkert, Walter. 1985. *Greek religion*. Translated by John Raffan. Cambridge, Mass.: Harvard University Press.

———. 1992. *The orientalizing revolution: Near Eastern influence on Greek culture in the early archaic age.* Translated by Margaret E. Pinder and Walter Burkert. Cambridge, Mass.: Harvard University Press.

Burnyeat, Myles F. 1992. Socratic midwifery, Platonic inspiration. In *Essays on the philosophy of Socrates*, edited by Hugh H. Benson. Oxford: Oxford University Press.

Butler, Judith. 2000. Circuits of bad conscience: Nietzsche and Freud. In *Nietzsche's French legacy: A genealogy of poststructuralism*, edited by Alan D. Schrift. New York: Routledge.

Cavell, Stanley. 1979. *The claim of reason: Wittgenstein, skepticism, morality, and tragedy.* New York: Oxford University Press.

———. 1988. Psychoanalysis and cinema: The melodrama of the unknown woman. In *The Trial(s) of psychoanalysis*, edited by Françoise Meltzer. Chicago: University of Chicago Press.

———. 1996. *Contesting tears: The Hollywood melodrama of the unknown woman.* Chicago: University of Chicago Press.

———. 2004. *Cities of words.* Cambridge, Mass.: Harvard University Press.

Clark, Maudemarie. 1994. Nietzsche's immoralism and the concept of morality. In *Nietzsche, genealogy, morality: Essays on Nietzsche's "On the genealogy of morals,"* edited by Richard Schacht. Berkeley: University of California Press.

Conway, Daniel W. 2000. Odysseus bound? In *Why Nietzsche still?*, edited by Alan D. Schrift. Berkeley: University of California Press.

Cox, Christoph. 1999. *Nietzsche: Naturalism and interpretation.* Berkeley: University of California Press.

Cunningham, John. 1988. Comedic and liturgical restoration in *Everyman. Comparative Drama* 22: 162–173.

———. 1993. The figure of the wedding feast in *Great expectations. Dickens Quarterly* 10: 87–91.

———. 1994. Comedic structure, Christian allusion, and the metaphor of baptism in *Great expectations. South Atlantic Review* 59: 35–51.

Derrida, Jacques. 1979. *Spurs: Nietzsche's styles.* Translated by Barbara Harlow. Chicago: University of Chicago Press.

Douglas, Mary. 1968. The social control of cognition: Some factors in joke perception. *Man* 3: 369–370.

Dudley, D. R. 1937. *A history of Cynicism from Diogenes to the sixth century A.D.* London: Methuen and Co.

DuPont, Damien. 2002. *The genealogy of morals*: Nietzsche's self-examination. Unpublished manuscript.

Fischer, Kurt Rudolf. 1977. Nazism as a Nietzschean "experiment." *Nietzsche-Studien* 6: 116–122.

Foucault, Michel. 1978. *The history of sexuality*, volume I: An introduction. Translated by Robert Hurley. New York: Vintage Books.

———. 1984. Nietzsche, genealogy, history. In *The Foucault reader*, edited by Paul Rabinow. Hammondsworth, U.K.: Penguin.

———. 2001. *Fearless speech*. Edited by Joseph Pearson. Los Angeles: Semiotext(e).

Freud, Sigmund. 1919. The "uncanny." In *Standard edition of the complete psychological works of Sigmund Freud*, vol. 17, edited by James Strachey. London: Hogarth.

———. 1935. Autobiographical study. In *Standard edition of the complete psychological works of Sigmund Freud*, vol. 20, edited by James Strachey. London: Hogarth.

Gilman, Sander L. 1975. *Incipit parodia*: The function of parody in the lyrical poetry of Friedrich Nietzsche. *Nietzsche-Studien* 4: 52–74.

———. 1987. *Conversations with Nietzsche: A life in the words of his contemporaries*. Translated by David J. Parent. Oxford: Oxford University Press.

Golden, Leon. 1973. The purgation theory of catharsis. *Journal of Aesthetics and Art Criticism* 31: 473–479.

———. 1976. The clarification theory of *katharsis*. *Hermes* 104: 437–452.

Gould, Stephen Jay. 2002. *The structure of evolutionary theory*. Cambridge, Mass.: Harvard University Press.

Gould, Timothy. 1998. *Hearing things: Voice and method in the writing of Stanley Cavell*. Chicago: University of Chicago Press.

Graham, Billy. 1966. God is not "dead." *U.S. News & World Report*, April 25, 1966.

Greenberg, Harvey Roy. 1993. *Screen memories: Hollywood cinema on the psychoanalytic couch*. New York: Columbia University Press.

Haar, Michel. 1977. Nietzsche and metaphysical language. Translated by Cyril and Liliane Welch. In *The new Nietzsche*, edited by David Allison. Cambridge, Mass.: MIT Press.

Habermas, Jürgen. 1987. *The philosophical discourse of modernity*. Translated by F. Lawrence. Cambridge, Mass.: MIT Press.

Hales, Steven D., and Rex Welshon. 2000. *Nietzsche's perspectivism*. Urbana: University of Illinois Press.

Hamacher, Werner. 1990. The promise of interpretation: Reflections on the hermeneutical imperative in Kant and Nietzsche. In *Looking after Nietzsche*, edited by Rickels. Albany: State University of New York Press.

Hatab, Lawrence. 1995. *A Nietzschean defense of democracy: An experiment in postmodern politics*. Chicago: Open Court Press.

Heidegger, Martin. 1982. *Nietzsche*, volume III. Translated by Joan Stambaugh, David Farrell Krell, and Frank A. Capuzzi. Edited by David Farrell Krell. San Francisco: Harper and Row.

Henrichs, Albert. 2004. "Full of gods": Nietzsche on Greek polytheism and culture. In *Nietzsche and antiquity: His reaction and response to the classical tradition*, edited by Paul Bishop. Rochester, N.Y.: Camden House.

Higgins, Kathleen. 1994. On the genealogy of morals—Nietzsche's Gift. In *Nietzsche, genealogy, morality: Essays on Nietzsche's "On the genealogy of morals,"* edited by Richard Schacht. Berkeley: University of California Press.

———. 2000. *Comic relief: Nietzsche's "Gay science."* Oxford: Oxford University Press.

Hillard, Derek. 2002. History as a dual process: Nietzsche on exchange and power. *Nietzsche-Studien* 31: 40–56.

Irwin, William. 2002. *The death and resurrection of the author?* Westport, Conn.: Greenwood Press.

Janko, Richard, translator, notes. 1987. *Aristotle: Poetics I.* Indianapolis, Ind.: Hackett Publishing Company.

Johnson, Dirk Robert. 2001. Nietzsche's early Darwinism: The "David Strauss" essay of 1873. *Nietzsche-Studien* 30: 62–79.

Kelly, Alfred. 1981. *The descent of Darwin: The popularization of Darwinism in Germany, 1860–1914.* Chapel Hill: University of North Carolina Press.

Kemal, Salim. 1990. Some problems of genealogy. *Nietzsche-Studien* 19: 30–42.

Kivy, Peter. 2003. Jokes are a laughing matter. *The Journal of Aesthetics and Art Criticism* 61: 5–15.

Klossowski, Pierre. 1997. *Nietzsche and the vicious circle.* Translated by Daniel W. Smith. Chicago: University of Chicago Press.

Kofman, Sarah. 1989. *Socrate(s).* Paris: Galilée.

———. 1993. *Nietzsche and metaphor.* Translated by Duncan Large. Stanford, Calif.: Stanford University Press.

Kuhn, Thomas. 1962. *The structure of scientific revolutions.* Chicago: University of Chicago Press.

Lacan, Jacques. 1977. Aggressivity in psychoanalysis. Translated by Alan Sheridan. In *Écrits: A Selection.* New York: Norton.

Lampert, Laurence. 1999. Nietzsche's best jokes. In *Nietzsche's futures*, edited by John Lippitt. New York: St. Martin's Press.

———. 2001. *Nietzsche's task: An interpretation of "Beyond good and evil."* New Haven, Conn.: Yale University Press.

Lawlor, Leonard. 2003. *The challenge of Bergsonism: Phenomenology, ontology, ethics.* London: Continuum.

Lingis, Alphonso. 1977. The will to power. In *The new Nietzsche*, edited by David Allison. Cambridge, Mass.: MIT Press.

Lippitt, John, ed. 1999. *Nietzsche's futures.* New York: St. Martin's Press.

Lovejoy, Arthur O. 1930. *The revolt against dualism.* New York: Norton Press.

Magnus, Bernd, and Kathleen M. Higgins, eds. 1996. *The Cambridge companion to Nietzsche.* Cambridge: Cambridge University Press.

May, Simon. 1999. *Nietzsche's ethics and his war on "morality."* Oxford: Oxford University Press.

McNeill, David N. 2004. On the relationship of Alcibiades' speech to Nietzsche's "problem of Socrates." In *Nietzsche and antiquity: His reaction and response to the classical tradition*, edited by Paul Bishop. Rochester, N.Y.: Camden House.

Méridier, Louis, ed. 1908. Grégoire de Nysse, *Discours catéchétique.* Paris: Libraire Alphonse Picard et fils.

Middleton, Christopher, ed., trans. 1969. *Selected letters of Friedrich Nietzsche.* Indianapolis, Ind.: Hackett Publishing Company.

Müller-Lauter, Wolfgang. 1999. *Nietzsche: His philosophy of contradictions and the contradictions of his philosophy*. Translated by David J. Parent. Urbana: University of Illinois Press.

Navia, Luis. 2001. *Antisthenes of Athens: Setting the world aright*. Westport, Conn.: Greenwood Press.

Nehamas, Alexander. 1982. Plato on imitation and poetry in *Republic* 10. In *Plato on beauty, wisdom and the arts*, edited by J. Moravcsik and P. Temko. Lanham, Md.: Rowman & Littlefield.

———. 1985. *Nietzsche: Life as literature*. Cambridge, Mass.: Harvard University Press.

———. 1987. Dangerous pleasures. *Times Literary Supplement* 437: 27–28.

———. 1996. Nietzsche, modernity, aestheticism. In *The Cambridge companion to Nietzsche*, edited by Bernd Magnus and Kathleen M. Higgins. Cambridge: Cambridge University Press.

Niehues-Pröbsting, Heinrich. 1996. The modern reception of Cynicism: Diogenes in the enlightenment. In *The Cynics: The Cynic movement in antiquity and its legacy*, edited by R. Bracht Branham and Marie-Odile Goulet-Cazé. Berkeley: University of California Press.

Novitz, David. 1996. Disputes about art. *The Journal of Aesthetics and Art Criticism* 54: 153–163.

Nussbaum, Martha. 1986. *The fragility of goodness*. Cambridge: Cambridge University Press.

Oliver, Kelly. 1994. Nietzsche's abjection. In *Nietzsche and the feminine*, edited by Peter J. Burgard. Charlottesville: University Press of Virginia.

Pappas, Nickolas. 1989a. Plato's *Ion*: The problem of the author. *Philosophy* 64: 381–389.

———. 1989b. Authorship and authority. *The Journal of Aesthetics and Art Criticism* 47: 325–332.

———. 1999. Psychoanalysis and film: The question of the interpreter. In *The death of psychoanalysis: Murder? Suicide? Or rumor greatly exaggerated?*, edited by Robert M. Prince. Northvale, N.J.: Jason Aronson.

———. Forthcoming. Morality gags. *Monist*.

Parkes, Graham. 1994. *Composing the soul: Reaches of Nietzsche's psychology*. Chicago: University of Chicago Press.

Pelikan, Jaroslav. 1993. *Christianity and classical culture: The metamorphosis of natural theology in the Christian encounter with Hellenism*. New Haven, Conn.: Yale University Press.

Perkins, Richard. 1997. An innocent little story: Nietzsche and Jesus in allegorical conjunction. *Nietzsche-Studien* 26: 361–383.

Pizer, John. 1990. The use and abuse of "Ursprung": On Foucault's reading of Nietzsche. *Nietzsche-Studien* 19: 462–478.

Pletsch, Carl. 1991. *Young Nietzsche: Becoming a genius*. New York: The Free Press.

Porter, James. 2000a. *The invention of Dionysus: An essay on "The birth of tragedy."* Stanford, Calif.: Stanford University Press.

———. 2000b. *Nietzsche and the philology of the future.* Stanford, Calif.: Stanford University Press.

Quinn, Arthur. 1982. *The figures of speech.* Salt Lake City, Utah: Gibbs M. Smith Inc.

Reed, Gail S. 1982. Towards a methodology for applying psychoanalysis to literature. *Psychoanalytic Quarterly* 51: 19–42.

Rickels, Laurence A., ed.1990. *Looking after Nietzsche.* Albany: State University of New York Press.

Ridley, Aaron. 1998. What is the meaning of aesthetic ideals? In *Nietzsche, philosophy and the arts,* edited by Salim Kemal, Ivan Gaskell, and Daniel W. Conway. Cambridge: Cambridge University Press.

Risse, Mathias. 2003. Origins of *ressentiment* and sources of normativity. *Nietzsche-Studien* 32: 142–170.

Rosen, George. 1975. Nostalgia: A "forgotten" psychological disorder. *Psychological Medicine* 4: 340–354.

Safranski, Rüdiger. 2002. *Nietzsche: A philosophical biography.* Translated by Shelley Frisch. New York: W. W. Norton & Company.

Sallis, John. 1991. *Crossings: Nietzsche and the space of tragedy.* Chicago: University of Chicago Press.

———. Forthcoming. "The flow of *physis* and the beginning of philosophy: On Plato's *Theaetetus.* In *Proceedings of the Boston Area Colloquium in Ancient Philosophy,* volume 20, edited by John J. Cleary and Gary M. Gurtler. Leiden: Brill.

Santas, Gerasimos. 1988. *Plato and Freud: Two theories of love.* Oxford: Blackwell.

Schacht, Richard. 1983. *Nietzsche.* London: Routledge.

———, ed. 1994. *Nietzsche, genealogy, morality: Essays on Nietzsche's "On the genealogy of morals."* Berkeley: University of California Press.

———. 1995. *Making sense: Reflections timely and untimely.* Urbana: University of Illinois Press.

Schrift, Alan D. 1995. *Nietzsche's French legacy: A genealogy of poststructuralism.* New York: Routledge.

———, ed. 2000. *Why Nietzsche still?* Berkeley: University of California Press.

Seitz, Brian. 1995. *The trace of political representation.* Albany: State University of New York Press.

Skowron, Michael. 2002. Nietzsches Weltliche Religiosität und ihre Paradoxien. *Nietzsche-Studien* 31: 1–39.

Solomon, Robert. 1994. One hundred years of *ressentiment:* Nietzsche's *Genealogy of morals.* In *Nietzsche, genealogy, morality: Essays on Nietzsche's "On the genealogy of morals,"* edited by Richard Schacht. Berkeley: University of California Press.

Staten, Henry. 1990. *Nietzsche's voice.* Ithaca, N.Y.: Cornell University Press.

Strong, Tracy. 1988. *Friedrich Nietzsche and the politics of transfiguration.* Berkeley: University of California Press.

———. 1996. Nietzsche's political misappropriation. In *The Cambridge companion to Nietzsche,* edited by Bernd Magnus and Kathleen M. Higgins. Cambridge: Cambridge University Press.

Sypher, Wylie. 1956. Introduction. In *Comedy*, edited by Wylie Sypher. Garden City, N.Y.: Doubleday.

Thiele, Leslie Paul. 1990. *Friedrich Nietzsche and the politics of the soul: A study of heroic individualism*. Princeton, N.J.: Princeton University Press.

Tillich, Paul. 1948. The escape from God. In *The shaking of the foundations*. New York: Charles Scribner's Sons.

Todes, Daniel P. 1987. Darwin's Malthusian metaphor and Russian evolutionary thought, 1859–1917. *Isis* 78: 537–551.

Vernant, Jean-Pierre. 1984. *The origins of Greek thought*. Ithaca, N.Y.: Cornell University Press.

Werman, David S. 1977. Normal and pathological nostalgia. *Journal of the American Psychoanalytical Association* 25: 387–398.

White, Richard. 1994. The return of the master: An interpretation of Nietzsche's *Genealogy of morals*. In *Nietzsche, genealogy, morality: Essays on Nietzsche's "On the genealogy of morals,"* edited by Richard Schacht. Berkeley: University of California Press.

Wiener, Philip P. 1963. The central role of time in Lovejoy's philosophy. *Philosophy and Phenomenological Research* 23: 480–492.

Wilcox, John T. 1997. What aphorism does Nietzsche explicate in *Genealogy of morals*, Essay III? *Journal of the History of Philosophy* 35: 593–610.

———. 1998. That exegesis of an aphorism in *Genealogy* III: Reflections on the scholarship. *Nietzsche-Studien* 27: 448–462.

Wilken, Robert L. 1984. *The Christians as the Romans saw them*. New Haven, Conn.: Yale University Press.

Yates, Peter. 2004. Nietzsche, Aristotle, and propositional discourse. In *Nietzsche and antiquity: His reaction and response to the classical tradition*, edited by Paul Bishop. Rochester, N.Y.: Camden House.

Zuckert, Catherine. 1976. Nature, history and the self: Friedrich Nietzsche's untimely considerations. *Nietzsche-Studien* 5: 55–82.

Index

abusio, 212

Acampora, Christa Davis, xv, 223, 247

Adam, 71, 164, 195, 222

Allison, David, 9, 79, 232

Ambrose, 240–241

Antisthenes the Cynic, 119

Apollo, 3, 6, 26, 42–43, 46–47, 52, 70, 215; the Apollinian impulse, 41–43, 56–57, 60–68; birth of, 47; Dionysus, his relationship to, 36, 42–43, 46–47, 50, 62–63, 66–68, 70; as father, 47, 63

aposiopesis, 9, 246

ascetic ideal, 105, 124, 208

asceticism, 115, 199–200

Aristophanes, 197; and Socrates, 76–77; in *Symposium* (Plato), 74–76

Aristotle, 50, 53, 62, 153; on metaphor, 129–131, 143–144, 155; *Metaphysics*, 36–37, 119, 184; *Parts of Animals*, 39; *Physics*, 197; *Poetics*, 54–59, 130, 143–144; *Rhetoric*, 130, 143

atavism, 248–249, 251

atheism, 40, 226–227

Augustine, 20, 220–221, 239–245, 252. *See also* confessional reading

bad conscience, 162

baptism, 69, 193–194, 210

Basel, 38, 170

Bataille, Georges, 183, 212

Bergson, Henri, xiii, 182–186, 189–192, 212

birth, 5–6, 11–12, 196–198; from Apollo and Dionysus, 47–48; as identification with child, 162–163, 226–227; impossible, 48, 52, 62–63, 196; mixed types, 200–201; Plato and, 73; in populations, 199–203; pregnancy, 5, 107, 162–163, 197, (elephantine) 219

Brandes, Georg, 12

Burckhardt, Jakob, 170–171, 189

Burkert, Walter, 37, 43, 47, 56, 71

Caiaphas, 107–108, 137–138, 157, 170

calculability of the human, 148–149, 247; the opposite, 223

caricature, 189

About the Author

Nickolas Pappas is associate professor of philosophy at the City College of New York. He received his B.A. from Kenyon College and his Ph.D. in philosophy from Harvard University. He is author of the *Routledge Guidebook to Plato and the Republic*, now in its second edition, and about twenty articles on Plato, Aristotle, aesthetics, and other topics. He lives in New York City with his wife and two daughters.